Masters Rowing

Volker Nolte • Wolfgang Fritsch

MASTERS *Rowing*

TRAINING FOR TECHNIQUE, FITNESS, AND COMPETITION

Meyer & Meyer Sport

British Library Cataloguing in Publication Data

A catalogue record for this book is available from the British Library

Original title: *Master Rudern: Das Training ab 40,* © 2010 by Meyer & Meyer Verlag

Masters Rowing

Maidenhead: Meyer & Meyer Sport (UK) Ltd., 2021

ISBN: 978-1-78255-210-9

Aachen, Auckland, Beirut, Cairo, Cape Town, Dubai, Hägendorf, Hong Kong, Indianapolis, Maidenhead, Manila, New Delhi, Singapore, Sydney, Tehran, Vienna

 Member of the World Sport Publishers' Association (WSPA), www.w-s-p-a.org

Printed by: Print Consult GmbH, Munich, Germany

Printed in Slovakia

ISBN: 978-1-8-78255-210-9

Email: info@m-m-sports.com

www.thesportspublisher.com

Contents

Preface

Rowing is a passion that has united us for many decades. Although our interest on the water now differs, with Volker still enjoying age-appropriate competitive training leading to quite successful masters racing, and Wolfgang engaging more in coaching master rowers, we continue to share our keen interest in sport research and coach education. Additionally, we look back with fond and inquisitive memories of many years of successful international racing and coaching that provided us with a wealth of personal experiences in our sport, not to forget our academic careers in sport science, particularly in rowing.

We shared over the years many studies and discussions about rowing, which finally resulted in the first edition of our book *Master Rudern – Das Training ab 40* being published 2010 in German. However, it was clear to both of us from the very beginning that this book must also be published in English, and we have always been convinced that an English edition would find its audience. We realize the amazing interest and need from competitive, as well as recreational masters rowers, in the English-speaking part of the world to gain access to a comprehensive collection of information about this topic in one place. We reviewed and corrected our German edition, brought everything up-to-date and translated it into English. This process also included some adaptations to the specific situations of rowing in English-speaking countries, especially North America, but we maintained the basic ideas and structure of our book.

It was very noticeable and surprising at the same time for us that masters rowing – at least in the technical rowing literature – has not been given very much attention, especially as it is enjoying increased popularity. There are a number of forums of discussion, particularly on the internet and also some articles based on personal experiences, but scientific studies that focus on the elder rowers are rare. Instead, many masters rowers and their coaches are left to copy training plans and coaching practices of high-performance rowers. Likewise, many masters rowers try to design their training by remembering their own workout practices that they experienced as high school or university rowers from decades earlier. Boat rigging also tend to work on the "principle of hope" and is often still geared to the glittering times of great flexibility and strong stamina.

Our perspective on masters rowing goes somewhat further. In addition to the training of the many competitive masters, older athletes who may no longer be found at FISA's big international masters events, but who have ambitions to maintain or improve their rowing technique, physical performance and health with the help of rowing practices, have been consciously included in this book. The latter group of masters rowers may be gearing up for smaller competitions with sometimes varying course lengths, or simply enjoying the camaraderie with their rowing friends. Our aim is to contribute to securing the quality of life, the physical performance and independence of all of these older athletes who follow our unique sport.

In this book, we want to provide basic information on how to do, but also expand by investigating masters rowing from a scientific point of view. Of course, we will share our hands-on experiences as rowers and coaches, and present best practices on what to do in our sport. We will go to great lengths to stay close to the practice and thus give all masters rowers, not only the competitive masters, many tips for learning and training. In addition to all this, we would like to pass on some scientific background of masters rowing and the training with older people. This is all done to help masters rowers enjoy this great sport for as long, as healthy, as enjoyable and as successful as possible. Our definition of masters rowers includes not only the ambitious regatta participants in the various age groups who want to achieve a rowing success through systematic training, but all older rowers who want to practice our sport with joy, purposeful and healthy. If masters athletes or coaches of elderly rowers are looking for ways to develop in rowing, they will find lots of tips, information and hints in our book.

In addition, we realize that the increase in the number of participants in competitive masters rowing continues to be unbroken. One clear sign for this is the steady growth in the turnout to national and international regattas of the masters. We will strive to give those rowers valuable information about how they can possibly make their training safer, more effective and even more enjoyable.

The enthusiasm of many adults for rowing and its diverse manifestations has increased enormously. Many clubs offer beginner courses for adults and older people who may not be racing but still want to improve their physical fitness and health by participating in rowing.

Our overall concern is therefore to make a contribution to securing the highest possible levels of quality of life, of general physical performance and of independence in the aging process with the help of rowing.

We both hope that the detailed chapters on "Aging Successfully" and "Learning to Row" – in addition to "Rowing Techniques" and "Training the Master Rowers" – will also be an enrichment for the reader.

The publication of this book has been a heartfelt wish for us for quite some time. All the more, we thank the direct and indirect participants in this book, because without their help the publication would certainly not have happened. First, there are the many master rowers and rowing partners who rowed and trained with us over the years and gave us plenty of inspiration for this book. Also, many volunteered for photo shoots. Your ideas and suggestions have found their way into this book.

In addition, we would like to highlight some of our supporters who have been very helpful as discussion partners and in the preparation of the manuscript, tables, and illustrations: Donald Peterson of the Canadian Center for Activity and Aging, and Charles Rice of the School of Kinesiology at the University of Western Ontario, Maria Martensen as a newcomer in rowing, as well as Julia Sonntag from the Department of Sports Science at the University of Konstanz. Special thanks are due to Liz Evans and Alan Oldham who helped to present the book in its English version.

Introduction

ROWING – PASSION FOR A LIFETIME!

For most rowers, their sport is more than a simple physical activity; it is a form of artistic expression. Rowing introduces participants to a culture that becomes for many, a way of life, something Craig Lambert (1999, p.12) describes so well in his book *Mind over water: Lessons on life from the art of rowing:* "We are out here in the darkness to reveal ourselves, to discover who we are. With the oars, we attempt things that we cannot do, we confront that which is beyond our capacities. *Mind over water.* The shells transport us into the unknown." Many, especially older rowers – both seasoned veterans and late-life beginners – wholeheartedly agree with this author. All by degrees become convinced of rowing's power to convey the essential qualities and abilities that bring meaning to a modern life: strength, endurance, tranquility, balance, coordination, perseverance, team spirit, joy of competition, mindfulness, purposefulness and concentration!

Regardless of their motivation to pick up an oar – or ergometer handle – adult rowing is a transformative experience. The combination of the social aspects of crew and team performance with its high demands on coordination and physicality, all in connection with sophisticated equipment, makes it comparatively unique within the sporting spectrum.

In rowing, adult athletes are known as "seniors" or "masters rowers". Formerly common terms such as, "old women" and "old men" have happily fallen out of fashion as has "veterans" to a large extent, although this term remains in use for specific age race categories at some United States regattas (e.g. Head of the Charles). Throughout this book, we will use the term "masters rower", as this is now the internationally recognized designation for athletes aged 27 years and upwards not racing in the open age category often called "senior".

Regionally, there are also races offered under the name of "masters" for rowers even below the age of 27 years, to give younger adults who enter the sport a chance to accompany club comrades to regattas and be competitive. Although we recognize this development, this book will focus on adults over the age of about 30 years with their age specific situations and challenges. According to our understanding, this includes rowing as a performance sport under oftentimes very competitive conditions, as well as a demanding fitness activity or as an exercise for recreation and healthy living. Thus, masters rowing can extend over an age span of 50 years and often longer.

Historically, rowing was one of the first sports to offer organized activity and competition programs for all ages from youth up to advanced age. This is not by chance: targeted, continuous pursuit of rowing can counteract, stop and even reverse most of the inevitable aging processes that happen over a life span and many studies confirm the health effects of rowing.

But the benefits of rowing are not just physiological. It improves a person's quality of life in general and has positive effects on the psyche. As a community sport, rowing provides a chance for meaningful social contact along with the shared experience of challenge and growth through common ventures such as traveling to regattas or touring destinations, as well as positive psychological stimuli to increase problem solving and gain self-confidence.

Sports for adults in the middle and later parts of their lives are becoming more and more popular, mirroring broader societal changes. These are caused by shifting demographics of the population, but also by the evolving landscape of both work and leisure. Sport is omnipresent and offers a variety of services particularly for older adults, especially under the premises of health and prevention. In the course of these developments, the number of physically active or sports-oriented adults has increased, while at the same time the diverse range of activities available is rapidly expanding

The authors are in this expanded sense themselves enthusiastic masters rowers, who even after more than 55 years in the sport continue to enjoy the activity, aim for their particular individual goals and (mostly) experience satisfaction. Add to that countless other positive experiences reaching from the sensations of "perfect strokes" with the accompanying "effortless" run of the boat, the wonderful interpersonal interactions, the magnificent experience of being in nature, to the awareness and enjoyment of improved physical performance. This encourages us, the authors, to keep taking on the ever-

increasing demands of our sport whether as coaches, instructors or athletes. We wish to contribute in our own way to the sport we enjoy so much in order for as many adults as possible to experience rowing with the greatest joy and personal satisfaction. In doing so, we are convinced that lifelong sports - especially rowing - have positive effects on health, performance and life expectancy, and thus significantly improve people's quality of life, even as they age.

This conviction is in line with developments in our society that are generally recognizable in sports for adults and older individuals: the "rediscovery of the own body", along with a changing sense of health and fitness; the need for authentic physical activity in the great outdoors; the desire for social connectedness and a sense of inclusion. All of this characterizes the attitudes towards physical activity and the shift in adults' approach to sports.

In the conscious configuration of leisure time and as a separation from the working world, sport has become an important factor in adults' lives, and thus contributes to society's evolving image of the typical "older person". The increasing variety of activities and sports provides tailor-made offers for all kinds of specific interests and goals, not only in terms of different sports and forms of exercise, but also individual motives. Offerings span from competitive performance sports to recreational activities that are geared towards community or nature experiences.

The current trend is for more and more adults to find rowing as their activity of choice through various club and community programs like adult learn-to-row courses or training camps. These individuals progress from learning the basic rowing movements to the intricacies of refining technique and then finally to enjoying all that this sport has to offer. Additionally, many former high school, college and high performance rowers continue in their sport beyond their adolescent years or come back after a number of years of absence from the sport.

Rowing's draw lies in its ability to open up disparate physical, psychological and social experiences at every age and for every level of ability. The sport is particularly attractive because of the way individual experiences can be linked and combined so that no two people experience rowing in the same way. Regardless of which stage in life a rower takes up the sport and the primary motivation – for health, recreation and well-being, or striving for peak physical performance and competition – rowing, with its varied perspectives and opportunities, is an ideal sport for all.

The phenomenon of adult aged competitive and performance sports now stands side by side with the important notion of lifelong physical activity for physical and psychological health. This becomes strikingly obvious when you look at the increasing rates of participation across all ages and ever higher levels of performance at masters rowers' races. The frequency and format of racing opportunities for masters is also on the rise around the world.

The significance of the topic requires a systematic exploration of the various ways that masters rowers learn, practice and train. It is also important that we consider what "successful aging" looks like and rowing's role in this lifelong pursuit.

This book is dedicated to adults of all ages who are practicing this sport and to those wishing to guide and support these masters as coaches and instructors. We are indebted to the vast range of perspectives and motivations that masters seek and find through the pursuit of rowing.

The authors are aware that, by the very nature of rowing as a sport of various experiences, the motivations and perspectives of each adult rower are many and complex. Even a masters rower, who trains and races systematically, may well have in mind the health benefits of the sport and find joy in the pleasures of a rowing tour with friends. On the other hand, the inveterate touring rower is as interested in improving and maintaining their technique as in building and maintaining the social connections afforded by their crew and club.

A Note on the Book's Structure

In this book, we take the perspective of all masters rowers, regardless of whether they are simply using it to pursue good health, or practicing the sport to maintain or improve their physical fitness, or occasionally seeking the outdoors and activities in the boat to relax and decompress, or are life-long, or once again or new competitors. Throughout the book, the authors investigate how rowing, with all its different perspectives, can contribute to "successful aging". To this end, special attention is given to topics related to learning strategies, rowing technique, rigging and sensible rowing training.

The first part of the book (chapters 1 and 2) will focus on the particulars of the physical transformations that accompany aging and how developmental conditions change over the lifespan in the context of successful aging. We will then turn our attention to take a closer look at some masters rower populations of special interest. The findings and evidence presented here serve as the basis for the following chapters.

The second part (chapters 3-5) deals with the subject of adult learning in terms of the rowing movement and considerations on whether and how it is still possible for older athletes to "perfect" their rowing technique - even for resolute competitors. Closely related to this is the individual adaptation of the rowing equipment to age-related restrictions and body dimensions. When discussing the specific physical developments of aging and the goals of masters rowers, the authors make reference, where appropriate, to insights from the experiences of high-performance athletes, something continued in the following chapters.

The third part of the book (chapters 6 and 7) focuses on rowing training for masters age athletes. We seek to answer questions including: What should the rowing training for masters look like? Which aspects should be emphasized? What should be considered regarding load and recovery? How can a rower maintain or increase racing performance or physical fitness over the mid and long term? The book's last chapter concludes with descriptions of planning, execution and design of training, races, regatta schedules and camps.

The final part of the book includes bibliographic references, useful (internet) addresses and a glossary.

Chapter 1

MASTERS ROWING

WHO IS A MASTERS ROWER?

At one time, the transition between performance as an elite athlete and participation as a master was thought to be one of inevitable and rapid decline as an athlete approached "advanced" age in their sport. This was experienced firsthand by one of the authors of this book while trying out for the German National Rowing Team a number of years ago. The National Coach at the time suggested that it would be better for the then 26-year-old rower to look for a career outside of elite rowing since his best performance years were behind him. Coaching efforts and the support of the German rowing system were focused instead on the next generation of younger athletes. This well-intentioned counsel was based on the realization that the average age of the most successful international rowers had been steadily declining; the best research of the day suggesting that humans reach their maximum rowing performance around 25 years of age.

Perhaps coincidentally, this was also the era that saw the official entry age for masters rowing races set at 27 years. It is notable that masters categories start at comparatively different ages across sports. Swimmers can race as masters as early as age 25, triathletes and basketball players have to wait until they are 30 years old, and it is only upon turning 35 that track and field athletes and volleyball players can be considered masters.

Today we know that even older rowers can achieve absolute excellence; indeed, our definition of the age of peak rowing performance must be advanced well beyond the age of 25 years. Sir Steven Redgrave is perhaps the most famous example of this deeper insight, who at the age of 39 won his fifth consecutive gold medal – one gold for each Olympics he attended from Los Angeles 1984 through to Sydney 2000.

This trend has continued in recent decades with ever more highly talented athletes not only participating in elite rowing races, but doing so successfully for far longer. The list of finalists, medalists and even winners – some well over 36 years old – at the World Championships and Olympic Games includes such names as: Ekaterina Karsten (Belarus), Rumyana Neykova (Bulgaria), Duncan Free (Australia), Iztok Cop (Slovenia), Olaf Tufte (Norway), Greg Searle (Great Britain), Lesley Thompson-Willie (Canada), Vaclav Chalupa (Czech Republic), to mention just a few. Jueri Jaanson (Estonia) won the silver medal in the men's double at Beijing 2008 at the age of 42 and in 2019 a 46-year-old James Cracknell (Great Britain) became the oldest winner of Britain's famous University Boat Race following Cambridge's victory over Oxford!

While such athletes are without doubt exceptional, their growing ranks are an indication that there is no fixed "expiry date" on the physical performance required to achieve top rowing results, as long as the athletes stick to an appropriate long-term training regime. In fact, research now suggests that factors such as decreasing motivation, higher vulnerability to injury and personal demands (job, family) have a greater impact on a person's diminishing performance than any age-related decline of physical abilities.

Although they are technically of the eligible age of masters rowers, these older elite athletes are clearly outside the scope of our current volume. **For the purposes of this book, we will define masters rowers as athletes around 30 years of age and older who are neither publically funded, nor full-time members of a high performance program, nor those who subordinate their career or education in the pursuit of high performance objectives.** While masters athletes can compete at quite a high level and participate in organized training at any age, **"successful aging"** in a holistic sense – rather than absolute peak athletic performance – is the main goal; master rowers' training, therefore, should strive to reach this goal in an age-related, meaningful manner.

1.1 TARGET GROUPS IN MASTERS ROWING

1.1.1 The Competitive Masters Rower

For many athletes, it is a natural transition from their time as high-performance rowers in high school, university or club programs into a competitive masters rowing program with little or no interruption. Other masters find their way back to rowing after taking years off from regular training and competing in "their" sport, which they had exercised more or less intensively as adolescents. Not infrequently you also find athletes who have only discovered competitive rowing as adults. The ever-increasing number of regattas specifically geared towards masters, and the continuously rising rates of participation in masters races, bear witness to the great popularity of rowing as a competitive sport for athletes of increasingly older age. These trends can be observed worldwide.

The competitive structure of rowing is divided into age categories to ensure as equal a "field of play" as possible within races. Traditional age categories with a focus on younger athletes are defined by an individual competitor's maximum age (see Tab. 1). The "Senior" category – often referred to as "open" – has no age limitations and is meant to be for rowers competing at the absolute highest levels both domestically and internationally. On top of this, masters rowing has emerged as a competitive system similarly subdivided into age groups, but ones based instead on the minimum age of either the individual rower or crew average in larger events (see Tab. 3). The flexibility inherent in this system allows for a wide range of combinations of athletes of different ages as long as all are above 27 years old.

Tab. 1: Age categories in rowing with their official names

Age	Age Categories in Rowing
Up to 14	Boys and Girls
15 – 16	U 17 or Junior B
17 - 18 *	U 19 or Junior A
19 - 22 *	U 23 (some countries also have the category U 21 = 19 - 20 years)
All ages *	Senior
27+ **	Masters (various age groups) men / women

*Indicates international age categories with official World Championships.

**There are already in some rowing nations even younger age groups (e.g. 24+). However, no specific reference is made to these age groups in this book.

Besides the thrill of competition, motivations for participation as masters rowers are as varied as the rowers themselves. Below are some of the main factors that attract adults of all ages to the sport of rowing.

1.1.2   The Fitness- and Health-Oriented Masters Rower

Rowing is an excellent way to maintain and improve fitness and physical health especially well-suited to aging adults. As a low impact, joint-friendly endurance sport, rowing meets the desires of many people wishing to enjoy the health benefits of physical activity, including the prevention of diseases and deficiencies that come with a sedentary lifestyle. Rowing also poses no major risk of injury to older adults when performed with proper technique. In fact, one major cause of injury – falling – simply does not exist in the sport since the rower is already sitting down. Furthermore, rowers can participate year-round in a sport that strengthens so many muscle groups and particularly targets aerobic endurance both on or off the water.

Fitness-oriented masters rowers try to increase their physical performance and their recovery abilities through systematically and methodically planned training. This group of athletes is less interested in measurable increases in competition performance or in specific training aimed towards regatta participation. Nevertheless, these athletes do have a kind of "performance idea" in their vision. Their training primarily serves to achieve individual physiological adjustments such as weight loss, strengthened musculature or improved endurance. At the same time these athletes achieve quite a number of positive psychological experiences, like increasing self-esteem, learning and mastering rowing's relatively complex technique, finding satisfaction in finishing a particular part of a rowing session, or enjoying a well-running boat and a well-drilled crew.

Primarily **health-oriented masters rowers** have similar goals. These adults seek the ability to continue meeting or exceeding the demands of everyday life as they age. The experience of the activity in itself, moving in nature, the benefits to physical and psychological well-being and strong social contacts are other important motivational factors. For the health-oriented adult, rowing offers a broad variety of activities in the great outdoors. They can meet for single rowing outings, as well as for pleasure tours over several days. Whatever the activity, they can choose their individual physical loads and mental expectations.

1.1.3   Socialization and Community

Rowing as a recreational sport carries with it the possibility to be active in groups with a wide range of age, gender and performance. Thus, it is possible that one can find fun, relaxation and conviviality with friends simply by involvement in this sport.

Rowing is practiced primarily in clubs, which satisfy further social needs of adult members. For example, they provide a meeting place, organize parties and events, and provide a second home for both younger and older rowers.

1.1.4   Balance and Recreation

Rowing is mainly practiced outdoors and many adult rowers feel a special connection to water and nature. Whether they participate in multi-day pleasure tours, short trips or exploration trips by boat, moving on local or unfamiliar water ways offers both relaxation and adventure. Rowing thus also serves as a balance to the everyday and professional life, promoting well-being as an adventure sport and as pure and simple recreation in the activity itself.

Tab. 2: Target groups in masters rowing

	Performance and competitive rowing	Fitness and health rowing	Recreational rowing, pleasure touring, rowing as balance and recreation
Main Motives	▶ Optimizing physical performance relating to age ▶ Competition, regattas, benchmarking	▶ Physical fitness, rowing as a means to improve health and physical performance ▶ Weight reduction	▶ Conviviality ▶ Fun ▶ Social connection and links in a club ▶ Group experience ▶ Nature experience
Competitions, Training, Organizational Forms	▶ Regatta travels ▶ Rowing races over various distances ▶ Ergometer races ▶ Training and competitions in other sports ▶ Mostly systematic training in preparation for competitions	▶ Occasional participation in competitions and pleasure tours ▶ Possibly training and competing in other (endurance) sports ▶ Training according to time restrains and motivation	▶ Club tours, pleasure tours, excursions ▶ No or almost no competitions ▶ Limited practices in other sports
Training / Rowing Frequency	▶ Regular and systematic training 3-6 per week ▶ Training camps, holiday sports	▶ Regular / irregular training approx. 1-4 per week ▶ Sometimes holiday sports	▶ No systematic training ▶ Outings in the boat about 1-3 per week
Importance of the Sport	▶ Rowing plays a very important role and is a priority in life ▶ Very keen interest in the sport and in knowledge relating to training, rowing technique, boat technique and material	▶ Rowing plays a minor role, but is a vital part of life ▶ Great interest in topics and knowledge about the sport and in connection with fitness, health, rowing technique	▶ Rowing plays no central role as a sport ▶ Great interest in social events, trips and in the connection of rowing with cultural aspects

	Performance and competitive rowing	Fitness and health rowing	Recreational rowing, pleasure touring, rowing as balance and recreation
Teams / Groups	▶ Relatively homogeneous performance groups and teams ▶ Occasionally changing of selected training partners, also outside the own club	▶ Heterogeneous as well as homogeneous teams and groups possible ▶ Alternating training partners	▶ Very heterogeneous groups possible, but usually the same groups

1.2   COMPETITIONS FOR MASTERS

Performance-oriented masters rowers try to maintain or improve their competitive performance through targeted and systematic training. The idea of competing is a high priority for these athletes and a major motivation for training. Masters races are governed by the same rules and competition regulations that apply to senior and junior rowing with a few notable adjustments discussed below. According to international regulations, masters rowing includes athletes from age of 27 to the ninth decade of life.

Every year, masters regattas are very popular events worldwide. Organized with great efficiency, racing schedules are usually much denser than regattas for younger rowers and offer plenty of races in short intervals. The international rowing association (FISA) is aware of these developments and for many years has had a standing masters committee, the FISA Masters Rowing Commission, whose purpose and activities are published on FISA's website and reproduced here:

1. **Purpose**

   1.1 To oversee and promote masters rowing in all its forms on a national and international basis.

2. **Activities**

   2.1 To organize the World Rowing Masters Regatta annually.

   2.2 In cooperation with other commissions, establish standard masters classes in other forms of rowing.

   2.3 To gather dates and locations of key international masters regattas for the international calendar.

   2.4 To publish written information.

   2.5 To consult with and advise the Youth Rowing Commission regard the Masters Fund for Youth rowing an the use of the resources of the Fund.
   (See www.worldrowing.com)

Competition-oriented masters rowing is enjoying growing international popularity and plays an important role within FISA, who organizes an annual worldwide event. Officially named the "World Rowing Masters Regatta", the event is not considered a true World Championships. This distinction, however, is not always present in the minds of some participants, who can — if only in their own minds — become "world champions" with a win in their race. Races are run with all heats being finals; there is no progression to a next round. The result of this is several gold medallists for each boat class and age classification. This annual event enjoys enormous popularity. For example, the 2017 World Masters Regatta in Bled, Slovenia saw 4,700 rowers competing in about 6,000 boats with 18,000 total seats filled.

The international rules of racing for masters rowing are well established and are based on age categories, which begin with the age of 27 as a minimum threshold to compete and then set at different age increments with a minimum average age:

Tab. 3: Age classifications for masters rowers

Category			Development phases (correspond to ...)
A	Minimum age	27 years	"Early adulthood"
B	Average age	36 years or more	
C	Average age	43 years or more	"Middle adulthood"
D	Average age	50 years or more	
E	Average age	55 years or more	"Late adulthood"
F	Average age	60 years or more	
G	Average age	65 years or more	
H	Average age	70 years or more	"Elderly person"
I	Average age	75 years or more	
J	Average age	80 years or more	
K	Average age	83 years or more	
L	Average age	86 years or more	
M	Average age	89 years or more	

There are also "mixed" competitions with equal numbers of women and men in each crew. Male and female coxswains can compete in all races regardless of crew gender. Coxswains also do not fall within the age restrictions and are therefore not counted in the calculation of the average age of a crew. Regardless of age, rowers are limited to only two races per day. Lightweight classes are only offered locally, but not yet internationally.

Master rowers typically race side by side over 1,000 m on a multi-lane buoyed course. As the format for the World Rowing Masters Regatta, this is the international standard. Shorter sprint races can be up to 500 m. Longer "head races" normally around 5 km (3 miles) are conducted as time trials with boats starting one after another usually on a narrower waterway such as a river.

Where numbers warrant, masters races of different age groups can be run as a combined heat. Most national rowing federations have developed their own system of handicaps in order to compare the relative performances of one crew relative to another in a different age group. Regardless of which system is used, the relative accuracy of these numbers is most reliable when comparing neighboring age groups. If required, three neighboring age groups could be run together. The following table published by the German Rowing Federation is valid for 1,000 m distance races and indicates the length of time an older crew needs to start ahead of a crew of a neighboring age category to create a fair race.

Tab. 4: Time advantage in seconds for 1,000 m distance races of a crew relative to a crew of the neighboring age category

Age Category	A	B	C	D	E	F	G	H	I	J	K
Boat Class											
4x/8+	0.0	2.0	3.0	5.5	5.0	6.0	7.0	8.0	9.0	10.0	12.0
2x/4+/4-	0.0	2.0	4.0	6.0	5.5	6.5	8.0	9.0	10.0	12.0	14.0
1x/2-	0.0	2.0	4.5	7.0	6.5	7.5	9.0	10.0	11.0	13.0	16.0

For example, if a Masters-C-4x, a Masters-D-4x, and a Masters-E-4x are going to start in the same race; then the Masters-E-4x will start 5 seconds before the Masters-D-4x, which in turn will be starting 5.5 seconds ahead of the Masters-C-4x. So, the Masters-C-4x ends up waiting a total of 10.5 seconds after the Masters-E-4x started. The winner is the one who is the first to cross the finish line.

The presented handicap table that we used because of its simplicity is only one of numerous tables that you can find. Certain regatta organizations use their own handicap tables to accommodate for specific distances or the specific local situation (e.g. current or course layout). Handicap numbers in all these tables are very similar and are based on related premises to account for the age-related differences.

Success in the masters categories can only be achieved with extensive and deliberate training, which is hardly inferior to that of the top senior rowers. It is not uncommon for ambitious and well-trained non-rowers to try their hand at ergometer competitions, since the (rowing) technical requirements take a back seat to raw physical abilities. Nevertheless, these competitions and the comparative scores provide good feedback for the performance-oriented masters rower.

Ergometer racing is a special form of rowing competition. National and international records are maintained for different age, weight and gender categories. The status of indoor rowing has also risen in recent years with FISA's introduction of a World Rowing Indoor Championships, granting official "World Champion" status to winners in each of these categories.

1.3   THE PROFILE OF COMPETITIVE MASTERS ROWERS

For years, the World Rowing Masters Regattas has been among the world's largest rowing competitions. Participation at this international regatta, ranging from between 2,000 and 4,700 rowers annually, is greatly encouraged by an expansive programme that now includes eleven different age groups and 17 different boat classes.

Seiler (2003) surveyed over 1,000 masters rowers through the FISA website. Thirty percent of respondents were women aged between 27-68 with a mean age of 43 years; and 70% were men aged between 27-83 with a mean age of 47 years. The majority of those surveyed were from Europe, followed by North America and Oceania. The study found that 41% of female respondents had their first competitive experience in the masters category, while 55% of the male and 35% of the female subjects were former elite senior rowers.

A look at the data from a geographical standpoint shows considerable differences when it comes to previous rowing experience for masters rowers. The numbers for Europe and North America provide a good contrast. European masters rowers were far more likely to have previous racing experience with more than 60% of males and about 50% of females being former elite senior athletes while just 7% were "late entrants". In contrast, 30% of males and 60% of females among the North American masters identified as "new rowers". While the number of late entry masters rowers continues to grow rapidly in North America, former elite senior rowers dominate the European masters rowing scene.

In total, over 50% of masters rowers have family members who are also involved in the sport. Tracing the path of how late entry masters who go on to compete internationally made their way to rowing is an interesting exercise. Many women in particular learned to row only after the age of 30 (41% of all female masters rowers compared to 13% of males). Allowing for differences in regional traditions and national strategies, it is normal for youth athletes to enter a sport either through their school or university. It is therefore striking that over 70% of North American masters got to know rowing as an adult through the club system. Yet in Europe, where the majority of masters have rowed since youth, teenage membership in rowing clubs is significantly higher, while university sports have traditionally played a subordinate role.

Seiler's survey also looked at training with questions like: How much do masters rowers train? Do they receive coaching? Which boat classes are mainly rowed in training? Regardless of age category, masters rowers completed between four and five training sessions per week, which equated to a weekly training volume of 4-11 hours (winter 4-7 hrs, summer 7-11 hrs). About 60% of women and 30% of men are coached on a regular basis and also value coaching. In practice, most of the training is done in singles (1x), followed by eights (8+) and fours (4+/-).

Grabow (1995) conducted a training volume analysis comparing the training efforts of masters rowers with senior rowers. Areas he looked at include: overall training, on-water training, strength and additional endurance training, as well as core training/stretching. His finding of 3-5 training sessions per week with an average of 4 hours of training in the winter and about 5-6 hours of training per week in the summer line up well with Seiler's data. Over the whole year, masters rowers thus train at about 30% of the volume of senior athletes ranging from about 34% in summer and 28% in winter. The really interesting thing, however, is how the distribution of distinct forms of training differs greatly from these averages (see Fig. 1).

Given that masters rowers trained overall only about 30% of the volume of their younger counterparts, it is astonishing that masters' actual on-water time during summer training was found to be about 39% of the seniors' in-boat training. This was due to the fact that the masters rowers in the study performed almost no strength training during that time of the year. While time on the water accounted for the bulk of summer activities, masters did, however, do a greater proportion of complementary endurance training during the same training period relative to younger rowers (65% of the proportion of that of seniors). Only the proportions of supplementary trainings were in the winter higher for the masters athletes than the average of the total training, which shows that the masters rowed relatively less on the water, but did relatively more extra trainings on land.

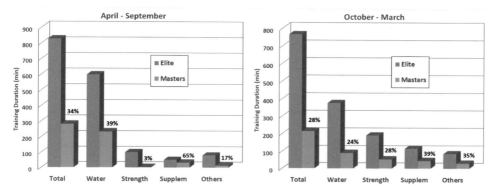

Fig. 1: Comparison of training volumes of elite and masters rowers for summer (April – September) and winter (October – March) seasons (mod. after Grabow 1995, 222-223).

The overall training effort of the masters rowers is, Grabow concluded, completely sufficient to satisfy both performance and health-oriented goals. Nevertheless, he criticizes the relative lack of strength training and the high intensities at which the older athletes in his survey performed their supplementary and specific endurance training. According to Grabow, the masters were training too hard.

The main motivation to compete in male masters races (41%) is a desire to keep rowing in a seamless transition from the senior category (Seiler 2003). Traditionally, many male rowers have just wanted to continue their competitive sport activities, while 35% of masters women started rowing simply as a form of physical activity and only later became enthusiastic about competing. Whatever their motivation, everyone understands that regular training has positive effects on health and physical performance. Ultimately, the goal of competing becomes the primary motivator for the majority of male (53%) and female (59%) masters rowers as the focus and highlight of daily training.

One frequent assertion against masters rowers is that they spend too much time on their training and not enough time engaged in helping to run their club. However, results of various studies do not support these allegations: After all, 85% masters rowers report involvement in a range of club activities, such as the important areas of coaching and administrative assistance.

The increase in dedicated masters rowers at national and international competitions raises some important questions that deserve careful and attentive consideration by rowing associations at all levels. Phenomena such as "rolodex racing crews", competition tourism, stress caused by over frequent participation in competitions that can result in medication abuse and even doping in masters-age sports need to be appropriately regulated or restricted by rules, information and education (Kreiß, 1995, p. 148).

In this context, one can observe developments that are already proving disruptive to the traditional club based structure of the sport. Chief among these is the rise of virtual clubs, whose membership consists only of selected masters rowers from different regions. Operating without boat houses or a central location, the normal community connections that come with a brick and mortar facility are no longer present. Such clubs may hire professional administrators and coaches to form and prepare highly competitive crews based on sophisticated procedures mimicking those of high performance teams. While the usually high price tag for memberships may guarantee a certain amount of success for ambitious top-masters, these clubs do not fit neatly into the existing model of club sports through the unnecessary professionalization of masters racing. These developments certainly offer a higher level of training, coaching and competitive experiences to those participating, but the long term consequences for the sport are not yet clear.

Chapter 2

SUCCESSFUL AGING AS A MASTERS ROWER

2.1   AGING, STAGES OF LIFE AND PERSPECTIVES OF OLDER AGE

Demographic changes of recent decades including a steady lengthening of life expectancy have shown a global increase of older relative to younger people. Researchers, therefore, are placing topics such as "older age" and "successful aging" more and more in the center of scientific discussions. Can sport – can rowing – contribute to maintaining or recovering quality of life and contribute to well-being in old age?

Parallel to the objective data that reveal this demographic transformation, the subjective narratives that society builds up around aging are similarly shifting. This means that aging in general is no longer only seen as a process of biological diminution; it is a complex development process affected as much by internal as external factors and can occur in many ways. Viewpoints that see aging merely as a deterioration process in which illness and neediness increase are losing significance.

We must, however, remember that the following factors about aging remain true. Aging is:

▶ universal and irreversible,
▶ negative in terms of reduced functional and adaptive capacities after the completion of years of development and growth phases,
▶ genetically-biologically determined, and
▶ takes place on biological, psychological and social levels (Dickhuth et al., 2007, p. 601).

We must also realize that aging can be observed from six different points of view (see Raeburn 2009, p.7-8):

1. Chronological age
2. Functional age
3. Biological age
4. Psychological age
5. Social age
6. Training age.

Development includes gains and losses in every phase of life. Successful development means maximizing developmental gains while minimizing developmental losses, relatively speaking. Of course, some biological abilities diminish with age. Yet **successful aging** in the face of this generally losing deal of biology includes on the one hand the art of living with one's own (biological) limitations while showing on the other hand how culture and mind can "outsmart" the body. Successful aging therefore means the ability to achieve an overall positive gain-loss balance sheet as you grow older and on into later life. This ability is determined by each person's unique nature and experiences and must therefore be seen on an individual basis.

This more complex consideration of aging from physiological, psychological and social perspectives enables a differentiated view of abilities and deficits. Thus, one can, in all three aspects of aging, elaborate on some improvements, constants, as well as increasing deficits (see tab. 5 and 6).

Physiological aging is understood as transformations of

▶ the vital capacity of the organism,
▶ its reserves to adapt and compensate,
▶ in the individual organ and functional systems.

From a physiological point of view, aging is a natural biological process in which changes in organs and decline in performance occur.

The lifestyle that a person leads and cultivates over the course of decades should not be underestimated in its significant influence on physiological aging. Alcohol, nicotine, poor diet – especially the lack of exercise associated with being overweight – inadequate stress on the body and a workplace related pollutant load are some of the risk factors and accelerators for physiological aging.

The issue of body weight is subject to age-related particulars: For example, the rate of mortality for 20- to 29-year-olds is lowest among those with a BMI (body mass index) of 21.4, while for 60- to 69-year-olds it is lowest for those with a BMI of 26.6 (see Fig. 2). Therefore, a BMI of 26 has quite a different meaning and health consequences for a 29-year-old relative to a 60-year-old. An increase in BMI is, within certain limits, nothing to be alarmed at; it all depends on the age of the person.

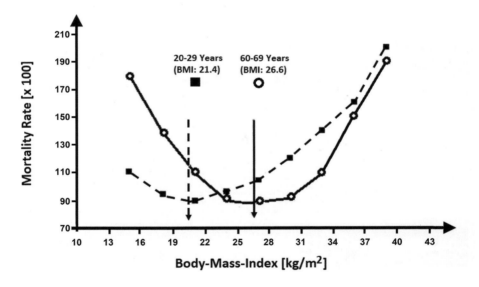

Fig.2: Relationship between mortality rate and BMI (mod. after Friedrich 2008).

Tab. 5: Influence on physical characteristics while aging

Increase despite aging	Constant even with aging	Decrease with aging
▶ Skill and experience (depending on the type and duration of the activity)	▶ Resilience to continuous load below the aerobic threshold	▶ Muscle strength ▶ Flexibility ▶ Speed ▶ Reaction time ▶ Resilience to short-term load above the aerobic threshold ▶ Vision ▶ Hearing ▶ Tactile sense ▶ Climate adaptability ▶ Coordination

A health-conscious and active lifestyle, which includes sport and exercise, in addition to appropriate preventive measures can have a considerably positive influence on the physiological aging process (see Kruse et al., 1999, p. 301). The principle applies that physical activity should not act as an additional stress factor, but should consist of well-adjusted load and recovery. One must carefully respect all the individual adaptations required in training for older athletes when setting the loads and must also consider a range of approaches to performance training. From a **psychological perspective** aging also presents both losses and wins on life's overall balance sheet. While it is true that the aging processes of the central nervous system result in negative transformations in sensorimotor, cognitive, and sensory functions, there are incredible psychological benefits that come with lived experience. Changes in psychological and cognitive functions are detectable, which have a positive influence on someone's quality of life. Most importantly, here too, one can simultaneously benefit from new forms of experience and minimize losses by engaging in physical training.

It is important to recognize that later life cognitive loss is directly impacted by the amount of cognitive training over the entire life. In this context it should be emphasized that physical training and exercise influence the sensorimotor and cognitive functions of the body in a positive manner (see Kruse et al., 1999, pp. 301f.).

Tab. 6: Influence of psychological characteristics and abilities while aging

Increase despite aging	Constant even with aging	Decrease with aging
▶ Experience ▶ Proficiency ▶ Judgment ▶ Ability to think positively ▶ Independence ▶ Capacity for teamwork ▶ Sense of responsibility ▶ Even temperament ▶ Steadfastness ▶ Maturity ▶ Positive attitude to work ▶ Safety Awareness	▶ General knowledge ▶ Ability to acquire and process information ▶ Concentration ▶ Long-term memory ▶ Resistance to short mental stress ▶ Learning ability	▶ Mental mobility and ability to change ▶ Speed of information acquisition and -processing ▶ Resistance to high continuous mental stress ▶ Ability to abstract ▶ Short-term memory ▶ Willingness to take risks

Social aging indicates the transformations over time in the social roles and functions of a person within society. Over the course of life, society defines certain expectations for different age groups regarding their roles and lifestyles. The majority of older people lead an independent life and their skills, abilities and experiences can benefit society.

Even if older people have to accept some restrictions over the course of their lives, the capabilities that arise for the individual in old age and for society cannot be denied. Older people often have a high level of competency and expertise, and they learn to handle limits better with age. They solve tasks more pragmatically and their life experiences make it possible to judge with greater sophistication.

The life stages of adults can be divided into three major sections:

1. Early adulthood,
2. Middle and later adulthood and
3. Late adulthood.

These stages are defined by Strass and Wilke (2006, p.16):

Early adulthood approx. 20-35 years

▶ Completion of professional education and beginning of employment,
▶ Detachment from the birth family,
▶ Assuming partnership, starting a family, taking on parental responsibilities,
▶ Increasingly "autonomous" participation in the leisure sector.

Middle and later adulthood about 30/35-60/65 years

▶ Progressive consolidation of a professional career,
▶ Further shaping a personally defined lifestyle in the leisure and consumer sector,
▶ Possible health problems,
▶ Changes in the workplace,
▶ Increased involvement in sport/rowing conflicts with the widespread notion that sport is a "thing for the young, but not for the old".

Late adulthood about 60/65-75+ years

Against the background of changing phases of life, late adulthood gives rise to a series of life and development tasks whose more or less "successful" handling should have a significant effect on life satisfaction in old age:

▶ Preparation and management of leaving the work force and the necessary reorientation of one's entire life organization,
▶ Readjusting the relationship with a partner,
▶ Coping with social losses through the eventual death of a spouse and other life companions,
▶ Transformation of leisure activities,
▶ Addressing the unrelenting "getting older", with its mounting health impairments and limitations of physical performance, as well as dealing with the finite end of life.

Successful and happy aging means strengthening your performance reserves so that longevity, physical and mental health, social aptitudes, personal action control and life satisfaction can be maintained as long as possible. In terms of functional capacity and everyday coping in old age, taking care in early adulthood – better yet in childhood and adolescence – can lay the foundations to counteract physical, psychological and social impairment of everyday life in late adulthood. For all that, this is a case where it truly is "better late than never" since getting active at any age has major benefits for an improved quality of life and rowing is an ideal activity.

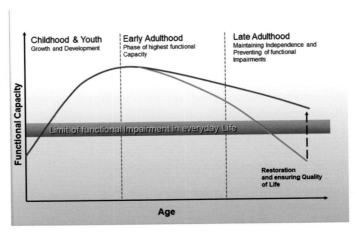

Fig. 3: Functional capacity and coping with everyday life (modified after Conzelmann 2004).

2.2   THE SOC MODEL: OPTIMIZATION THROUGH SELECTION AND COMPENSATION

Successful aging is for Baltes and Baltes (1990) a social structure in which age is not static but modifiable and changeable. Their "Selection, Optimization and Compensation" (SOC) model (see Fig. 4) seeks to constructively disrupt the aging process to compensate for emerging shortcomings and deficiencies and to select specific behaviors to optimize aging. Regardless of chronological or biological age, the following findings, when formulated as principles, appear to be the decisive criteria:

1. Human aging leaves room for modifications (Principle of Variability)
2. Development does not occur in a straight line, but is rather accompanied by inconsistencies (Principle of Discontinuity)
3. Aging is subject to individual, age-normative, social and historical influences (Principle of Contextual Relativity)
4. Humans can simultaneously develop in many different directions (Principle of Multi-Directionality)
5. Humans are malleable and can still change in old age (Principle of Plasticity)

Success in advanced age is measured by different criteria than in younger stages of life. Strategies for successful aging can be for example:

▸ A "healthy" lifestyle: regular activities, healthy diet, regular training, steady practice, moderate alcohol consumption, nicotine abstinence, etc.
▸ Further education
▸ Cultivating social networks, as well as
▸ Maintaining self-reliance and independence

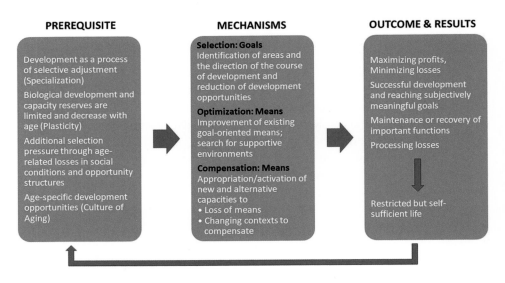

PREREQUISITE	MECHANISMS	OUTCOME & RESULTS
Development as a process of selective adjustment (Specialization) Biological development and capacity reserves are limited and decrease with age (Plasticity) Additional selection pressure through age-related losses in social conditions and opportunity structures Age-specific development opportunities (Culture of Aging)	**Selection: Goals** Identification of areas and the direction of the course of development and reduction of development opportunities **Optimization: Means** Improvement of existing goal-oriented means; search for supportive environments **Compensation: Means** Appropriation/activation of new and alternative capacities to • Loss of means • Changing contexts to compensate	Maximizing profits, Minimizing losses Successful development and reaching subjectively meaningful goals Maintenance or recovery of important functions Processing losses Restricted but self-sufficient life

Fig. 4: The psychological model of successful development: Selection, Optimization and Compensation, following Baltes and Baltes (1990).

Selection

We select opportunities that are ideal for us: We focus on specific areas of life that are of high priority to us and that combine environmental requirements, personal motivation, skills and biological performance capacities.

For example:
Working out, rowing, club involvement

Optimization

We seek resources to do things as well as possible: We strive to improve our selected path in life and try to maintain or maximize existing resources and competencies at the highest level possible:

For example:
Providing professional expertise and experience in club engagement, participation in social club life, developing or expanding training/coaching skills, expanding knowledge in sports, regular health and fitness training

Compensation

We are looking for new ways to get closer to our goals: We adapt as masters rowers to limitations and failures of certain functions as they occur.

For example:
Fewer races, rowing in more stable boats, more crew rowing, combining rowing with other areas like culture, culinary events, reduction of training duration and/or intensity

Although the Baltes and Baltes model does not explicitly focus on movement, sports specific capacities and development reserves, it is clear that the physical demands and experiences that come with rowing are opportunities to optimize an individual's course of life. What's more, rowing can also function as a special compensatory support as adults get older. It is well established that humans are much better off if they:

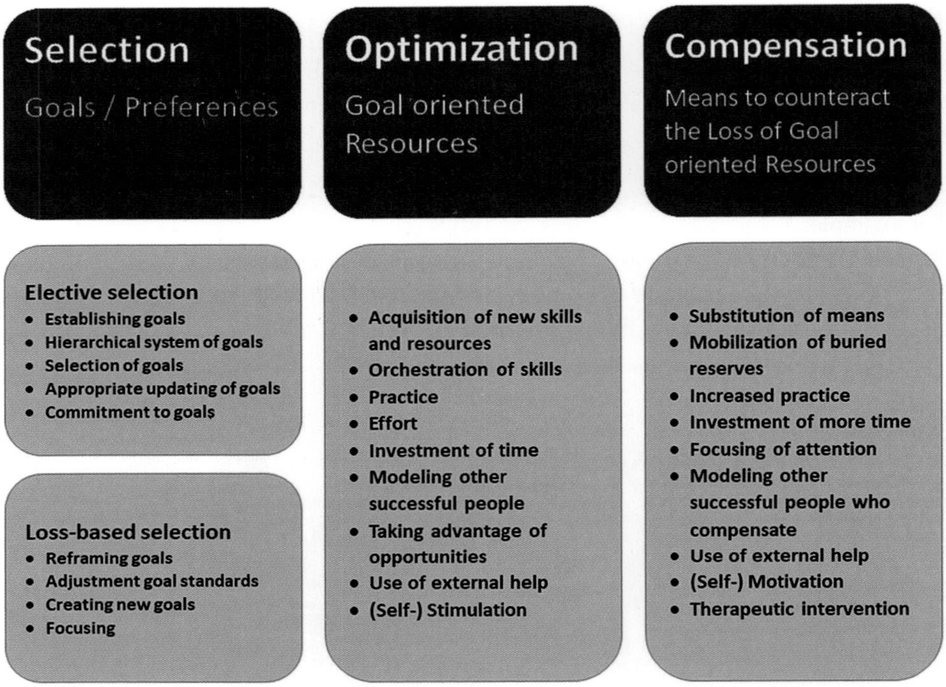

Selection	Optimization	Compensation
Goals / Preferences	Goal oriented Resources	Means to counteract the Loss of Goal oriented Resources

Elective selection
- Establishing goals
- Hierarchical system of goals
- Selection of goals
- Appropriate updating of goals
- Commitment to goals

Loss-based selection
- Reframing goals
- Adjustment goal standards
- Creating new goals
- Focusing

- Acquisition of new skills and resources
- Orchestration of skills
- Practice
- Effort
- Investment of time
- Modeling other successful people
- Taking advantage of opportunities
- Use of external help
- (Self-) Stimulation

- Substitution of means
- Mobilization of buried reserves
- Increased practice
- Investment of more time
- Focusing of attention
- Modeling other successful people who compensate
- Use of external help
- (Self-) Motivation
- Therapeutic intervention

Fig. 5: Model of selective optimization and compensation (after Baltes & Baltes, 1990).

- ▶ select, optimize and compensate,
- ▶ focus on areas where expansion is possible,
- ▶ accept losses,
- ▶ take advantage of losses,
- ▶ limit themselves to a few goals, but pursue them enthusiastically, and
- ▶ search for suitable compensation options.

Selection, optimization and compensation are key factors in taking-up and maintaining physical activity. In particular, rowing can be a great help through its rich diversity and its variety of objectives. Important goals can still be achieved in the course of life despite the loss of abilities, for example physical performance (see tab. 7).

Tab. 7: Strategies for physical activities

	Goal-Relevant Resources Exist	Goal-Relevant Resources Are Lost
Goal Setting	**Elective Selection:** Developing, drafting and selecting personal goals	**Loss-based Selection:** Rebalancing your own goals or creating new goals
	"In terms of my physical activities, I've defined my goals clearly and stuck to them".	"If a time comes when I cannot be as physically active as I used to be, I was just thinking about what other physical activities I can do instead".
Goal Tracking	**Optimization:** Acquisition and use of resources to achieve the desired results	**Compensation:** Acquisition and use of resources to maintain a once-achieved level in the face of a loss of resources
	"I have made every effort to realize my plans to be physically active".	"When I could not be as physically active as before, I have increased my efforts to continue to be active".

Developmental tasks of middle-aged adults in the social domain can be:

▶   Taking on social responsibilities
▶   Establishing and maintaining an economic standard of living
▶   Helping young children grow into responsible and happy adults
▶   Taking up age-appropriate leisure activities
▶   Shaping the relationship with a partner as an individual
▶   Accepting of and adapting to the physiological changes of mid life
▶   Learning how to deal with aging parents

Even with a decline in physical strength and mental reserves, successful aging remains oriented toward certain life missions. The retention of skills or learning of new activities, such as competitive rowing, remains possible at a relatively high level in old age despite "increasing biological vulnerability". Yet this is only possible through the process of selection and compensation such as, for example, limiting exercise duration or lowering training intensities. Development should never be taken only to mean the attainment of gains through purely positive changes in certain abilities, but rather always as specialization, which goes hand-in-hand with the loss of certain possibilities. Capacity and development reserves become increasingly narrowly limited in old age. Successful aging is only possible if the three adaptation features, namely Selection, Optimization, Compensation are being fully utilized (see Baltes and Baltes, 1990).

2.3 SPORT ACTIVITIES IN OLDER AGE

2.3.1 Age-Related Changes in Sport Activities

The topic "Sport in older age" currently generates great scientific interest, which Conzelmann (2004) attributes to the following reasons:

1. The demographic development, with the disproportionate increase of older people in our society
2. The problems of physical inactivity or sedentary lifestyle
3. Social changes, such as:
    ▶ The relationship between work and free time,
    ▶ The increasing differentiation of sport,
    ▶ Sport as a leisure activity and
    ▶ The transition of the image of age.

As for the fitness status of older people, the gap between those who exercise and those who do not is increasingly widening. On the one hand we encounter a rising number of active, energetic older people, who regularly engage in sports activities; on the other hand, there is an increasing number of older adults, who are frail and/or overweight due to lack of exercise. The following questions are of the upmost interest:

How do sports activities affect...

1. Life expectancy?
2. Physical fitness in old age?
3. Psychological well-being in old age?

Health, physical fitness and well-being are desirable for every adult looking to survive and thrive into very old age and are understood as important criteria for "successful aging". Boeck-Behrens and Buskies describe adequate mental and physical stress – the good sort of stress provided by exercise – as the best "fountain of youth" (2002, p. 282) and adults and older persons should consequently have an interest in exposure to it. Comparisons between trained and untrained people show that with trained individuals we find:

▸ A significantly higher maximum oxygen uptake,
▸ Differences in performance continuously increasing with age, and
▸ A significantly lower drop in performance.

A similar situation is found in the distribution of the "lumbar back pain" syndrome: Untrained people suffer more often from back complications and the number of untrained people with back pain increases significantly with advancing age compared to those who are trained.

Roughly speaking, age-related decline in performance is reported from about the age of 30 on, although individual organ systems are affected differently. Longitudinal studies looking at groups representing the general population show a decline in performance after 30 of about 5% per decade of life. From the age of 65-70 years, however, the decline is even larger.

In addition to the decrease in muscle mass, reported to be about 1-2% per year from the age of 50 on, one can observe a loss of contractile properties of aging muscles. Individual muscle fiber cross-sections shrink and in particular fast-twitch muscle fibers (type II) deteriorate. The consequence: Reduction of the ability to exert physical power, but also a loss of coordination (Dickhuth et al., 2007, p. 606).

Due to age, the nerve transmission velocity also decreases. As a result, the cognitive functions such spatial and temporal orientation become restricted. In addition, motor skills become less precise, slower and "less smooth". Above all, coordination and speed are affected.

These changes also manifest as a decline of aerobic capacity, a decrease of muscle strength, as well as considerable limitations in mobility, dexterity and coordination. All this accumulates to a loss of physiological functions that come along with age, which are associated with a lower ability to adapt to training stimuli and increasing the need for longer recovery after purposeful physical activity. While age had been the traditional culprit, researchers are increasingly divided on how much of the decline in motor skills is in fact age-related – and thus cannot be influenced – and how much is attributed to inactivity and lifestyle. It could well be that the lack of available time due to work and family life, changes in lifestyle, psychological strain, or decreasing motivation to be physically active are in fact the real causes of the above stated decline in performance, rather than immutable age-related physiological changes.

Independent of the presented discussion, one can clearly detect that performance sport in old age experiences an enormous boost in popularity both qualitatively and quantitatively. The emergence of a mosaic of lifestyles and a growing focus on personal body image have contributed greatly to this development. Yet the motivation to become active goes beyond a narrow focus on competition. Seeking better health, general improvements in physical endurance and fitness, experiencing nature and, especially in rowing, meaningful social interactions are all important motivations for sports participation.

It is only by recognizing these resource enhancing features of sport that one can explain its increased attraction to people without prior engagement in physical activities and the large number of late entries of older persons into sport. This is particularly true in rowing. The improved health and increased life expectancy that comes with an active life style thus allows a greater number of people to be active more often. Because of this development, more people are therefore able to benefit from overall increased mobility, better health and the ability to enjoy an independent life style for longer.

In a Swiss study on sport in older adults, Lamprecht and Stamm (2001) found a significant reduction in sport activities after the age of 60. When they looked at participation numbers in purely competitive sport, the decrease was already evident from an age of 40 years. If one uses a broad definition of sport and includes more diverse forms of movement, such as yoga, fitness classes and aerobics, it becomes obvious that women are significantly more active than men. By contrast, one finds that males are involved to a greater degree in more effort and achievement oriented activities that would be defined as 'sport' in the more traditional sense.

The two Swiss authors report that people progressively enjoy spending more time in their private homes with increasing age. This kind of retreat is however less prevalent for people participating in outdoor sports within team sports, also seeming to counter this sort of preventable isolation.

Health is by far the most important motive for older people to participate in sport, followed by physical experience, attitude towards life, social contacts, expression of emotions and adventure, which could include competitions. In most situations, however, performance goals and above all the desire to benchmark lose their influence as motivations for participation in sport as a person ages.

Studies that look at the availability of free time per day and the subjective assessment of one's personal health show that most people could easily engage in a sporting activity. Lamprecht and Stamm (2001) cite the role of other life priorities along with exaggerated perceptions of what is required to undertake sports as causes for people's sedentariness. Inactive people often perceive sport as a time-consuming and overly strenuous activity.

Is sport a universal remedy for successful aging? Numerous factors for subjective feelings of well-being in old age can certainly be positively influenced by sport, even though sport in and of itself does not have such an overarching effect (Conzelmann, 2004):

▶ Sport is not a "one size fits all" solution: Specific effects are only possible through selective interventions.
▶ There is no universal "older person". People vary because of
   1. Different genetics, environmental conditions, life experiences and biographies,
   2. A variety of pathological influences interfere with "normal" aging.

It was argued in older publications that people over the age of 70 cannot achieve any significant training effects through physical activity. Meanwhile, new research shows that physical activity and sport can, regardless of age, influence health and physical performance in a positive way thus confirming the assumption of life-long plasticity.

Raeburn (2009, p. 17) states that elderly people who participated in endurance sports and team sports in their youth are at lower risk of high blood pressure, but emphasizes that ongoing activities have a more protective effect than previous ones. This means that people must not only count on activities that they did earlier in their lives. It is much more important to continue to stay active. Interestingly, these findings do not apply to the same extent equally to power sports.

We can now contrast the 'negative' cycle of aging and the decline of certain body functions described above at the beginning of the chapter with a positive cycle. Thus, physical activity is the basis to maintain performance on a high level so that you can age successfully.

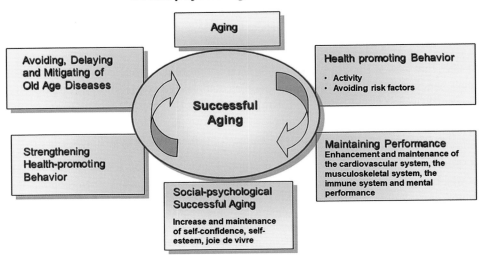

Fig. 6: The positive cycle of chances in the face of aging
(mod. After Boeckh-Behrens and Buskies 2002, P. 310).

In summary:

▶   Sports activities can improve physical fitness at any age and thus have a positive effect on the gain-loss balance.

▶   Life-long athletes are most likely to succeed in using the SOC model because of their multifaceted sport experiences.

▶   Movement, performance and health represent only a few of motivations to engage in physical activity. Others, such as self-awareness, conviviality, etc., should also be considered for sport in old age (Conzelmann, 2004).

2.3.2   Sport Performance at Older Age

Through proper training, high levels of physical performance can be maintained longer than previously thought. Moreover, maximum performances can be maintained or achieved far longer in life through correspondingly high training efforts. For the vast majority of people, however, whose training must be rooted in realistic commitments of time and energy, a steady loss of performance must be expected (as later described in

Tab. 10. Longitudinal analyses show that on average the human performance curve peaks at the end of the third decade of life and then steadily decreases with increasing age. The FISA Masters Classification would therefore seem to be justified, beginning with the first age category A at the age of 27 years.

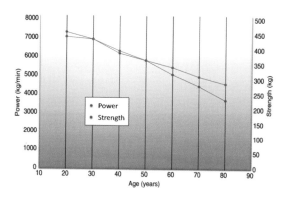

Fig. 7: Longitudinal data of strength and power of men depending on their age (from: Journals of Gerontology, Series A, Biological Sciences and Medical Sciences by E.J. Metter, cited by Spiriduso et al., 2005).

Longitudinal analyses, however, whether they look at power, strength or endurance are tracking the change of the average performance of a large population; they cannot capture the time-dependent development of a single athlete or the theoretical maximal potential for human performance. The third decade of life is usually when people undergo considerable lifestyle transformations due to significant changes in personal and professional conditions. For most people, performance losses are influenced by these circumstances, which all but erase the availability of the large volume of time previously used for quality training. Other priorities beyond sport take center stage for the vast majority of people.

The diminishing performance capabilities of people after the age of 30 shown in longitudinal studies need most often be attributed to disuse or underutilisation of body organisms and is not necessarily a consequence of getting older.

The overall world best times for 2,000 m on the rowing ergometer reflect this phenomenon to some extent. These records are achieved by very dedicated individuals who train diligently over long periods of their lives. Since these exceptional results do not represent the "average" person, they do not influence the results of longitudinal studies. Interestingly, the data for these world's fastest individuals show that the absolute record times are achieved by athletes in the age categories 20-29 and 30-39 years. After that point, the best times in each age category begin to slow down, gradually at first and then more sharply after the age of 55 (see Fig. 8).

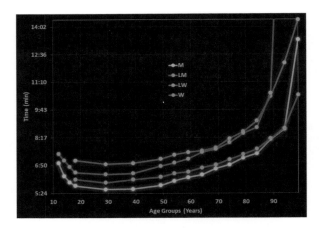

Fig. 8: Illustration of the record times for 2,000 m
ergometer rowing for all ages (accessed on May 9, 2019 from:
https://www.concept2.com/indoor-rowers/racing/records/world/2000).

Is it possible to achieve training and learning effects in old age and in untrained persons?

It seems almost intuitive that consistent training throughout one's life is a good thing. If an athlete were to maintain their training throughout their life, even with an age-related decline of physical performance comparable to non-active athletes (about 5% in each decade of life), their performance would still remain at a significantly higher level in old age. This means that a person who continues to engage in physical activity remains better equipped to handle all day to day tasks of living that become more difficult in the final decades of life.

Increased sport and other physical activities are associated with longevity and well-preserved functioning into very old age. It can be demonstrated that regular exercise leads to functional improvements even in old age (see Conzelmann, 1997). The necessity of sports related activities in old age is generally confirmed by many studies, although their exact impact varies from person to person and is dependent on "genotype, age, the respective ability, level of performance, and gender" (Tittlbach, 2002, p. 82).

The decrease of athletic performance can also be influenced by the body's gradual loss of sensory abilities such as "hearing" and "seeing", as well as temperature and thirst sensation. The factors that impact a person's proprioception are the same as those affecting their performance through a loss of sensation and fine-tuning (Dickhuth et al., 2007, p. 607).

Endurance performance in old age

The human capacity for endurance decreases in the second half of life. The following changes and related impact are seen as the main causes of physical and athletic performance losses with regard to the cardio-pulmonary system:

Tab. 8: Causes of decline in endurance capabilities

Changes	Impact
Reduction of vascular elasticity	▸ Increase of blood pressure ▸ Slowing of the circulatory reflexes ▸ Increase in work for the heart ▸ Lower maximum heart rate
Reduction of lung elasticity	Pulmonary functions show increasing limitations
Reduction of blood flow in the peripheral musculature	▸ Loss of metabolic capacity ▸ Decrease in maximum oxygen transport capacity
	In general: **Decrease in endurance capacity**

While there is only a slight decrease in aerobic endurance capacity for an untrained middle aged adult, this erosion of endurance speeds up from about the age of 45 years. Gender also seems to play a role. Tittlbach (2002) notes regarding the differences between women and men, that men have a relatively higher endurance capacity through to their fifties; after that point, women experience slower rates of decline so that ability levels eventually equal out. This author also notes an approximately 10% decrease per decade of life between the ages of approximately 30/35 and 60/65 years (2002, p. 53).

Even low levels of training intensities are enough for the relatively untrained to improve their aerobic capacity well into old age. A 30-90 min endurance session 1-3 times a week is sufficient for performance gains. While one finds a loss of maximum oxygen uptake in middle and late adulthood, this decrease has been much less in men with well-trained endurance (5% per decade) compared to a 9-10% decline in untrained men (Tittlbach, 2002, p. 54).

In general, aerobic endurance can be trained throughout life and it appears that equivalent endurance training leads to comparable adaptations at any age (Tittlbach, 2002, p. 54): In a study that compared training adaptations in 24- and 65-year-old men and women no differences were found in the development of absolute maximum oxygen uptake after challenging endurance training. These findings support other studies already showing that women and men of any age react positively to endurance training.

Endurance training effectively counteracts the aging processes of the cardiovascular system, indicating that aerobic activities should be used preferentially over anaerobic activities as one ages. In addition, the proportion of localized and static endurance exercises should be reduced, all in favor of more general, aerobic dynamic endurance training, such as rowing. For older athletes, these general principles are not only performance and health enhancing, but also reduce the risk of injury.

Regular and systematic endurance training can lead to the following positive effects, even in old age:

▸ Automatic transformation and economization of the heart's work
▸ Reduction of heart rate during rest and exercise with simultaneously higher stroke volume under given load
▸ Increase of the cardiac output
▸ Maintaining elasticity of the ribcage
▸ Increase in respiratory minute volume, spare capacity and vital capacity
▸ More effective oxygenation of skeletal muscles
▸ Lower stress hormone release with reduction of sympathetic stimulus
▸ Improving the flow properties of blood
▸ Reduced risk of thrombosis
▸ Positive effect on fat metabolism

In order to benefit most from the positive effects, attention must always be paid to the appropriate intensity; the vast majority of activities should be long and slow with moderate tension and a focus on relaxation. Endurance-oriented health training contributes to maintaining and improving physical performance. Due to the manifold adaptations of the organism, adequate endurance training helps to maintain and increase quality of life especially in older people. Likewise, endurance training can counteract the biological aging processes and increase life expectancy.

Overall, endurance training improves physical performance and with it the ability to cope with the day-to-day demands of life in old age. This results in improved quality of life, significantly slowing down the onset of aging.

Here too, rowing seems an ideal fit for health and fitness, especially given the ease of controlling just how much force to apply and the cyclically used muscles – these are all important features of any health focused physical activity.

Rowing is an excellent way to improve and maintain general aerobic endurance at all ages. The maximum heart rate decreases almost linearly with increasing age. Fig. 9 shows heart rates during maximal and submaximal (at 2 mmol/l lactate) loads as a function of age as described by Grabow (1995), based on 6 or 4 min all-out rowing ergometer tests for masters.

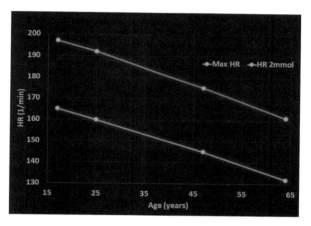

Fig. 9: Heart rate during rowing at two different intensities (Max HR = maximum heart rate and HR 2mmol = heart rate at 2 mmol/l lactate threshold) as a function of age (Grabow in Fritsch, 1995, p. 221).

Health focused endurance training for masters should be performed primarily at intensities that build up to a maximum of 2 mmol/l lactate in blood. Long training sessions, like a pleasure tour over several hours, should be done at even lower intensities.

Since most masters athletes will not have the chance to get training feedback based on lactate production, sport scientists provide easier to use measures that everyone can apply. Hartmann et al. (1997, p. 130) presented a simple method to assess extensive endurance training load for older rowers through heart rate (HRext). They suggest the following rule of thumb:

$$HRext = 170 - (0.8 * age)$$

Another simple method uses maximum heart as a starting point to control and design general aerobic endurance exercises. An athlete's training heart rate is derived at an approximate range of 65-80% of their maximum heart rate (Oschütz & Belinová, 2003, p. 164, Tab. 15). Once a rower knows their maximum heart rate (HRmax) during rowing, achieved for example during competition, the authors propose to use the formula specifically for rowing:

$$\text{HRext-rowing} = \text{HRmax} * 0.75$$

Hartmann et al. (1997) presented the following heart rate values as guidelines for the different age ranges as average values for extensive, aerobic rowing loads. Please note that these numbers represent average values and individual values will of course vary:

Average HRext	for 30-year-olds	approx. 145 beats / min
	for 40-year-olds	approx. 140 beats / min
	for 50-year-olds	approx. 130 beats / min
	for 60-year-olds	approx. 120 beats / min
	for 70-year-olds	approx. 115 beats / min

To cover all possible intensity ranges for endurance training, we propose the following based on percentage (%) of maximum heart rate (HRmax):

Target	Intensity Range based on % of HRmax
Recovery	<60-65% of HRmax
Aerobic training	65 - 75% of HRmax
Extensive endurance training	70 - 80% of HRmax
Intensive endurance training	80 - 85% of HRmax
Maximum aerobic endurance	85> 90% of HRmax
Speed Endurance	Not applicable

It is important to note that only healthy athletes with regular medical checks should undertake training. The numbers indicated here, like any calculation of heart rate ranges, are only guidelines; the most accurate assessments of training heart rates are achieved through specific tests by trained medical personnel.

Strength abilities in old age

Preserving and promoting strength in old age is just as important as a focus on endurance. Studies show that maximum strength decreases only marginally by about 4-5% per decade up to the age of 45. Strength loss, however, speeds up between the ages of 45 to 80 to about 12-15% per decade (see Tittlbach, 2002, p. 62). Similarly, to endurance loss, decreases in strength abilities start earlier in women, but then slow down in comparison to men, reaching the same numbers for both genders in late adulthood. All told, there is an overall decline in strength of about 30-40% from the onset of adulthood through to old age (see Tittlbach, 2002, pp. 57-62).

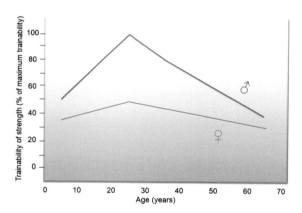

Fig. 10: Trainability of strength as a percentage of maximum trainability (mod. after Hettinger in Weineck, 2000).

The ability to train strength differs significantly in the various age ranges: women and men can best improve their strength abilities between the ages of 20 and 30 years. Higher levels of testosterone give men a greater ability to train strength over the entire lifetime (see Fig. 10).

When it comes to different types of strength, the overall decline in strength endurance of about 50-75% from the age of 25 to old age far outweighs the decline in maximum strength and explosive strength (about 20-30%).

A significant loss of strength is associated with a decrease in muscle mass due to the loss of muscle fibers, which become thinner in old age, as well as from a reduction of the cross section of the overall muscle. Muscle fibre thinning is mainly attributed to the reduction of stimuli and a potentially reduced ability to recruit motor units (see Oschütz & Belinová, 2003). In addition, there is an age related decrease in the amount of available ATP, creatine phosphate, and glycogen, all essential stores of energy for strength deployment. A drop in testosterone levels in old age is also believed to contribute to loss of strength, as this sex hormone has a protein-building effect.

Decreases in strength can lead to a weakening of the trunk musculature that may result in poor posture and back problems. For the most part, the loss of muscle strength comes down to a lack of training. This effect not only reduces a person's ability to perform everyday life actions, such as climbing stairs, lifting objects or certain leisure activities, it also leads to a general reduction in quality of life and general capacity for action. Strength training and especially strength endurance training prevents age-related muscle atrophy and orthopedic symptoms significantly.

For rowers, strength endurance should receive the largest share of time devoted to strength promotion due to its great affinity to endurance training. This applies to general training sessions outside of rowing, as well as specific rowing training sessions. Transferring this realization into masters rowing, it raises the question: What is effective and efficient for the older athlete, where large muscle groups, especially the trunk, leg and hip muscles should already be sufficiently developed?

There is a strong correlation in rowing between the strength that an athlete can exert repeatedly during the drive and boat speed. Rowing requires a persevering, fatigue-resistant use of strength in the cyclical course of its movement. This rowing-specific strength endurance is determined by the qualitative and quantitative demands placed on specific parts of muscle groups and their coordinated use. Strength endurance plays a decisive role not only in masters racing, but also in health- and fitness-oriented training, since functional posture and joint stability need to be maintained by muscles even under longer or repeated mechanical strains.

Strength training offers a range of possible variations:
1. Variations in the selection of exercises
2. Order of exercises
3. Number of repetitions without rest (which is then called: set)
4. Specific number of repetitions for one muscle group
5. Load/Resistance
6. Speed of motion
7. Intensity, usually expressed as % of one maximum repetition (1 RM)
8. Speed at which one set is performed
9. Rest between sets
10. Training frequency - number of weight training sessions per week

Coordinative skills in old age

The rowing movement is a highly coordinated skill requiring technical proficiency to effectively manage boat and oars in diverse environmental conditions. Specifically, rowers must possess and execute the skills of balance, rhythm, sequencing and synchronisation of body movements and be able to differentiate all feedback (Schmidt, 2003).

Ability to balance

Balance in rowing is finding a stable equilibrium in the boat, so that no rolling of the boat occurs which leads to the elimination of additional forces that cause resistance. Examples of such additional resistance include: rocking the boat or touching the water with the rowing blades during the recovery.

Ability to use rhythm

Rhythm in rowing is expressed through the harmony of all movements. During the stroke cycle, rhythm is the consistently optimal alternation between tension and relaxation even as intensity and stroke rate rise and fall.

Ability to sequence and synchronise body movements

The coordination of movements of all body parts comes down to motor skill. In rowing, an example is the spatial, temporal and dynamic sequencing of leg, trunk and arm work.

Ability to differentiate all feedback

Differentiating the available feedback is what rowers often call "feeling". "Boat, water and blade feeling" is fine tuning the movements of all individual parts and of all phases of the rowing motion. This is responsible for optimizing the use of all efforts to propel the rowing system, energy preservation, consistency or - when needed - changes in force application and slide movement.

Ability to adaptation and transition

Adaptability and the capacity to transition from one rowing situation to another is essential in order to respond appropriately to diverse situations such as the specific demands rowing in changing crew combinations, different boat classes, changing wind and current conditions, as well as to the tactical manoeuvers of competitors.

As with the physiological abilities, there is also an age-related decline in coordinative abilities. Children and adolescents improve their quality of coordination as more demands are put upon them. Although trainability of coordination remains as one grows older, the ability of the physical systems to learn new coordinative tasks and athletic techniques slowly decreases with age (see Table 9).

Yet, due to a complex structure, these processes are not completely understood. What we know is that coordinative abilities begin a gradual age-related decline between the ages of 35 and 40. The decline intensifies from the age of 45 and really accelerates from the age of 60/65 (Tittlbach, 2002, p. 70). These declines differ in various sub-categories of coordination. For example, coordinative performances under time pressure with a high demand on energy output decrease more than coordinative performances of precision movements that demand fine motor skills (Tittlbach, 2002, p. 70).

Tittlbach (2002) and Oschütz and Belinová (2003) identify the following factors as the primary cause of these declines in coordination performance:

▸ Age-related neuronal changes
▸ Aging processes of all organs and tissues
▸ Inactivity
▸ Poor flexibility
▸ Faster fatigue of the central nervous system

Tab. 9: Development of the coordinative performance over a lifetime
(mod. after Roth and Winter, 1994).

Development of coordinative performance over a lifetime	
Stage of Development	**Coordinative Abilities**
Childhood to about pubescence	Largely linear performance **increase**
Pubescence to adolescence	Interference, **slowing of increases,** instability and readjustment
End of adolescence until the beginning of early adulthood	**Further improvements,** individual manifestations
Third to fourth decade of life	Training-dependent **preservation** or relative conservation
Fourth, fifth and sixth decade until death	Gradual and finally irreversible **involution**

Beyond specific coordination training, any other form of physical activity can significantly slow down the age-related decline in coordinative abilities. Even older, untrained individuals between the ages of 60-82 years showed significant improvements in neuromuscular function including balance, hand-arm coordination and response time after five months of gymnastics, swimming and dance training (Puggaard et al., 1994, p. 47). This demonstrates that whether focusing on general coordination or taking an interdisciplinary approach to training, either one presents an effective, cost-efficient and safe method of prevention of decline in older adults.

It is important to realize that an activity focused just on one sport, such as rowing, presents a relatively one-sided coordinative stimulus, even though the rowing movement, like swimming, dancing and cross-country skiing, demands relatively high coordinative abilities.

Well-developed coordinative abilities support the development and economization of physiological abilities. They also help the body to sustain movements and training loads of longer durations, allowing for fast and appropriate reactions thus reducing the risk of injury.

The development and training of general and rowing-specific coordinative abilities is a fundamental and indispensable part of all learn-to-row and training programs. While developing coordinative abilities leads to better rowing – and better living – the opposite is also true, that the sport of rowing is particularly suitable for advancing coordinative skills in middle and late adulthood.

Agility in old age

The concept of agility includes elasticity as well as flexibility, so that muscles, tendons, ligaments, joint capsules and joints need to be included in this discussion. Agility is dependent on anatomical, neurophysiological, energetic and psychological factors, which is why it cannot be clearly labelled as entirely physiological or coordinative.

Chemical and structural changes in the aging body lead to a decrease in the elasticity of tendons, ligaments, fascia and most especially of musculature. The support structures of the body are affected by degenerative changes to the joints, damage to the cartilage (arthrosis) and reduction of friction-reducing synovial fluid, the result of which can be quite painful.

Hollmann and Liesen (1986, p. 344) speak of significant degradation of flexibility in healthy persons from 45-55 years on, while more recent studies note a decline in agility from as early as 25 – 30 years on with reductions of 3-5% per decade (see Tittlbach, 2002, p. 75). Thus agility is the motor capacity in humans that starts declining the earliest, although an individual's gender and the elasticity of their tendons and ligaments seems to play a role. Higher estrogen levels and their resultant higher fat content as well as lower tissue density due to higher water content in the musculature, bestows women with a better lifelong agility than men.

Nevertheless, it seems that agility is also trainable well into old age. Yet the importance of this ability must not only be seen in the context of sport. Reduced agility can lead to significant restrictions in general mobility and a subsequent reduction of quality of life. Additionally, along with overall strength, agility plays an important preventative role against imbalances caused by shortened or insufficiently strengthened muscles. Maintaining and improving agility promotes general well-being and can contribute to overall body awareness. Agility and agility training are often underestimated in training for rowing at all ages, not only masters.

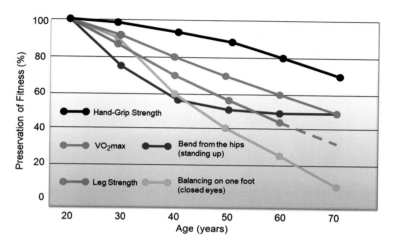

Fig. 11: Age-related change of selected parameters of physical performance (Modified after Kuroda, 1989).

While signs of aging can be seen in all motor skills, they occur in varying degrees (see Fig. 11). For example, strength and endurance abilities show relatively low changes both internally and in comparison to other motor skills, yet the changes seen in coordinative performance are significant. All age-related decreases, especially when it comes to motor skills, are only worsened by inactivity.

It remains to be noted:

All motor skills can be trained all life long and can always be positively influenced by appropriate sports activities.

2.3.3   The Contribution of Rowing to Successful Aging

Rowing as both a sport and lifestyle provides everything needed for successful aging with regard to physiological-functional, psychological and social matters all combined in a single activity. Regardless of a person's phase of life or goals for participation in the sport, rowing in its broad context beneficially mobilizes and optimally utilizes individual spare capacities (see Table 10). Rowing is as much of a method of successful aging as it is a goal. Far from being a problem for successful aging, masters rowing is instead a life-long solution.

2.3.4 Rowing Performance at Old Age

Recent decades have seen a rise in the number of rowers reaching Olympic finals and even medaling beyond their 35th or even their 40th birthday. Examples of these once rare, but increasingly "normal" accomplishments are as mentioned before rowers like Hansen, Chalupa, Redgrave, Cop, Jaanson, Lipa, Neykova, Carstens and many more. This means that these athletes show that highest performances can be maintained much longer than previously believed.

Tab. 10: Rowing during adulthood – Spare reserves in masters rowing
at different life phases.

Sport Goal	Early Adulthood	Mid/Late Adulthood	Late Adulthood
Compensation/ Well-being	▶ 1-3 x rowing per week ▶ Pleasure rowing ▶ Supplementary training	▶ 1-3 x rowing per week ▶ Pleasure rowing ▶ Rowing and culture ▶ Supplementary training ▶ Active vacation ▶ Club involvement	▶ 1-2 x rowing per week ▶ Pleasure rowing ▶ Rowing and culture ▶ Supplementary training ▶ Active vacation ▶ Club involvement
Fitness/Health	▶ 2-4 x rowing per week ▶ Different sports ▶ Supplementary training ▶ Improve rowing technique (skiff, racing shells, etc.) ▶ Sports- /Ski-camps	▶ 2-4 x rowing per week ▶ Strength and Supplementary training ▶ Improve in other sports ▶ Improve rowing technique (skiff, racing shells, etc.) ▶ Sports-/Ski-camps ▶ Club involvement ▶ Coach/Learn-to-row instructor	▶ 2-3 x rowing per week ▶ Strength and Supplementary training ▶ Other sports ▶ Improve rowing technique ▶ Sports-/Ski-camps ▶ Club involvement ▶ Coach/Learn-to-row instructor
Performance/ Competition	▶ 3-6 x training / week ▶ Rowing racing ▶ Ergometer competitions ▶ Supplementary/ Additional training ▶ Training camps, Active holidays ▶ Sports-/Ski-camp ▶ Coach	▶ 3-5 x training per week ▶ Rowing racing ▶ Ergometer competitions ▶ Crew rowing, Technique ▶ Supplementary/ Additional training ▶ Training camps, Active vacation ▶ Sports-/Ski-camp ▶ Coach/Learn-to-row instructor	▶ 2-5 x training per week ▶ Less racing ▶ Ergometer competitions ▶ Crew rowing, Technique ▶ Supplementary/ Additional training ▶ Active vacation, Sports-/Ski-camps ▶ Club involvement ▶ Coach/Learn-to-row instructor

Rowing ergometer performances of masters

Indoor rowing offers near lab-like conditions for analyzing the cardiovascular and muscular systems of participants. From 1990-94, Seiler, Spiriduso and Martin (1998) collected national and international indoor rowing competition results from rowers in 29 countries. Using these results, from 2,487 men between the ages of 24-93 and 1,615 women between the ages of 24 and 85, the researchers developed a relative rank for performances based on age and gender.

The study was designed to capture the time differences in the then standard 2,500 m race distance between women and men, as well as the age-related changes in rowing performance. The peak performance for men was achieved in the age group 24-29 years and for women in the age-group 30-39 years. The results also showed that among the rowers observed, men between the ages of 40-60 were able to maintain their performance quite well and relatively better than women. In this age group, men were on average only 11% slower than the fastest male rowers while the women in the same age group were about 20% slower than the fastest female rowers.

The ergometer manufacturer Concept2 that produces the standard equipment for international indoor rowing training and racing maintains an up to date list of all World Records achieved on their machines for all kinds of distances, weight classes, age groups and abilities. The most popular record distance nowadays used is 2,000 m. The record numbers are very informative and we can use them to see trends in the performance of athletes of all ages. The Concept2 listings use their own age categories. The first two age categories that we are interested in are 10 years long, while from 50+ years on, age categories change every five years. With the vast amount of data available thanks to several decades of new results, some differences from the findings of the older study above have become apparent.

First, the fastest absolute times for 2,000 m regardless of gender and weight category are now held by athletes in the 19-29 years age group (see Fig. 8). Absolute times relative to the 2,000 m World Records for each age category show distinct differences between women and men in the open category (see Fig 12a). The difference between the absolute record times and the records achieved in the next older group of 30-39 old athletes is at first for women and men virtually the same (2.8 sec slower for women and 2.9 sec slower for men). From then on, however, the women's times are in average 17 seconds slower relative to the men's best time differences in the later age categories. The difference is in relative measures for men in the age category of 55-59 years 9.9% slower than the fastest absolute men's time, while women are 11.0% slower than the top women's result. This is a distinct shift from the data 30 years ago which means that women seem to be catching up to men in maintaining their rowing performance; like their male counterparts, women are staying faster longer.

In fact, if you calculate the decline in race times from age group to age group as percentages of the best time in the preceding age group, you can see that all rowers' categories slow down at a fairly consistent rate (see Fig. 12b). There are, of course, small variations in the different age groups, but these balance out over the years. It is interesting to see that up to the age of 69 years, race times for all categories slow down on average by 2.4% every 5 years. Race times then slow down from age 69 – 84 years by 5.4% followed by considerably higher loss in performance after that age.

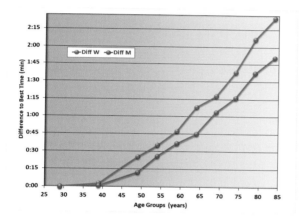

Figure 12:

a.) Absolute differences of 2 km rowing ergometer world record times in the open weight category from women (W) and men (M) of different age groups to the absolute best records.

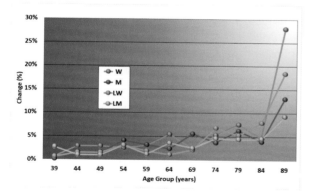

b.) Percentage slowdown in 2 km ergometer race times from age group to age group. Attention: Since data was only recorded for a 10-year increase in the age group of 39 – 49 years, the 5-year change was calculated by dividing this increase in half (LW – lightweight women; LM – lightweight men).

We need to remember that aging is only one of several conditions that influence the decline in performance. Besides aging, other factors such as physical conditions, endurance capacity, training habits and competitiveness play influential roles. The best times for LW for example only slow down on average by 1.8% every five years between the ages of 35 – 69. We then see a more pronounced slowing down of 6.7% every five years between the ages of 70 – 84 years. Studies of other endurance sports, such as running and cycling, reinforce these findings.

Age alone is a modest indicator of rowing performance in the heterogeneous population. Other factors, such as body size, training duration and technique, create greater variability. With age, much seems to be possible through diligent training, regular rowing and participation in additional sports. Regardless of the potential for physiological growth and maintaining performance, rowing's particular focus on coordination is important in old age. This applies especially for late or lateral entry rowers, who are equally represented in competitive racing as well as in rowing for fitness and health.

Longitudinal study of Olympic rowers

Hagerman et al. (1996) examined nine rowing silver medalists from the 1972 Olympic Games over a 20-year period. Subjects were tested in 1972, 10 years later in 1982 and again 10 years later in 1992. Physical parameters such as height, weight, etc. were recorded at each assessment. Activity levels were defined for each individual participant, based on the number of training sessions per week and competitions per year.

Strength and cardiorespiratory and metabolic stress were recorded during a 6 min full-out test to simulate the 2,000 m on-water race duration. In 1972, a mechanically braked Lyon rowing ergometer was used. In subsequent assessments in 1982 and 1992, testing was conducted on Concept2 Indoor Rower models A and B respectively. Power (W), lung function/ventilation (VE), oxygen uptake (VO2) and heart rate (HR) were recorded.

The study found that rowers' weight increased in the years 1972 to 1992 from an average of 87.4 kg to 93.8 kg ($p < 0.05$). Body fat mass increased significantly ($p < 0.01$) from 12.3% to 15.6%. The levels of activity following the 1972 Olympic Games were quite different among the subjects. Training before 1972 was naturally very high for all subjects in duration and intensity. There was a dramatic change in training habits for all study participants, especially in the first ten years after the Olympic Games. Training frequency was reduced from an average of seven training sessions per week in 1972 to 3.6 training sessions per week in 1982, and then in 1992 to 3.1 sessions per week.

A significant decrease in the lactate tolerance was also detected. While the athletes in 1972 were able to tolerate an average of 14.4 mmol/l, only 7 mmol/l could be reached in

1992 tests. The measured lactate concentration in the blood decreased by 25% between 1972 and 1982 and again by 64% between 1982 and 1992.

It became clear that the physical factors that are important for aerobic performance decreased with age as subjects got older. While this decline can be slowed by regular endurance training, most subjects performed regular endurance training in the post-Olympic years and still experienced a significant decline in fitness. It was noticeable that for these elite Olympic rowers, the level of fitness decreased significantly every 10 years, while their average body fat mass increased. Body fat mass increased rapidly in the first decade after the Olympics, while anaerobic capacity declined significantly only in the second decade. From this study alone, however, no conclusions can be drawn on the aging processes of the general population. The Olympic rowers were at a very high level in terms of physical performance during their high-performance phase, and it seems reasonable to see that training volumes and intensities were dramatically reduced after the rowers reached their peak performance. As a result, performance also decreased.

Masters rowers in comparison

Yoshiga (2007) compared selected body characteristics (body fat content, fat-free body mass) and cardiorespiratory variables (VO2max, oxygen pulse, lactate, maximum heart rate, maximum respiratory minute volume) between older and younger rowers, as well as similar persons of the general non-rowing population of equivalent size and weight.

Tab. 11: Selected body characteristics of masters rowers in comparison to other populations (mod. after Yoshiga, 2007, p. 116).

Characteristics	Masters rowers	Older "normal" persons	Young rowers	Younger "normal" persons
Age (years)	64 ± 4	65 ± 3	22 ± 2	23 ± 2
Body Fat (%)	18 ± 4	23 ± 4	12 ± 4	17 ± 4
Fat-free Body Mass (kg)	56 ± 5	53 ± 5	61 ± 4	57 ± 5
VO2max (l/min)	3.0 ± 0.4	2.2 ± 0.3	4.2 ± 0.3	3.1 ± 0.5
VO2 at 4 mmol/l Lactate (l/min)	2.6 ± 0.3	1.8 ± 0.3	3.7 ± 0.4	2.7 ± 0.5

(continued)

(Tab. 11, continued)

Max. Heart Rate (1/min)	176 ± 13	166 ± 9	198 ± 8	201 ± 9
Heart Rate at 4 mmol/l Lactate (1/min)	163 ± 12	157 ± 11	177 ± 12	177 ± 11
Maximum O2 Pulse (ml/beat)	17.2 ± 2.3	13.5 ± 2.0	21.6 ± 1.8	15.4 ± 2.5
O2 Pulse at 4 mmol/l Lactate (ml/beat)	17.0 ± 0.9	11.5 ± 0.9	20.7 ± 1.0	15.0 ± 1.1
VEmax (l/min)	117 ± 17	74 ± 13	162 ± 18	84 ± 17
Lactate at maximum Load (mmol/l)	8.3 ± 1.0	7.9 ± 1.1	10.9 ± 1.1	10.0 ± 1.2
Rowing Performance 2,000 m Concept2 (min)	8:09 ± 0:16		7:11 ± 0:12	

In terms of body-related characteristics (body fat and lean body mass), it is notable that masters rowers reach measures comparable to that of younger individuals who did not row. Although body fat content generally increases with age, fat-free body mass decreases at the same time due to loss in muscle mass. Masters rowers, however, succeed in maintaining or attaining many performance characteristics of younger non-rowing individuals (see Tab 11).

The same applies to aerobic capacity: Here, too, the measures of VO2max and VO2 at 4 mmol/l lactate that the older rowers reach correspond to the levels found in the younger persons. The oxygen pulse and the respiratory minute volume of masters rowers are even higher than the average measures of untrained younger persons. Only in two measure do masters rowers not match or outpace younger non-rowers: maximum heart rates and lactate at maximum load values.

A comparison of older competitive rowers, younger competitive rowers and highly accomplished younger competitive rowers shows that masters rowers are comparable with junior rowers in body-related characteristics and cardiorespiratory variables (Yoshiga 2007). Compared to highly accomplished, well-trained rowers, however, larger differences become obvious (see Tab. 12).

Tab. 12: Competitive masters rowers in comparison with younger and highly
accomplished younger rowers (mod. After Yoshiga 2007, p. 117).

Feature	Competitive masters rowers	Younger competitive rowers	Younger highly competitive rowers
Age (years)	62 ± 2	21 ± 1	22 ± 1
Height (m)	1.74 ± 0.04	1.72 ± 0.04	1.81 ± 0.04
Body Mass (kg)	72 ± 5	71 ± 6	80 ± 8
Body Fat (%)	17 ± 3	17 ± 4	11 ± 2
Fat-free Body Mass (kg)	60 ± 5	59 ± 4	71 ± 5
VO2max (l/min)	3.3 ± 0.4	3.1 ± 0.3	5.1 ± 0.4
VO2 at 4 mmol/l Lactate (l/min)	2.5 ± 0.4	2.5 ± 0.4	4.4 ± 0.4
Max Heart Rate (1/min)	176 ± 5	188 ± 7	189 ± 7
Heart Rate at 4 mmol/l Lactate (1/min)	149 ± 11	165 ± 12	175 ± 8
Maximum O_2 Pulse (ml/beat)	19.5 ± 2.1	17.6 ± 1.8	26.9 ± 2.2
O_2 Pulse at 4 mmol/l Lactate (ml/beat)	16.8 ± 0.9	15.6 ± 1.1	25.1 ± 1.0
VE_{max} (l/min)	121 ± 15	126 ± 13	178 ± 10
Lactate at maximum Load (mmol/l)	8.4 ± 1.0	9.8 ± 1.6	10.3 ± 1.8
Rowing Performance 2,000 m Concept2 Ergometer (min)	8:15 ± 0:14	8:14 ± 0:13	6:27 ± 0:07

According to Yoshiga's research, the performance of masters rowers over 2,000 m on the rowing ergometer correlates very strongly with lean body mass, maximum oxygen uptake, maximum respiratory minute volume and leg extension strength (see Fig. 13).

Not only high performance rowing, but even basic, regular rowing training for older adults provides a high preventive effect on health. Rowing at any level helps to keep essential, body-related characteristics, such as body fat content, fat-free body mass and cardiorespiratory parameters, in good condition. The use of large muscle groups achieves both cardiorespiratory, as well as muscular training effects. And by the way: Rowing has a low injury rate!

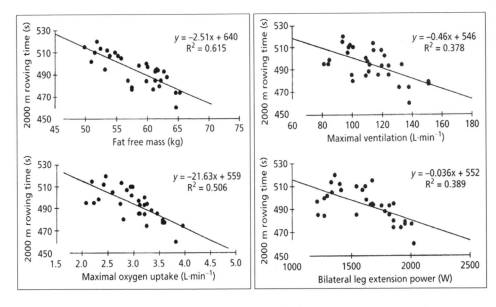

Fig. 13: Ratio between 2,000 m rowing performance and fat-free mass, VO2max, maximum respiratory minute volume and leg extension strength in masters rowers (mod. after Yoshiga 2007, p. 122).

Chapter 3

LEARNING TO ROW

3.1   HOW ADULTS AND OLDER PEOPLE LEARN TO ROW

The growing involvement of interested, ambitious adult rowing beginners presents both opportunities and challenges for clubs. We know that learning to row requires expert guidance. This places higher demands on a club's resources in terms of organization, equipment, as well as personnel, but also requires competence and expertise to teach rowing in an engaging way.

Older people generally possess the same components and processes of motion regulation as younger people when they learn rowing. The big differences come down to life experience, possible time in other sports and individual goals.

It is important that we distinguish between three broad types of learners when it comes to adult rowers 1) those beginners experiencing rowing for the first time; 2) those currently rowing who seek to acquire better rowing technique; and 3) those relearning the

movement after many years – maybe even decades – away from the sport. Although the latter group can draw on some previous experiences with the sport, they usually still have to learn rowing anew, as some physical and coordinative conditions may have changed. This is different from the second group of masters rowers who hope to correct technical "mistakes" to improve their ability to compete or to participate in health training whether in a crew or individually.

Improving skill in rowing – or at least maintaining it – is a goal shared even by former high performance rowers, who often come to masters rowing with decades of experience. For rowers at any level, technique can change due to short-term performance fluctuations and "fitness crises", which can have a negative effect on a crew's coordination. Gradual disease or age-related changes and some degradation processes such as diminishing mobility or coordinative losses are difficult to avoid. In a sense, all masters rowers are in a literal race against time to compensate for these processes through the conservational learning of skills.

Acquiring good rowing technique starts with the first stages of a learn-to-row program. A good instructor can help with this process, but should always make clear to beginners that they are responsible for their own rowing skill development.

Motor learning is harder for older people than for adolescents and young adults, especially when cognitive processes between visual input and the body's motor response to mediation are needed. Individual differences and age-related changes like weight gain, increasing lower mobility or lack of strength, while they don't prevent learning new skills, can often limit physical performance in old age. This needs to be taken into consideration by both learners and instructors.

Learning prerequisites differ greatly between adult rowing beginners and must therefore be considered in choosing the proper learning methods:

1. Do the adult novice rowers have experience in learning other sports and skills?
2. Which learning prerequisites (e.g. general coordination ability, physique, etc.) do the novice rowers have?
3. Are the cognitive and psychological prerequisites given? How can novices receive new information? Do they have the necessary patience and stamina for the new seating position?
4. How ambitious and motivated are the beginners to learn rowing?
5. Are external conditions considered, like the adequate type of boat (racing shell vs. touring boat), boat class (single vs. crew boat), rigging, available water conditions, and crewmates with different body sizes?

Lifelong learning abilities include motor adaptation processes like strength and endurance. In general, older adults that exercise regularly have a similar learning performance to younger adults during tasks as long as they have no time pressure, no high power or no speed requirements (see Brach and Schott, 2003, p. 465). These elements of performance must therefore be carefully evaluated before including them in the learning process.

"Old adults learn at the same rate and in the same amounts, they just perform slower, with less accuracy, and more variability" (Spiriduso, 1997, p. 107).

Although introducing the correct rowing motion is the primary goal when working with beginners, effective adult learning is more than just providing a sufficiently good enough rowing skill. The following are broader goals for any adult learn-to-row programs that focuses on the possibilities and contributions that rowing provides for successful aging:

1. To help learners experience the fascination and diversity of our sport.
2. To learn fundamental rowing skills which ensure the safety of both athletes and equipment when rowing, the execution of the rowing movement by the individual, as well as the coordinated teamwork of rowing together in a crew.
3. To convey the knowledge of rowing operations, equipment handling and boathouse skills, including training and health related skills.
4. To develop a feeling for the rowing movement and the boat, as a prerequisite for the expansion of rowing skills and independent growth.

The specific approach to teaching a beginner must be adapted to the individual's learning conditions and any external circumstances, paying close attention to the club setting and water situation. The intention of this learning process must not only be to succeed as quickly as possible, but to make rowing lessons an unforgettable fun experience and adventure.

▸ Can high level rowing skills be maintained in old age?
▸ Which strategies can be used to compensate for the degradation processes of rowing skills?
▸ How should practice be designed, which teaching method should be used, and what are the constraints?

Learning to row requires committed practice and active engagement with the rowing movement both cognitively as well as physically. It is also helpful to provide mechanical and motor context for the adult learner to recognize "why" and "how" footstretcher settings, positioning of the slides, rigging of boat and oars connect and contribute to the rowing movement. These mechanical settings do not guarantee good rowing technique, but they help to develop a feeling for the movement and the boat. Overall, the learning process, the optimization of the rowing motion, the effectiveness and economization of the rowing technique, the interaction in the crew, as well as the feeling of an efficient rhythm seem very complex actions and need adequate time.

The motor coordination ability and learning processes are for the most part self-organized functions of our body. Learning in this context means that the learners themselves must actively experience and discover the general rules that underlay the specific tasks, the

persons involved and the surrounding environment. The search and discovery process can be based in between the continuum of blind trial-and-error learning and targeted strategies (see Wiemeyer 2003, p. 417).

Beginners first seek stable solutions, which initially limits their movement alternatives. With increasing certainty, they are looking for further free expression of movement. It shows in this training process clearly, what is not feasible for the learner and where progress is possible through practice. It is undisputed that learning and improving technique can be achieved more easily and more effectively when athletes are fitter.

Learning is usually influenced by previous experiences. If they hamper the formation of new patterns of coordination, these must be overcome through disruption (Wiemeyer, 2003, p. 417). Balance exercises in the boat are a good example of this in rowing since they do not belong to the previous movement experiences of adult beginners.

Many outstanding coaches and rowers never stop thinking about how to work on optimizing their rowing technique so that individual and crew performance improvements can be achieved.

3.2   METHODOLOGICAL NOTES

How can the learning and training process in rowing be fostered among adult and older beginners based on the described objectives?

3.2.1   Equipment Requirements and Teaching Organization

Coaches and instructors have first and foremost to prepare their training sessions in a way, that safety for the rowers and boats is guaranteed. They need to know the local water conditions and observe weather forecasts to make sure that they can run lessons in a safe way. Specific club safety rules need to be followed and in case of any uncertainties, one should always err on the side of safety. Nevertheless, it is the task of the instructor to teach the adult and older rowers to understand the safety precautions well enough that the rowers can be included in the decision making processes to run the training sessions safely.

All beginners need to be educated in making sure they are prepared to learn rowing safely. Athletes must be able to swim and should have a health clearance from their family doctor to ensure they can participate in all rowing activities. Any health or mobility restrictions need to be declared to the instructor, so that they can adapt the training session if possible.

In our opinion, it makes no difference whether someone starts with sweep rowing or sculling. One finds arguments and best practices for both. However, it would be ideal – and this is what we recommend – to offer both kinds of rowing at the beginner stage to expose the learners to the entire range of rowing movements.

Generally, beginners in North-America take their first rowing strokes in either quads or eights racing shells or in wider, more stable single scull boats. In Europe, gigs or C-boats are used, but the learning steps are very similar. The new trend of coastal boats may provide another set of relatively stable rowing boats that can be used in learn-to-row programs. For most rowing clubs, the ultimate situation would be to have beginners learn rowing in a racing singles, but this can only be done in ideal circumstances: very small instructor to athletes ratio, instructors in motorboats, availability of suitable and well rigged single sculls and safe, clean and warm water conditions.

One instructor per beginner boat is an ideal starting point. On water with low-traffic and no current, it is conceivable that one instructor with a motorboat might take care of two to a maximum of three boats. If the situation allows that the instructor accompanies the beginner boats in their own single, it has the advantage that they can use their own rowing to demonstrate and explain the proper movements to the beginners. If coxed boats are used for the learn-to-row sessions, it is advisable to have the instructor in the coxswain seat.

If beginners learn rowing in singles, they need to get their first instruction at the dock where they try handling the scull that is in the water with very light movements before they putter around in the immediate vicinity of the dock. It is important to keep in mind that this process requires a certain "agility" as well as courage from the beginner. Make sure that the width of the single – and with this, its stability – is appropriate for the learner's situation.

It is absolutely essential to ensure that the boats are optimally rigged for the appropriate target group. A boat with the oarlock height that is proper for 10- to 12-year-old students, will not be suitable for 40-year-old men. This also applies to the span, the footstretcher setting and the oar, as well as the inboard length.

Some features are important to be remembered for teaching older adult athletes:

1. Clearly defined and appropriate reference targets need to be presented,
2. Practice times need to be planned to last longer and
3. All athletes need to be kept excited and motivated so that they stay with the program.

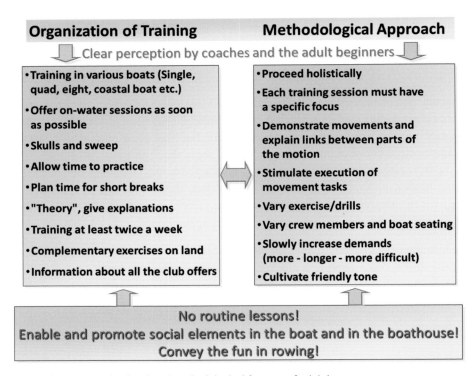

Fig. 14: Organizational and methodological features of adult learn-to-row programs.

It must be a stated goal of the learn-to-row program for adult athletes that they will be guided to become independent from instructors who must strive to make themselves "redundant" as training progresses.

The group composition, the individual performances of the learners and their personal interests determine the contents of each practice.

A movement's or activity's relevance, rather than exact execution of prescribed movement patterns, should be the main goal of the learning process. For example, it is more important to teach that the blades need to be completely squared before placed in the water, instead of an exact timing when the squaring occurs during the recovery. Additionally, the technique required to row forward in a straight line is not the only thing to learn as a beginner. All necessary skills to move a boat safely to a designated point of destination need to be taught, like boat maneuvers (i.e. turning or backwards rowing) or handling of all possible situations that may occur (i.e. emergency stopping, steering with the oars, rowing in rough water conditions).

Holistic approach

Rowing should be taught in an accurate and reliable way. The overall movement is far more than the sequential linking of part movements. Especially in rowing, movements only obtain their specific character in the complex interaction of individual components, whereby the definite and specific task is retained in its core. Of course, the rowing stroke can be "segmented", which means that its parts can be practiced in isolation and then layered together step by step. However, this method should mainly be used by advanced rowers and to learn fine skills.

For example, the entry or the release can be practiced in isolation to further perfect an already learned movement or to optimize it for race-specific purposes. This method is less important in the learn-to-row environment. Research has shown that novices had more long-term success learning rowing in eights when rowing exclusively full strokes and with all rowers at once compared to their peers that were using part strokes and part crew (McLaughlin, 2004).

Overall, make sure that the character of a "smooth" rowing motion is maintained in the learning process.

Variable practice (tasks and situations)

Experiences should be offered in as many different ways and areas as possible in order to destabilize early coordination patterns and install new ones. It makes perfect sense to switch tasks to avoid too much repetition of the same practice before moving on to the next exercise variant. For example, a change can be made by practicing a turn followed by balance exercises and then the next time doing a turn followed by backward rowing.

Practicing in random order

It makes sense to do the exercises in random order rather than in a block order, which could possibly lead to a delay in the motor learning process. Such a delay could ingrain movement patterns that may work well in specific situations, but lack the flexibility of context needed to adjust when anything changes. Therefore, exercises of various elements should be mixed like boat maneuvers such as backwards rowing, pausing with blades off the water and turning. They do not even always have to build upon each other.

Instructions

If specific experiences in the learners are lacking, the most suitable instructions are those that promote a search and discovery process like metaphors, information about expected principles, learning aids and visual landmarks. A stern rigger can serve as a visual orientation mark for the catch and a metaphor can facilitate the perception of movement, for example "execute the release as if your hands follow the outside of a small ball".

Exercises should be selected and offered in a way that learners can execute them immediately and with ease.

Also, be aware that there are individual preferences with regards to how information is best received. Depending on the individual, either visual, auditory or tactile information show best results in the learning process. This means that some athletes react best when they see what they should do. This could be done through pictures, graphs, videos or demonstrations of the rowing movement. Other athletes prefer to hear what they should learn, which can be presented by descriptions of the movement or explanations of the biomechanics of rowing. Other athletes need to experience how it feels when a movement is performed in a specific way. Finally, some rowers learn best, if they get a mixture of visual, auditory or tactile information. Instructors need to find out which learning style suits their beginners best and then act accordingly. This reflection bears a lot of opportunities, since it opens a vast variety of teaching ideas that can be used successfully.

Leave the learner with ample time to practice and to experiment!

The ultimate goal of a learn-to-row program is not to learn in record time, but to provide a joyful, motivating experience. This, by the way, applies to adults as well as youngsters.

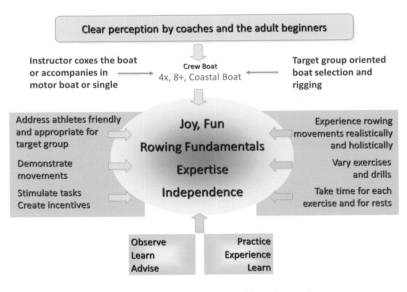

Fig. 15: Organization and methodic of learning rowing.

Familiarize yourself with the equipment and its treatment

Before the beginner steps into a boat, we recommend a tour through the club boathouse. The stored equipment there can be used to explain vividly the different types of oars and boats, as well as the various boat classes. Also, it is easy to put a boat in stretchers, so that the design features, as well as the function and use of individual parts, such as sliding seats, footstretchers, riggers, oarlocks and of course oars and sculls, can be illustrated. It is also interesting to mention the changes that boat design and equipment development have undergone in the modern sport of rowing's nearly 200-year history.

Further information should refer to the proper transport of the oars and boats to the dock or water. Oars need to be brought to the dock first before the boat and should be carried with the blades in front of the athletes, so that they can see them and avoid bumping them into any obstacle. Also, to avoid risk of damage or injury, each rower should be reasonable about how many pairs of sculls oars they carry (i.e. instructors should adapt the rule that only a maximum of two oars are to be carried). They need to be placed on or close to the dock in a way that they are out of risk of being damaged.

Since the rowers are at the dock and in the process of bringing the oars to the water, they need to plan which part of the dock will be used later on to put the boat in the water. The size of the boat has to be taken into consideration, and, if possible, the boat will need to get in the water on the lee side of the dock (facing away from the wind). Having made this decision, the rowers now get back to the boathouse to carry the boat.

It is advisable to store the beginner boats at an appropriate height in the boathouse so that they can be reached easily. An eight at the highest rack, for example, endangers the boat below when novices try to lift it onto their shoulders.

To carry the boat, rowers of about the same height should face each other on opposite sides of the boat and spread out along the boat. Each club has developed its own best transport options for the boats dependent on the terrain around their boathouse. Some clubs can step straight out to the docks that are on the same level as the boathouse, whereas other clubs have to walk down a hill or stairs to get to the docks. The experienced instructor knows about these specific situations and assigns the rowers according to the best place on the boat to carry it. Of course, this has to be taken into account.

You first carry the boat in your hands out of the boat bay and then lift it up on to your shoulders to carry it to the dock. Rowers walk the boat alongside the dock close to the side where the boat will be placed in the water. The boat then needs to be lowered to waist-height and turned to the floating position, with the inside of the boat now facing up. The rowers hold on to the boat at features that allow a solid grip like the gunwale, rigger or cross bars. Rowers on the water side of the boat walk around to the other side of the boat between the other rowers and get a solid hold of the boat. The rowers step close to the edge of the dock before lowering the boat into the water. Keeping the fin and rudder away from the dock is very important in this process and the instructor should help with this by holding and controlling the boat near the fin until the beginners are experienced enough to do this safely on their own.

Two people (could be two rowers or the coxswain and the instructor, for example) need to be assigned to hold the boat securely next to the dock while the other rowers fetch the oars. The boat needs to be held in a position close to the dock without getting in contact with the dock. This applies for the next steps of the process, too, until the boats floats freely on the water.

Before putting the oars in the oarlock, beginners need to distinguish port and starboard oars which is normally done by a piece of colored tape (red for port which becomes the scull for the right hand or the oar on the right side of the rower when sitting in the boat; green for starboard). Sometimes the first letter P or S is imprinted on the oar sleeve. Also, rowers have to realize that the oarlock needs to point towards the stern of the boat to work properly.

The instructor demonstrates the placing of the sculls or oars into the oarlocks, pointing out to place port and starboard oars on the correct side of the boat with the oarlocks turned towards the stern of the boat. Oars are inserted into the oarlock at the narrowest point of the shaft close to the blade and then gently pushed into the oarlock until the collar touches the inside of the oarlock. The gate of the oarlock then has to be screwed tightly to secure the oar.

Oars facing the water are placed across the gunwales until the rowers get into the boat.

The next step in the learning process is how the novices **get into the boat** and **set their footstretchers** correctly. When boarding, it is important to remember that you only step on the parts of the boat designed for this. There is a specific stepping place between the two slides to carry the weight of the rower. While holding both of the scull handles or the sweep oar with the water-side hand, the water-side foot steps onto the stepping place. Be sure to keep the sliding seat on the bow side of this stepping foot so that the rower can sit down easily. The other hand steadies the rower by holding on to the rigger or the gunwale. It has proven to be useful for the beginners to step into the boat one after the other while the instructor on the dock holds onto the boat.

The setting of the footstretchers is best done when the boat is pushed off the dock and floats freely on the water. With the oar handles tightly wedged between the trunk and thighs of the rower's bent legs, the rowers now loosen the footstretcher fasteners (either wing nuts or levers). The footstretcher can be adjusted longitudinally (to the bow or stern) according to the length of the rowers' legs. The following are good measures for setting the footstretcher: When the rower sits in the release position, the end of the scull's handles should just brush the tummy in sculling boats, while the end of the inboard of a sweep oar should just reach as far as to the outer side of the rower's trunk. For this procedure, also refer to Fig. 37 and respective explanations.

Tab. 13: Component 1 – Familiarizing yourself with the equipment and its handling

Sub Goals	Technical Terms	Notes and Corrections
Information: Basic types of boats and rowing; appropriate rowing gear	Costal rowing boats, pleasure boats, racing boats, sculls, sweep oars, oarlocks, riggers, sliding seats, stepping place, slides, footstretcher	Rowing clothes? Storage of boats
Oars (Sculls and sweep oars, port and starboard), fins, rudders	Blade, shaft, sleeve, collar, handle, rudder, steering cables, tiller bar	Storage of oars
Handling of equipment, carrying boats	Bow, stern, gunwale, riggers	Boat care, positioning of rowers while carryingw
Putting boats in the water and taking them out	Keel, fin, rudder, edge of the dock	Pay attention to fin and keep the boat off of the dock. Know which part of the dock to use.
Placing the oars in the oarlocks	Port, starboard, oarlock, gate	Are oars on the correct side of the boat? Oarlocks in the correct position? Blade on the dock turned with convex curvature up? Gate properly fastened?
Getting in and out of the boat	Stepping place	Oar(s) held properly? Oarlocks closed? Seat position? Only step on to proper parts of the boat.
Adjusting each rowers' work place	Inboard, footstretcher, footstretcher screws	Footstretcher screws fastened? Check the correct setting in the finish position (see Fig. 37).

Rowing Commands

1. Hands on the boat – lift!
2. Up on the shoulders – ready – up!
3. Ready to walk – walk!
4. Let it run! Or: Way enough! (This command is also used to stop the rowing motion).
5. Down to the waist – ready – down!
6. Roll the boat towards the water (the boathouse or similar) – ready – roll!
7. Get ready to get into the boat – get in!
8. Push off the dock – ready – push!
9. Count down when ready, starting from bow!
10. Get ready to get out of the boat – get out!

Observation Tasks:

▶ How do the experienced rowers carry their boats out of the bay to the dock?
▶ How do they place their boats in the water?
▶ How and with what commands do they use to step into the boat and push off?

Reminder for correctly putting the oars in the oarlock:

▶ Red = Oar for the right hand = Port; Green = Left-hand side of the boat = Starboard
▶ Oarlock/Gate screw points towards the stern of the boat

Check in to board the boat:

▶ Oarlock – Scull – Sliding Seat – Footstretcher (OSSF)

Finding the balance

The boat is now on the water and the rowers are in the basic or safety position. This is when the rowers sit in the boat with their legs straight, oar handles and hand above the thighs with the blades turned flat on the water so that its concave curvature points to the sky. Rowers generally return to the basic or safety position whenever they finish an exercise or in any case of uncertainty or confusion. Having blades flat on the water is also an ideal place to begin balance exercises. These will let the beginner experience how tippy a rowing boat is while gradually gaining a sense of security. For example, if the rowers hold their oars in the safety position, the instructing coxswain can try to tip the boat by shifting their weight side to side, first carefully, then more vigorously – unsuccessfully of course. The rowers can actually stabilize the boat in a balanced position by holding the oar handles at a uniform height. On the other hand, they can also push all handles down to the gunwale and rock the boat from side to side.

Learning how up and down handle movements influence that balance of the boat is essential before moving on to more advanced exercises. Keeping blades flat on the water, rowers can rock the boat to starboard by lifting the port handles and then to port by lifting the starboard handles.

Tab. 14: Component 2 – Securing the balance

Sub Goals	Technical Terms	Notes and Corrections
Basic or safety position	Handles, inboards, blades	Are the blades flat on the water (concave side up)? Position of the inboards over the thighs; are hands/handles at same height?
Balance and rocking exercises	Gunwale, blades	Are oarlocks closed? Are the blades flat on the water? Is the boat outside any shipping/traffic route of other boats?
Feel the position of the blade	Squared and feathered blade position	Are finger and hand position correct?
Rowing forward and backward with one hand/side only and alternating	Squared blade, catch/finish position, entry, release	Position of the blade in the water, hand position, fingers? Path of hands? Rowing hand moves above the resting hand in sculling.

Forward rowing

Try the following exercise first, with one rower and one oar alone, then add more rowers/oars. Straighten the arms out! The next step is to square the blade, place it into the water and pull the handle easily towards the body. This way one can feel the correct blade position in the water or the right path of the blade in the water. When sculling with both hands, there is an overlap of the hands during the middle part of the drive and recovery. To avoid bumping hands, moving the left hand above the right hand with the hands slightly staggered so that the right hand is closer to the body. After practicing the stroke with one oar only and just with the arms, it is time to include the trunk and legs in the movement. It is important that the instructor pays attention to the beginner using the correct hand position or grip on the oar. Beginners tend to adjust their hand position after feathering the blade, which leads to an incorrect grip of the handle when the blade is squared for the next stroke. The proper grip is achieved when the blade is squared and only the fingers hold the handle, the palms of the hands do not touch it. This means that the wrist remains flat; the back of the hand and top of the forearm form a line.

Fig. 16 shows some examples of proper grip during the drive. It all starts in the recovery, when the hands should be as relaxed as possible without losing control and the handles are held only with the finger tips. This leads to a hand position during the drive with straight arms and flat wrists. The handle of sweep an oar is held a little tighter with the inside hand (hand closest to the oarlock) that also turns the oar to feather and square while the outside hand is held extremely loose.

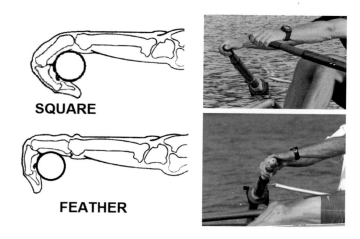

SQUARE

FEATHER

Fig. 16: Proper grip on the rowing handle.

These first exercises are designed to give the beginner some experience moving the blade through the stroke and generate a perception of the movement that can be repeated. All these exercises can be done individually, then in pairs and very soon with the whole team.

It is advisable at the beginning of the learning process to have the blades dragging lightly on the water during the recovery. This gives a relatively stable position of the boat and enables the rower to feel the hand heights and control the balance of the boat.

While for example the single gives immediate feedback of how well the blade is squared and feathered, this is not necessarily the case in a larger boat with more rowers involved. Therefore, a lot of importance must be placed on the correct grip. The forearms tend to tighten up easily and the wrists bend. Therefore, cues, small breaks and going back to the initial exercise rowing with one hand on the square can be very helpful.

At this stage of the learning process, it is important to teach steering the boat with the oars. The beginners need to experience what happens when the oars on one side of the boat pull with more effort. They should then realize that they can do this to influence the direction of travel. This skill along with the other component 2 exercises means the rowers can now head for a destination.

This component of exercises also includes the ability to decelerate the moving boat relatively quickly, i.e. stopping by lightly squaring the blades from a safety position and then pushing the handles upwards at the same time. This manoeuver is done on one or both sides of the boat. Start with stopping the boat lightly before trying to stop more vigorously.

Tab. 15: Component 3 – Forward rowing

Sub Goals	Technical Terms	Notes and Corrections
Turning the blades: Squaring and feathering	Squaring and feathering of the oars; entry and release	Hand position
Rowing with constantly lengthening the slide	Finish, catch, drive, stroke, slide	Tightening the core, posture? Hand positioning, grip, hand path, blade work, using the slide, length of slide
Small changes of travel direction by pulling more on one side	Pulling more on port or starboard	Exaggerated movements? Entry, stroke length
Stopping, slowing down	Stopping, braking	Position of the blade, sensitive/metered braking
Rowing towards a fixed target	Keeping course	

Rowing Commands

1. Sit ready – Attention – Go!
2. Harder on port (or: starboard)!
3. Let it run! or Way enough!
4. Blades down on the water!
5. Kill (or check) the run!
6. Stop – stop!

Tasks

▶ Regarding the grip: Close your eyes and square and feather the blades several times. Are grip and blade position still correct?
▶ In the single: Head for a specific destination! When is it best to turn around? How do you orient yourself on the water?
▶ Row a large circle by pulling only on port then starboard. This is called a "360".
▶ At the command of the coxswain/instructor: Stop the boat! In the crew boat: Do this alone, in pairs, etc. and then all together.

The next step is to perform the most important boat maneuvers. Based on the previous experiences, the first of these should be **rowing backwards**, which, similar to forward rowing, is introduced by constantly lengthening the stroke. In doing so, the stroke starts at the finish position and the handles are pushed away from the body towards the catch. The blade should be in a reversed orientation with the concave curvature pointing to the stern of the boat. Coxswains have to hold the rudder in the neutral position! Otherwise, the rudder could be damaged by the water pressure acting on it, from the wrong side, so to speak.

Forward and backward rowing form the basis of a turn, which can now - depending on the comprehension and learning ability of the rowers - be introduced in different variants and sub-steps. The oars on one side of the boat need to be rowed forward while the other side are rowed backwards. This can be done alternating or together, without and with slide. However, it is advisable to make this a fun exercise: take the time for smaller forms of play and even competition for this learning step.

The next step is the independent **pushing off and getting back to the dock** without the help of the instructor. At first, the instructor steers the boat and grabs the oars on the dock-side of the boat and pushes or pulls them while standing on the dock. It then becomes the task of the learners to try and find different ways to push off the dock and get back to it that are appropriate to their abilities. These maneuvers need to be explained and repeated frequently to give the beginners a chance to learn them properly.

Tasks

▸   Row backwards towards different targets.
▸   Turn the boat by rowing three strokes forward on port (starboard), then three strokes on starboard (port) backwards, then two strokes each, finally one stroke at a time!
▸   How many strokes are needed for turning the boat 180 or 360 degrees?
▸   Try out different ways to push off and land back at the dock.
▸   Build an obstacle course (e.g. push off the dock, forward rowing for 100 m, stop, backward rowing for 30 m, turn to port, forward rowing for 30 m, stop, turning to starboard, rowing a figure eight-shaped course, getting back to the dock) and repeat it several times.

Tab. 16: Component 4 – Boat maneuvers

Sub Goals	Technical Terms	Notes and Corrections
Backward rowing with both sides while continuously increasing stroke length	Squaring, feathering, push from the finish	Blade position, grip, hand path
Turning to port and starboard	Turn	Uniform speed for the forward and backward movement
Pushing off and getting back to the dock	Wind, waves, current	Proper approach angle, stopped too early / too late? Conditions not observed?

Rowing Commands

1. Everyone backwards – Ready? – Go!
2. Turn to port (starboard) – Ready? – Go!
3. Let it run! Lean to starboard (port) and blades up on port (starboard) – up!

Coping with situations

Anticipation and practice are essential to handling all sorts of situations in rowing. In general, rowers gain a greater degree of security through regular preparation and rehearsal. Exercises such as balancing the boat with the blades off of the water ("flying"), stopping the boat, taking the hands off the handles or standing up in the boat improve rowers' abilities in various water conditions. For a club with a dock, good preparation might also include pushing off and landing with the boat on the shore (beaching), without using a dock. This task should be done for the first time guided by the instructor. Beaching is necessary at certain regattas or for day trips and pleasure tours that start or end away from a boathouse as well as in emergency situations.

The handling of specific situations also includes navigating through narrow stretches of water, where the oars must be turned parallel to the boat or the blades pulled in towards the oarlock, reacting to ship waves (in general, rowing boats are turned parallel to the oncoming waves and rowers take the safety position), switching seats on the water, as well as landing along different types of shore lines.

Tasks

▶ Standing up in the boat.
▶ Switching seats in the boat.
▶ Turning the oars parallel to the boat.
▶ Pulling in the blades towards the oarlock.
▶ Lying down in the boat.
▶ Passing a narrow spot (through a bridge, a row of buoys).
▶ Getting out and re-entering the boat at a beach.

Tab. 17: Component 5 – Managing situations

Sub Goals	Technical Terms	Notes and Corrections
Advanced balance exercises	Clean rowing (blades off the water during recovery), "Flying"	Release motion correctly done? Speed sufficient?
Rowing in waves	Big hand circles at the end of the release, clean release, boat parallel to oncoming, large waves (e.g. from motorboats)	Safety position? Secure distance to the ship/ boat that generates the waves, as well as to the shore? Boat parallel to the waves?
Change of seats in the boat	Boat shoulders, gunwales, stepping place	Safety position, only step on secure parts of the boat and not into the boat
Passing Narrows	Oars alongside (parallel to) the boat, pulling oars in	Sufficient speed/momentum? Holding on to the handles
Re-entry into a single after capsizing	Port, starboard	While in the water, grab both handles with one hand and push into the boat! Push upper body across the boat and then swing legs around to sit in the middle of the boat.

Rowing Commands

1. Big circles!
2. Oars – long!
3. Oars – in!

Steering, Commanding a crew

Every beginner should take the opportunity to lead a crew as a **coxswain**. In addition to steering (directing the course of the boat; keeping or changing its direction), they must use **rowing commands** to ensure **crew and boat safety**. Learn-to-row novices in particular can benefit from the experience of **heading** towards a particular target while considering various influences (wind, waves, current, size and load of the boat, rudder design, etc.). They quickly become aware of the necessity and **function of the rowing commands**.

The coxswain need to heard by all crew members and, therefore, need to raise their voices or use amplifying equipment, especially in eights. Calling loudly and using electronic equipment must be practiced, and the coxswain has to check with the rower farthest away that this rower can hear the commands.

Although coxed boats (fours and eights) are the norm in most club operations, 'coxless' crews should also know the steering rules. This applies to boat types, where steering is done by pulling more with one of the sculls (singles, doubles), and shells equipped with foot controls that attach to the rudder operated by one rower (coxless pair and four, and quad).

Steering with the rudder generates centrifugal forces on the rowers so that the boat rolls in the opposite direction in which the boat is turning. A coxswain should therefore announce any changes in course direction so that the rowers can adapt their balance. Changing travel direction and steering should be planned ahead by the coxswain, and longer turns are preferable to sharp, abrupt ones. If possible, sudden steering maneuvers should be avoided.

The following steering rules are definite:

1. A change of direction by a rudder is only possible if the boat is faster than the surrounding water.
2. Steering always means a loss of speed. Therefore, one should steer as little as possible.
3. The ideal rudder deflection is approximately 25 degrees. One achieves a high steering effect at this angle with little additional water resistance.
4. When steering, keep the rudder in the angled position during the whole stroke. Depending on the desired change in direction, the rudder should be angled only lightly and only until the new direction is reached.
5. The steering wire should not be looped around the coxswain's body. The wires are held – especially in a racing shell – with the hands on top of the boat's gunwale and should be constantly under tension. This is especially true for rowing backward.
6. For long and high waves, the boat must be turned parallel to the waves. The rowers take the safety position.
7. Pushing off the dock and landing should always be performed against the current or against the wind, whichever is stronger.
8. If you can use both sides of the dock, push off on the leeward side of the dock and land on the windward side.
9. While landing, make sure you approach the dock with appropriate speed and angle. This means that you need a little speed to be able to steer with the rudder and/or the oars and that the angle is such that the steering finally turns the boat parallel to the dock at the end of the landing maneuver.

Tasks for learning to become a coxswain:

▶ Direct a crew without using a rudder, using only the rowing commands for all maneuvers, as well as pushing off and landing at a dock.
▶ Which rowing commands do you know?
▶ Steer towards specific target points without hitting them (buoys, posts, other boats, docks).
▶ Rowers should take the coxswain position once in a while.

Tab. 18: Component 6 – Coxing

Sub Goals	Technical Terms	Notes and Corrections
Knowledge of the rowing commands	Rowing commands, amplifying equipment	Can you be heard by all? Acting appropriate in the actual situation?
Knowledge and application of traffic rules and the proper steering maneuvers	Leeward and windward side of the dock; Traffic patterns and buoys; Strength of current and wind	Angle of the rudder too large? Sudden pull on the rudder? Is the steering process planned long enough ahead of the target?
Pushing off and landing on the dock as coxswain with rowing commands	Current and wind; Lee and luv	Plan the proper angle toward the dock and the appropriate speed of the boat.

Turning in flowing waters

You can perform a turning maneuver both with and against the current. With the current, it is easiest to stop by burying the oars on the side that is closest to the shore. This turns the stern of the boat into the current, which assists the turning process. The best way to turn against the current is by stopping on the side of the boat that is closer to the middle of the river or the main current. This brings the bow of the boat into the current, which again helps with the turn. It is important to note in both cases that the boat drifts down the stream with the current while turning. Rowers must plan to have enough room to perform the turn and avoid possible collision with upcoming obstacles.

Docking with and without wind

It is best in calm waters to approach the dock at a relatively sharp angle. As the boat nears the dock, the waterside oars brake the run, pivoting the boat into a parallel with the dock. With solid grip of the waterside oars, that side's handle(s) is(are) pushed down into the boat, slightly lowering that side and raising the dockside riggers of the boat. The dockside blades are lifted up off the dock and the rowers reach out with their hands to catch the dock and bring the boat in gently so the delicate hull is not touching the dock. The coxswain gets out first, grabs the boat and stabilizes its position just off the dock. They then give the command for the crew to step out of the boat. In coxless boats, the bow rower takes charge. The rowers stepping out of the boat use the same procedures as getting into the boat, but in reverse order.

If it is possible to land on both sides of the dock, one must observe the direction of the wind. Choosing to land from the windward side is ideal since the wind helps to push the boat towards the dock. In strong wind, however, there is greater risk of damage from being pushed too quickly against the dock. Approaching the dock at a shallower angle from a further distance is important in windy condition and rowers need to be especially aware when holding the boat away from the dock.

Landing on the leeward side of a dock is more difficult since the wind is pushing the boat away from the dock. This approach may require several attempts, but reduces the risk of boat damage in high wind.

All docking maneuvers need loads of practice and the instructor should help in the beginning from the dock catching the oars and/or the riggers of the boat to help guide the boat through a safe landing.

After docking the boat, the hull needs to be securely held off the dock ideally by the rowers, but the instructor should help in the beginning of the learning process.

Rowing Commands

1. Coxswain getting out!
2. Untie and count off when ready!
3. All crew, one foot back on the stepping place ... Ready? – Up and out!

Getting the boat out of the water, onto slings and back into the boathouse

Oarlock gates will be opened, rowers remove their oars and bring them to a secure place on or close to the dock. The boat has to be held securely off the dock during the whole time. Rowers distribute themselves along the boat in the same order they brought the boat to the dock. They lift the boat out of the water and bring it to slings in front of the boathouse to clean the boat before it is put back into the boathouse. Special care must be taken when lifting the boat out of the water that no part, but specifically the rudder, does not touch the dock. Each club has their own rules how the boats have to be cleaned and in which direction (bow or stern first) being placed back into the boathouse.

Further care must be taken when placing the boat back on to the respective racks in the boathouse. The boat must not touch any parts of the boathouse, as well as any other boat. At the same time, the boat must not hit or be hit by any other boats, especially by oarlocks.

Rowing Commands

The following commands are for the carrying procedure where the boat is lifted right over the heads and then down to the shoulders; this is a more advanced maneuver, and beginners should proceed with the reverse process described previously, placing the boat into the water.

1. Hands on.....up and over the heads ... Ready? – Up!
2. Split right/left and down to the shoulders ... Ready? – Down!
3. Up and over the heads! Roll slowly into slings!
4. Hands on.....up and over the heads... Ready? – Up!
5. Walking slowly into the boathouse watching the riggers!
6. On to the racks!

Rowing should be an independent experience for adult beginners and a motivating encounter with the sport. Additional offers of the club, such as club-integration, social events with the learning group, as well as with all club members, or the offer of exciting day trips should complement the learning of rowing skills (components of learning rowing). Also, stimulating methodical concepts with large variations in the selection of exercises, along with information about all the different possibilities that our sport offers are a must in the learn-to-row program.

Many clubs provide enrichment opportunities to their advanced beginners as well as their ambitious competitive rowers. Examples include additional lessons to learn sculling in a single or training camps for which an experienced or well-known guest coach could be hired. They could offer video analyses, biomechanical testing, ergometer tests possibly with spirometry or individualized training recommendations.

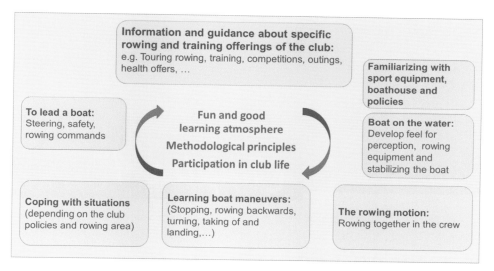

Fig. 17: Foundation/basic course – Elements of rowing learning (mod. according to Fritsch, 2006 and Fritsch, 2014).

Chapter 4

IS THERE STILL ROOM TO IMPROVE TECHNIQUE?

Masters rowers, whether competitive or ambitious fitness rowers, are always keen to work on their technique. Many realize, however, that successfully changing well-established patterns of movement is difficult. This indeed is a special challenge.

If you are a long-time rower, you have at some time or other had to make peace with your individual movement traits or even flaws; you may even feel comfortable with having your own "unique" style. You get around reasonably well, can row tolerably well together with others in crew boats and may even get somewhat annoyed when "well-intentioned" advice is given to you from crewmates or outsiders regarding your personal rowing technique. In most cases, you are already quite aware which of your movement errors should be corrected – you've heard the same feedback many times before. You have even attempted to work on them. Yet correcting the flawed motion has proved neither quick nor effortless enough; relapse into the familiar technique just seems inevitable. For example, masters rowers often allow their feathered blades to settle back on to the water after the release, which may contribute to a sense of greater stability. Perceptions aside,

the reality of dragging one blade more than the other on the water puts a shell more easily off balance along with a predictable decrease in boat speed, problems compounded in rough water. External feedback, while it can lead to successful changes in the moment, cannot be the only solution since on their own, masters rowers too often fall back into old patterns. This is, of course, an imaginary scenario, but will certainly fit some of the readers' experiences.

Adult novice rowers are absorbed by many challenges as they progress through the steps of rowing presented in chapter 3. Learning a correct rowing technique can often revert into a "survival strategy" on the water. For example, it often seems easier for beginners to speed up the slide during the recovery, reducing the time for the boat to be unsettled, even providing a little extra time at the catch to square the blades as they prepare for the entry and drive. Executing these movements more slowly, by contrast, is significantly more difficult for the beginner, yet taking time to ingrain the correct pattern ultimately results in a smoother and more integrated stroke. This transition from simply learning the movement patterns to an effective rowing technique deserves special attention.

Fundamental to lasting learning is the motivation of the masters rowers to work seriously on their technique, as well as an understanding of the physical-biomechanical context. Athletes must be convinced that improved technique is indeed beneficial. This also implies that there needs to be a consensus within a crew and with the coach about the "correct" rowing technique – or at least an agreed upon range of effective and efficient movement patterns.

The study of pictures or video recordings of highly skilled Olympic crews or current top teams is helpful, but only reveals how this particular team or individual rower organized a good technique for themselves and what works best for them. Such polished performances rarely provide insight into how they got to this point and certainly not how it feels to them. We might justly ask whether these top rowers would row with a different style, if they were to row in a different crew or in different conditions?

Is there a special rowing technique for masters rowers?

The effort to acquire good technique or at least improve a rower's existing technique is worthwhile for all age groups and performance levels. Proper technique plays a vital role in any rower's overall performance, although "performance" can mean very different things to individual athletes or even for the same athlete at different times. Generally speaking, the goals of the rowing technique are:

- ▶ Optimal use of the individually applied work for maximum propulsion in the water
- ▶ Minimize all resistant forces on the boat
- ▶ Coordinate the individuals' performances to maximize team performance
- ▶ Reduction or even prevention of injuries
- ▶ Increase the overall experience of rowing in all its components (nature, team, social aspects, competition, etc.)

With these goals of rowing technique in mind, it is clear why all rowers indeed search for constant improvement in skill, regardless of age and performance level. There are, however, certain differences in actual rowing technique that must be acknowledged and applied when it comes to rowers at different stages of performance. That being said, before elaborating any specific features of correct rowing technique for masters rowers, we must first describe the general features of effective rowing technique.

Despite the defined concept of an "ideal" rowing technique, individual differences in athlete stature and fitness demand a range of acceptable variation within the standard. These variants can be called rowing styles and are often successfully used in training and competition. In the following description, however, we will confine ourselves to the general concepts, not only because of the large number of possible styles, but also because the most effective variations are by definition included within the ideal.

The reference to various medical restrictions implies that athletes with pre-existing or emerging injuries should row only after consulting their physician and/or physiotherapist. So, if for example a rower suffers back pain while rowing, they need to see a physician to investigate the underlying causes of the complaint and to get the "green light" to return to specific rowing training.

Rowing well considerably increases the experiential value of our sport. Not only because using correct rowing technique reduces the risk of injury and thus ensures long term and uninterrupted participation in our sport, but it's also simply more fun to row in a crew with technically competent crewmates that fit well together! Well beyond the enjoyment of racing alone, the regular experience of team unity, light run of the boat, effortless propulsion, boat speed, the sounds of a synchronous crew in a speedy shell, and ease of effort in coping with adverse or changing water conditions can bring tremendous satisfaction and improve self-esteem.

4.1 GENERAL CHARACTERISTICS OF CORRECT ROWING TECHNIQUE

Correct rowing technique is designed to facilitate the most efficient translation of rower-generated forces into boat speed, and to minimize all resistance on the boat and the crew. This is true for every rower in every age and in every boat! Although 60-year-old recreational rowers are no longer aiming for absolute maximum speed, they will still try to row technically correct, so that the boat will achieve an optimal run for the forces applied. In this case, the rowers will glide in a balanced boat and as a cohesive team, so that the movement is experienced as smooth, technically savvy and just "fast". This is enjoyable for the whole crew.

To describe correct rowing technique, the following important biomechanical principles can be established:

1) Impulse = long effective rowing stroke

Since we are dealing with intermittent propulsion in rowing, the overall rower-boat system loses speed during recovery. As a result, the rower has to re-apply a propelling force during the drive in order to return the lost speed to the system (i.e. bring the system rower-boat back up to speed). The stronger the propelling force and the longer the time that this force acts during the drive, the higher the speed increase achieved. The overall system gains momentum during the drive! This is a physical law and it is described by impulse.

$$I = F * \Delta t = m * \Delta v = M$$

With:
I = propelling impulse; F = propelling force on the blade;
Δt = duration that the propelling force acts on the blade;
m = mass of the whole system rower;
Δv = speed that the overall system gained through propulsion;
M = momentum of the overall system

The same mechanical law, of course, applies to the recovery. It is here, however, where we must account for the opposite directed impact from the resistance forces of water and wind on the boat, oars and athletes. These act in opposition to the propelling forces and are therefore expressed as negative in our equation. This means that the resulting change in speed is negative, meaning the overall system loses speed during the recovery.

Since the mass [m] of the total system is constant, the propelling impulse [I] is a direct measure of the rate of the increase in speed [Δv]. Rowers must therefore try to maintain a high force on the blade for as long a time as possible. This can only be achieved if the effective stroke length is correspondingly large. Since the oar angle is limited at the finish, a long stroke can only be achieved at the catch. And it is generally true that the faster the boat, the larger the catch angle must be.

To take full advantage of this biomechanical principle in rowing it must, however, be applied individually. On the one hand, shorter stroke length can be compensated for with an increased stroke rate, on the other hand, the optimal stroke length for a slower boat is shorter than for a faster boat (e.g. a pair vs. an eight). Additionally, the stroke length must be adapted to the physical conditions of the masters rower. Physically stronger rowers can choose a larger catch angle and will be able to move faster with it. Yet, if the strength abilities of a rower are limited or the build of the rower restricts the reach, a stroke with too large a catch angle can feel like torture. In such a situation, a "long" rowing stroke is neither effective nor desirable.

a.) Catch position   b.) Finish position

Fig. 18: Example of a correct stroke length, which allows an optimal impulse.

2) Minimum vertical movement of the Centre of Gravity (CoG)

The trunk movement around the hips, the up and down of the hands as well as the bending and stretching of the legs over an entire stroke all contribute to the up and down of the position of the rowers' overall mass which we call Centre of Gravity (CoG). This movement of the CoG requires energy that the rowers must generate through their energy supply and is therefore no longer available for propulsion. For this reason, it is important that rowers minimize the vertical movement of the CoG without limiting the stroke length.

This is achieved above all by moving the upper body as horizontally as possible and the hands as linearly as possible. To this end, the trunk begins to swing on the drive only after the legs have stretched open half way. As a result, the lowering of the legs' CoG almost counters the raising of the trunk's CoG so that the overall CoG movement remains effectively horizontal. The moment the legs are stretched out, the trunk finishes the swing and the arms bend only as far as the blades in the water can generate propulsion. The CoG of rower lowers during this last part of the drive, and this vertical movement needs to be limited with a restricted lean back of the trunk, for example.

The recovery starts with stretching the arms, followed shortly after by swinging the trunk forward and then bending the legs. The legs begin flexing slowly, so that the hands can pass over the raising knees so as not to interrupt the horizontal path of the hands. Then the successive movement of arms, trunk and legs is more accentuated at lower stroke rates and overlaps more at higher stroke rates. The final swing forward of the trunk in the recovery is again coordinated with the bending of the knees so that the center of gravity performs as little vertical movement as possible.

Fig. 19: Movement of the CoG during an entire stroke.

It can often be observed that rowers attempt to extend the stroke artificially at the finish with a large trunk swing to the bow, which we will call lean back. Too much lean back, however, is counterproductive, not only because it unnecessarily uses energy through a significant vertical movement of the CoG, but also because it creates breaking resistance as the blades cannot be extracted cleanly from the water. The faster a rower moves the boat, the less lean back is required. Clean bladework at the finish is an excellent indicator of a correct degree of trunk lean back.

3) Continuous horizontal movement

When exceptional teams perform at a high level, it often looks as if they "glide along with ease". Their movements seem supple and effortless. This phenomenon comes from the fact that top performers row without unnecessary extra movements, have clean bladework and prefer a "round" or "smooth" rowing motion. This means they move continuously and avoid any pauses or extra acceleration.

Rowers who perform their horizontal movements continuously reduce unnecessary energy consumption, especially on the recovery. Each pause in the movement costs time and results in the need for higher acceleration of the CoG at a later point, all at the expense of more effort.

In addition, any horizontal acceleration of the rowers' CoG during the recovery has a negative effect on the boat speed. Any acceleration of the rowers' CoG relative to the boat will affect the boat's movement by a factor 3 to 8, depending on the boat class (this factor is calculated by the weight of the rower divided by the weight of the boat). Thus, the movement of the rowers' CoG adds a significant component of speed changes on top of the existing variations in boat speed caused by rowing' intermittent propulsion. These increased boat speed variations have a considerable impact on the boat's resistance in the water which slows the overall system even more, resulting in the rowers needing to work harder.

4) Correct sequencing of the main joints - coupling of involved muscle groups

The rowing movement is mainly performed by four joints: knees, hip, shoulders and elbows, **supported by the corresponding muscles**. Because the feet are firmly connected to the boat by the footstretcher, flexing and stretching the knee joint creates movement of the hips relative to the boat. The hip joint along with the spine causes flexion and extension of the trunk, which causes the movement of the shoulder relative to the hip. The shoulder and elbow joints cause the flexion and extension of the arms and thus the movement of the hands relative to the shoulder. These three main motions together cause the movement of the hand relative to the boat, which ultimately causes the movement of the oars and thus the propulsion.

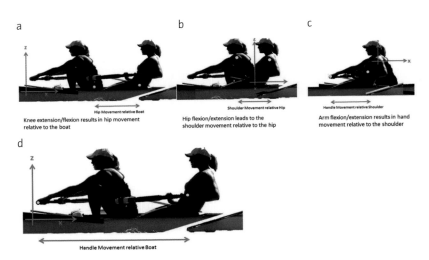

Fig. 20 a-d: Coordination of joint movements. The flexion and extension of the three main body joints (fig. a, b, and c) cause the overall movement of the hand relative to the boat (fig. d).

The coordination of these joint movements must respect the previously mentioned principles; to ensure this, a clever sequencing with partial overlap (coupling) must be performed. This succession of joint movements during the drive prolongs the power delivery and thus extends the duration of the drive, leading to a larger impulse. But this also engages the stronger muscle groups (legs and back) at the beginning of the drive when the transformation of the rowers' power is most efficient and therefore, larger forces on the handles are applied for logical reasons. The weaker arm muscles are saved for the final pull when the force on the inboard has to decline anyways. The joint movements, however, must also overlap a little so that the speed of the hand relative to the boat can be maintained. In general, a sequencing of the drive follows the pattern:

Legs − Trunk − Arms

The recovery movement follows the reverse pattern: arms − trunk − legs. We see again an overlap of the joint movements to maintain the hand speed relative to the boat, but the general movement sequence persists which means that the legs start moving last. This ensures that the handle can pass over the knees uninterrupted before the knees lift up when bending. As a result, the hands can be moved horizontally from the finish without the knees getting in the way. Likewise, the early swing of the trunk leads to a proper preparation of the trunk's position early in the recovery, which reduces the lunging movement into the catch.

Proper sequencing of the joint movements during the recovery provides several further benefits. It is the basis of a movement pattern that creates a nice, continuous flow that is easy to follow in a crew. Also, coupling correctly reduces the horizontal velocity of the rower's CoG and sets up the overall system for the least amount of energy loss and thus for the best conservation of speed and a better boat run.

Finally, by keeping all movements as horizontal as possible, the vertical movement of the rowers' CoG is reduced. This has the added benefit of helping to avoid any dropping of the shoulder into the catch, which normally results in lowering the hands and thus skying of the blades.

The correct timing of joint movements is shown graphically in the following Fig. 21. You can not only see the sequencing of movements, but also see the speed magnitudes.

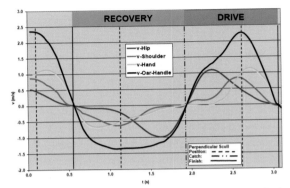

Fig. 21: Velocity distribution and coordination of the movements of the four main joints along with the resulting speed of the hand relative to the boat.

v-Hand:
Resulting speed of the hand relative to the boat.

v-Arm:
Velocity of the hand relative to the shoulder caused by the arm movement (Fig. 20c).

v-Body:
Velocity of the shoulder relative to the hip caused by the rotation of the trunk around the hip (Fig. 20b).

v-Leg:
Velocity of the hip relative to the boat caused by the leg movement (Fig. 20a)

5) Effective Bladework through proper hand path

The blade force is the only force that can propel the overall rower-boat system and optimum propulsion requires that the rowing blade be moved properly through the water. The speed of the boat, the oar angle relative to the boat, the angular velocity of the oar around the pin, and the blade depth play significant roles in this process.

The blade at the end of the oar shaft is directly connected to the boat via the oarlock, so that blade and oar always move with the boat. The rower's hand movement relative to the boat causes the oar to rotate about the pin. Boat velocity and the angular velocity of the oar around the pin together ultimately produce the movement of the blade relative to the water. The oar rotation is a direct result of the rower's power applied to the handle, which determines the achievable boat velocity. This in turn is limited by the rowers' ability to generate power.

The correct entry of the blade into the water is one of the most difficult movements in rowing. Several components, such as the present boat velocity, desired boat velocity, the rower's physical abilities, vertical and horizontal velocity of the hand, but also the actual oar angle, must be coordinated. Added to this are the environmental influences of wind and waves, which must be taken into account. The final movement is so complicated because all of the components influence each other. The blade must enter the water in a way that it can take full advantage of the length of the stroke at the catch and that it can build up the propulsive force of the water on the blade surface as quickly as possible.

One possible aid for assessing the quality of the entry is to observe the splashes on either side of the blade. If the entry is carried out correctly, only slight, V-splashes are formed at the blade's point of entry (see Fig. 22a). That is, on both sides of the blade there are small splashes of water that go away from the blade and form a V-shape. Large splashes of water towards the bow have a braking effect and indicate too slow vertical and/or horizontal movement of the blade. Conversely, large splashes of water to the stern are a sign that the entry was started with an air strike. Either the blade was too far from the water at the catch and/or the horizontal movement was too fast relative to the vertical movement: in both cases, the rower started the drive movement without the blade being in the water.

Along with the speed of the boat and the rotation of the oar in the oarlock, the blade depth determines the position of the blade to the oncoming flow of the water. Blade depth must be chosen so that the hydrodynamic processes on the blade can develop optimally, but also that the entry and release of the blades can be carried out in the shortest possible time. For these reasons, it is important that the blade must be completely covered by water, if optimal propulsion is to be generated. If the blade is submerged too deeply, it requires unnecessarily wasted additional force to push it lower in the water at the catch as well as to lift it out at the release. The following pictures give an impression of the correct blade depth during the drive.

a) First part of the drive – just after entry

b) At perpendi – cular oar position

Fig. 22 a-c: Examples of rowing blades with correct blade depth.

c) Last part of the drive – beginning of release

Performing a proper release is just as difficult as a proper entry. Once again, the rower must comply with and coordinate the components already mentioned for the entry. Although it is necessary to try and keep "pressure on the blade" as long as possible, the blade ultimately must be "rowed out" of the water. It is simply physically impossible to break off the force abruptly at the end of the drive and simultaneously lift the blade perpendicularly out of the water, as some people suggest.

In reality, one needs a certain amount of time to release a completely covered blade (see Fig. 22b). Good rowers can achieve this in about 0.1 seconds. During this time, a moving boat covers 0.2 to 0.6 m depending on its speed and this movement must be regarded when taking the blade out of the water. If the rower would attempt to keep the blade covered until the finish position, the rower would catch a major crab. Instead, the rower needs to start the release motion about 0.1 to 0.3 m in front of the body. The easing of the pulling force must be coordinated with the vertical movement, so that a fluid release can occur without power loss or boat deceleration. This phenomenon is very well displayed in the images in Fig. 23, which give an idea of the time elapsed and the distance traveled by the blade required for a clean extraction from the water.

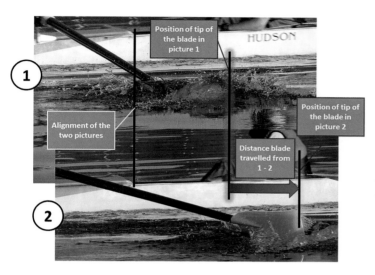

Fig. 23: Impression of the duration of the release and the distance travelled by the blade in order to extract it cleanly. The two pictures are about 0.1 s apart and horizontally aligned at the front point of the rigger. The horizontal distance that the blade travels during the release is indicated.

Whether or not the release was carried out correctly can again be seen by observing how the water reacts as the blade is extracted. Ideally, there are no splashes, but this is extremely difficult. In reality, the rower must be careful to keep the splashes as small as possible and as vertical and symmetrical as possible. Splashes in one direction alone (forward or backward splashes) always indicate an incorrectly coordinated or overly fast or slow release.

Fig. 24 describes schematically how the hand should move relative to the boat during a complete stroke. This two-dimensional plot of the end of the handle is called the *handcurve*. **The vertical movement of the hand must be minimized.** It should be just so large that during the drive, the blade is correctly covered with water (highest hand level) and during the recovery, the blade is only as far away from the water as needed for clean guiding of the blade off the water and a complete squaring of the blade to be carried out without the need to lower the hand towards the catch (lowest hand level). This vertical movement can be as small as about 0.20 m (or around the width of half of the rower's blade) in properly rigged boats.

Having said this, **the horizontal movement of the hands should be maximized** and is, depending on the size of the rower, approximately 1.3-1.6 m finish to catch.

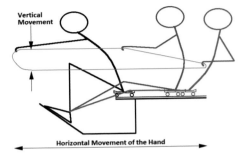

Fig. 24: Representation of the ideal handcurve during a complete rowing stroke.

6) Balance and stability: Work in the middle of the boat!

Technically good rowers always have good balance. All movements are carried out so that the boat is stabilized, allowing the rowers to fully apply their power without disturbing the boat's run. In addition, a balanced boat reduces the potential for injury. An unstable boat forces the rowers to engage in lateral compensatory movements of the spine. Such movements place major strain on individual vertebrae and intervertebral discs; when additional loads are applied as in the case of taking a stroke at pressure, the risk of injury is increased.

Balance and stability are therefore an essential part of good rowing technique and should always be integrated into technique training. To this end, the rowers should work in the middle of the boat and reduce unnecessary sideways movements. This is certainly easier to do in sculling, as all movements are performed symmetrically to the middle of the boat. When sweep rowing, the hands and thus arms and shoulders rotate from the center out towards either port or starboard at the catch. This "leaning movement" should be done through a natural rotation in the trunk and an additional turning in the shoulder. The head also participates in this body and shoulder rotation, but if possible should remain close to the center of the boat (see Fig. 25). The center of gravity (CoG) remains over the keel line.

Fig. 25: Example of correct work in the middle of the boat, which simplifies the balance of the boat.

7) Synchronous movements for cohesive teamwork

A rower's perception of the relative difficulty or ease of rowing in a boat with others is heavily influenced by whether a team is coordinated and in sync. From diverse body movements and sliding seats' speeds to different stroke lengths and the uncoordinated application of power, such instances of non-coordination are immediately registered by team members and cause the rowing to feel "heavy".

A team, therefore, must set as a priority goal to row as synchronously as possible. Although research has shown that certain small differences in individual team members' force curves may be advantageous (in particular, for example, in the coxless pair), it also confirms that rowers with different body dimensions are best served by adapting to each other. Ultimately, the spatial-temporal movements of all team members must be consistent. Thus, the entry and the release are fixed points in time within the stroke cycle that must happen simultaneously for all rowers in a given boat, regardless of individual differences in size, shape or power output. Body movements must be synchronized in time, so that power need not be unnecessarily expended on compensating for poor crew coordination.

Fig. 26: Synchronous motion, example 1: The blades of an eight during the entry.

Fig. 27: Synchronous motion, example 2: Body positions and bladework during recovery.

4.2 DOES THE TECHNIQUE OF THE MASTERS ROWER DIFFER FROM THAT OF THE ELITE ROWER?

It is almost impossible for a lay person to distinguish the master rower's technique from that of the elite rower, since the same technique principles described above apply to both groups. The expert, however, can make out the subtle differences. These must also be taken into account when designing focused training for older persons in the sport, especially when creating effective learning environments.

When examining how the masters rower differs from the elite rower, two fundamental considerations must be taken into account. On the one hand, we can expect certain age-related changes: a decline in neuronal performance with age, a reduction in muscle mass, a reduction in mobility, an increase in the body fat percentage of the total mass and an increased vulnerability to injury. On the other hand, the decline in a masters rower's performance is linked to the fact that they complete fewer training sessions per week with very different intensities. These differences, which may occur alone or together, lead to a physiological reduction in reaction and movement speed, as well as stroke length, strength and power. This necessarily results in reduced boat speed for the masters rower.

The consideration of these relationships is evident. It requires adapting the biomechanical principles to the level of performance and/or the age of the rowers, without, however, questioning the principles in general. Still, as we find very widely distributed proficiencies in masters rowing, the differences shown below must be adjusted individually for the various performance levels within the masters rower population. In principle, however, it can be said that masters rowers:

▶   Shorten their catch angle
▶   Have a smaller force increase in the first part of the drive
▶   Reach their maximum force later in the drive
▶   Achieve a lower peak force
▶   Row at lower stroke rates

These differences have the positive effect of lowering the risk of injury for the older rower. The reduced catch angle improves the masters rower's body posture, so that less strain on the lumbar spine occurs. The lower peak force reduces stress on the entire body, the shoulders, spine and knees. As a result, the body is better protected against injury.

Fig. 28: Improved posture through limited trunk lean forward at the catch.

Fig. 29: Reduced peak force later in the stroke reduces the strain on the knees and spine.

The general diminution of a person's maximum performance with age goes hand in hand with reduced movement speed and acceleration. In rowing this leads to a decline in the maximally achievable force on the inboard along with a slower, less powerful drive. The average speed of the boat slows down, reducing the effective maximum stroke length and the need for speed of the entry. That is, the masters rower no longer needs to aim for the same catch angle and does not have to take up pressure as quickly. With the lower stroke rate and boat speed, the point of peak force application is often shifted more towards the perpendicular position of the oar.

A comparison of the oarlock forces (force curve) between the elite and masters rower looks as follows:

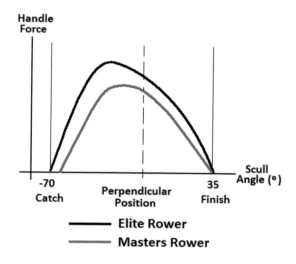

Fig. 30: Optimum handle force curve of the master rower in comparison to the elite rower.

Finally, masters rowers tend to adjust their stroke rate to their performance and boat speed. Here, they choose a stroke rate where the rowing feels light and fluid and the run of the boat is still guaranteed.

4.3 IS THERE A PROTECTIVE TECHNIQUE FOR FITNESS-ORIENTED MASTERS ROWERS?

Rowing is an ideal sport for people of all ages. It offers the full range of sports activities in delightful settings with plenty of challenges for every skill and performance level. Each masters rower can choose their own goals in our sport and find their own personal satisfaction.

The most important goal for all rowers should be to maintain or even increase good health. Here, too, rowing offers an ideal array of activities as long as some basic conditions are met. While practicing our sport, stamina, strength and coordination are trained simultaneously, while the load on bones, cartilage, tendons and ligaments is relatively low. In this regard, the benefits of rowing are clear.

Nevertheless, overloading can occur, especially if an athlete is not properly prepared or has some pre-existing conditions, both unfortunately a regular reality in masters rowing. Some examples to illustrate this are:

▶   An athlete decides to start rowing again in the spring, although little or no training was done during the winter.
▶   The athlete has gained weight and is now overweight because of an unhealthy lifestyle.
▶   Due to wear or injury, the athlete is in poor health.

In all of these cases, it is easily possible for a rower to become overloaded, resulting in overuse or injury or worse.

At this point we remind again of the importance of

▶   Regular health checks
▶   A realistic assessment of the athlete's performance level when choosing the proper training volume and intensity! Of course, this realistic assessment also dictates the choice of rowing technique

All of this starts with the proper choice of equipment. Today's boat and oar manufacturers offer a wide variety of rowing equipment so that every rower can choose the most appropriate fit for their individual needs. Additionally, it is of the highest importance that each boat is optimally rigged (see chapter 5). Then each masters athlete should choose the rowing technique best adapted to their respective situation and based on the principles described above. In general, the following notes apply with a "protective technique" in mind. Slower boat speed, low preparation and/or pre-injury are all factors that will influence the extent to which technique should be adapted, as illustrated here:

▶   The overall length of the oars significantly impacts the load on the rower and should therefore be shortened.
▶   While the horizontal footstretcher position should always be set in reference to the rower's optimal finish angle, the catch angle can be shortened by limiting knee angle and/or lean forward at the catch in order to optimize the overall length of the drive.
▶   Reducing the forward lean of the trunk at the catch allows the rower to gain a body posture during entry that is more protective of the back in particular.
▶   High peak forces should be avoided and the overall pulling force can be reduced: **the main impulse should come from the legs.**
▶   The peak force should occur more in the middle of the drive rather than the beginning of the drive.
▶   Stroke rates should be reduced without affecting the flow of movement.

4.4   BALANCE, MOVEMENT COORDINATION AND BOAT FEEL IN OLDER AGE

Balance, movement coordination and boat feel are the effects of underlying and vastly more complex internal human functions. Several parts of the central and peripheral nervous systems are involved in the execution of any movement: sensory systems, motor systems and cognitive systems. How these different systems interact with each other depends on the task and the environmental demands. Spirduso et al. (2005) emphasize that the performance of these nervous systems decline with age if they are not being appropriately stressed.

Due to complexity of these interactions, a performance loss in one of these systems may not affect balance and coordination of movement much. If, however, several systems are influenced by age, noticeably significant changes can occur.

Thus, it is clear that each rower should expect a loss of balance and coordination of movement with age and that these losses will affect boat feel. It is easy to see that rowing in a sleek racing shell at high stroke rate in rough water can then lead to circumstances ranging from complicated at a minimum up to excessively challenging to the point of overloading a masters rower. Such heavy overload can take all pleasure from our sport.

How can coordination, balance and boat feel be maintained?

First of all, it is important to do appropriate exercises to prevent the loss of coordination. On the other hand, it is possible to improve the coordinative abilities of an athlete. Proper training must therefore always be a controlled challenge to the rower, not only physiologically, but also in terms of technique. Thus, masters rowers should always try to include sessions in their training that challenge their physiology as well as their coordination, such as rowing in different types of boats or in challenging water conditions.

This, however, requires a realistic assessment of the rower's technical and physical abilities. It is absolutely correct and important as a 50-year-old beginner with little physical training to get into a single and try to improve their skills in this boat. Yet it may be that the boat could be a wider, more stable recreational shell, and rowing should be tried first in fair weather. Similarly, a somewhat out-of-shape former competitive rower could of course try few sets of "power strokes" with their teammates in a racing eight, as long as the stroke rates are kept within realistic limits and the overall load remains in line with the rowers' health.

The feeling of "the perfect stroke" to which everyone aspires can be experienced in any type of boat and at any speed. It does not require ultralight super oars or boats! There is no need for a stroke rate of 45 per minute, or to be in the highly accomplished team of super-humans that meets for 12 training sessions a week. A properly rigged coastal rowing four, filled with friends who are focused, but relaxed, trying to get the technique right, co-operating well with each other at 20 strokes per minute, can provide a rowing experience just as – and possibly more – satisfying.

4.5   WHAT EXERCISES CAN IMPROVE MY ROWING TECHNIQUE?

Special exercises, often correctly called "drills" or "games", not only serve to improve rowing technique, they can also break up a longer training session and add an aspect of fun. Of course, it is advisable to choose exercises that will invigorate and enhance the row. These exercises are intended to remedy the technical problems that are currently occurring or to serve to provide variety and joy. Doing a drill just for the sake of doing a drill does not make much sense because the rowers will lack the motivation to focus on the main goal of the drill – if such a goal is even present. Conversely, sensibly selected drills quickly show success and inspire the rowers to aim for new challenges.

Here are a few tips that should be followed to successfully use "games" (see also Trono, 2001 and Vernacchia, McGuire & Cook, 1992, p. 107):

▸ Rowers need to understand the purpose for which a particular exercise is being done. This motivates them and allows them to concentrate on the essentials of the exercise. They also understand better how to transfer the newly learned skill into the normal rowing motion.

▸ The coach must take into account the learning phase that the rower is in when choosing a specific drill. It is important for beginners, that the exercises are simple, yet challenging for their skill level. The athletes need to understand the task and the conditions need to be such that the exercise can actually be carried out (e.g. little wind, no waves). Sufficient breaks and enough time to repeat the exercises are very important. Coaches need to observe that drills are not repeated for too long of a time to not mentally overload the learner which will make the exercise inefficient. With increasing skill, the drills can be run as a competition.

▸ The selection of a drill also depends on the type of learner. As mentioned in chapter 3, some people learn better with auditory aids, others with visual and some with kinesthetic ones. Auditory learners respond best to verbal explanations, keywords, or boat sounds. Visually-oriented learners, on the other hand, need to see how a movement is performed and what their own movement looks like. Video analysis is a preferred learning tool for such learners and recordings from expert teams give them good models of the correct movements. Viewing recordings of their own rowing allows a good comparison with the "ideal movement". Kinesthetic learners must perform and feel the movement and its changes in order to know which movement is right or wrong. Instructors must allow kinesthetic rowers to experience a range of many different types of movement. That said, for most people, the best method of learning will be a unique blend depending on the current situation and past experience. Instructors should strive, therefore, to develop a range of possible methods for providing explanation and feedback to find what works best for the individual rower.

▸ The "tasks" must be challenging, but attainable, so that they lead to a sense of achievement for the rowers. An ideal drill is one where the simple act of executing it successfully will automatically lead to improvements in the desired skill within the overall rowing movement.

Drills are designed to help the athlete perform a specific exercise correctly, make it easier, improve the feel, and simply make loads of fun. They usually over-emphasize a certain movement, promote the concentration on the targeted movement or allow the rowers to better feel a specific part of the movement. Only imagination limits the variety of possible drills and it is important that rowers and coaches let their ingenuity go wild and develop new exercises. This makes rowing training interesting and entertaining. The following examples are initial ideas intended to stimulate further thought and can only give a hint of the infinite variety of possible exercises.

Exercises to improve specific parts of the rowing motion

The following exercises are presented to help improve certain targeted movements. Of course, this is just a selection of all possible exercises and the imagination of the reader should know no bounds. To the contrary, we encourage the reader to develop their own variations or completely new exercises. You can further increase the level of difficulty by combining two or more of them. So, you can for example row in sculling with a wide grip and on the square at the same time; or in a sweep boat with one hand only, pausing every three strokes and lightly slapping the outside of the boat with the free hand during the pause.

Basically, any exercise should be approached in a relaxed manner as a complete and continuous rowing motion and the intensity should gradually be increased (i.e. first at low stroke rate and then increasing the speed). While doing this, the beginner needs to be given sufficient time to experiment with the exercise and is always assisted in the process by plenty of encouragement.

Of course, individual parts of the movement (e.g. arms only rowing) can be practiced in isolation from the overall movement at an advanced performance level. This does not contradict the suggestion that the rowing movement should always be executed as a whole, "round" and continuous movement. It should be noted, however, to what extent the isolated exercises have a positive effect on the overall rowing technique. They certainly always improve the sensory perception of movements.

Tab. 19: Exercises to train technique.

Targeted Skill	Beginner Exercise
Balance	**In the moving boat:** ▶ Pause every third stroke for 1-10 s with hands over knees ▶ Rowing only with the inside hand (sweep rowing) ▶ Wide grip – in sculling: hands about 15-20 cm from end of the handles; in sw Outside hand remains at the end of the handle, inside hand moves 50-60 cm the end of the handle

Advanced Exercise

In the moving boat:

▶ Pause every third stroke for 1-10 s
  - At the finish position
  - At the catch
  - With squared blades

▶ Performing an "air stroke" every third stroke (normal rowing motion without putting the blades in the water; Blades are feathered and do not touch the water)

▶ Full 360° rotation of the oars about their longitudinal axis during recovery (Caution: This exercise is very difficult!)

(continued)

(Tab. 19, continued)

Targeted Skill	Beginner Exercise
Balance	▶ Cross grip in sweep rowing – inside hand moves to the end of the handle while outside hand moves about 30 cm away from the end of the handle; arms cross over ▶ Opening the hands during recovery - hands are stretched out on top of the handles ▶ Lightly tapping the outside of the boat with the outside hand during the recovery ▶ Rowing with squared blade during half-boat rowing

Advanced Exercise

▶ Rowing with very low stroke rate with blades off the water during recovery
▶ Start with squared blades

(continued)

(Tab. 19, continued)

Targeted Skill	Beginner Exercise
Balance	**Boat sitting still:** ▸ Rhythmical immersion and emerging of the squared blades in the finish position while balancing the boat (Bobbing) ▸ Rocking the boat (lightly): Moving hands up and down with blades flat on the water ▸ Passing a ball over their heads from one rower to the next
Team coordination	▸ Overemphasis of individual parts of the rowing movement (e.g. exaggerated pulling towards the finish; large lean back; especially quick catch) ▸ Rowing with eyes closed ▸ Quick release and hands away ▸ Rowing with half crew ▸ Rowing with different stroke length (full, ¾, ½, ¼, without slide)

Advanced Exercise

Boat sitting still:

▶ Balancing with blades off the water
▶ Standing up in the boat

▶ Start at the finish position; then releasing the (squared) blades out of the water and moving into the catch position without touching the water; then balancing there

▶ Rowing with high and highest stroke rates; half slide, full slide
▶ Rowing with eyes closed and changing stroke rates
▶ Start with eyes closed
▶ Changing the length of the stroke on every stroke on the coach's or coxswain's call

(continued)

(Tab. 19, continued)

Targeted Skill	Beginner Exercise
Handling of the oars	▶ Rowing with different grips, e.g. wide grip, hands crossed, rowing only with thumb and index finger, underhand grip ▶ Delayed feather (release with squared blade until it is out of the water, then feathering) ▶ Rowing with the back side of the blade (blade turned 180) ▶ Backward rowing
Speed of movement	▶ Increase stroke rate in rowing with shortened stroke ▶ Increasing stroke rate every 5 strokes at ½ slide until an agreed stroke rate is reached, then 10 sprint strokes with full slide and full effort ▶ Overly fast entry, release or recovery ▶ Starts or short sprints (e.g. 10 strokes) ▶ Rowing in a larger boat or with experienced rowers
Rhythm	▶ Change of stroke rate on call of the coach in short succession ▶ Continuous change back and forth of stroke length (full slide, ¾, ½, ¼, without slide, ¼, ½....) ▶ Excessive use of force at low stroke rate ▶ Listening to sounds of the boat
Bladework	▶ Part crew rowing ▶ Starting with a very low stroke rate (~15/min) and slowly increasing by two strokes/min every 10 strokes ▶ Rowing with constant observation of one's own blade ▶ Rowing with "wide grip"

Advanced Exercise

- Continuous change of grip from stroke to stroke without changing the rhythm
- Take turns rowing with oars only on one side of the boat with the other side on the feather (air stroke) not touching the water
- Full rotation of the oar about its longitudinal axis during recovery – (Careful: difficult exercise!)

- Increase stroke rate in rowing with shortened stroke with blades on the square
- Increasing stroke rate every 5 strokes at ½ slide until an agreed stroke rate is reached, then 10 sprint strokes with full slide and full effort with squared blades
- 100 m race
- Contest: Who achieves the highest stroke rate without shortening the stroke?

- The same exercises as on the left, only with eyes closed

- Rowing at extremely high stroke rate (> 36/min)
- Competition: 10 strokes from a standing position and who gets furthest? With and without setting a stroke rate

(continued)

(Tab. 19, continued)

Targeted Skill	Beginner Exercise
Bladework	▸ Wrap white tape around the oar shaft 30 cm from the blade end of the shaft, so you can better see how far the shaft goes into the water during the drive and then correct blade depth ▸ Rowing a circle by using only oars on one side of the boat (e.g. port), while the other side (in this case starboard) is held flat on the water to stabilize the boat; the rowers watch and control their blades (the drill is called "360's") ▸ Backward rowing ▸ Row carefully not making any noise with the blade during the drive
Catch and entry	▸ Squaring the blades early ▸ Consciously fast entry ▸ Rowing with inside hand only in sweep ▸ Rowing with a wide grip ▸ Half crew rowing with consciously quick entry and building pressure quickly in first part of stroke ▸ Produce intentional back-splashes during entry ▸ Deliberate fast sliding into the catch for the last 10 cm of the slides and emphasizing quick entry and "lock on" ▸ Listening for the sound the blade makes at the entry, which can be emphasized through quick hand movement

Advanced Exercise

▶ Rowing with shortened stroke length (½ slide) and increasing stroke rate every five strokes

▶ Starting from a stand-still at the finish with squared blades in the water, then pushing the hands towards the stern to give the boat some backward speed; at the catch wait a split second until pressure builds on the front of the blade, then perform a strong stroke starting with a push of the legs. (Careful: Start with a small catch angle and maintain good posture!)

▶ "Russian Catch" – rowing only the first 25% of the stroke through leg extension, without using the arms or trunk; with and without feathering the blades

▶ All exercises to the left with eyes closed

(continued)

(Tab. 19, continued)

Targeted Skill	Beginner Exercise
Release and Finish	▶ Overemphasizing the last part of the drive
	▶ Rowing at low stroke rate (~ 15-20/min) with extra resistance (e.g. half crew; pulling a can behind boat; bungees wrapped around boat)
	▶ Rowing with longer oars (longer outboard!)
	▶ Rowing at low rates (15-18/min) and overemphasize the release motion
	▶ Bobbing – moving squared blades up and down in finish position
	▶ If bobbing is mastered, add after 10 times bobbing the release, recovery and one drive on the call of the coxswain – execute at slow movement speed
	▶ Overemphasis of the final part of drive at low boat speed and low stroke rate
	▶ Rowing with feet out of the shoes
	▶ Follow the blade with your eyes, specifically watching the splashes on the blade during release

Advanced Exercise

- Rowing with squared blades and maintaining boat speed or even trying to increase boat speed
- Increasing boat speed while maintaining a steady low stroke rate (SR 15/min)
- Delayed feather: Release the blades on the square and only feather when hands passed the knees

The exercises in Tab. 19 give masters rowers and their coaches a great list of ideas for how to work on certain parts of technique. The use of such drills is usually more successful than simply calling for a specific change. They let the rower experience and feel how the targeted technique works while engaging in an exciting and challenging exercise. Using a series of drills with levels of additional complexity (see Tab. 20) helps in several ways. First, the rowers start with a simple drill to get the first feedback and experience the movement. Secondly, the challenge of increasing difficulty motivates the rowers and further ingrains the basic movement being learned or, as is more often the case, corrected. Thirdly, this approach takes any boredom out of learning technique.

The following examples were used by the authors in a previous presentation (Fritsch & Nolte, 2018, 62):

Tab. 20: Series of drills with levels of additional complexity.

EXAMPLE A	
1. Easy	Normal rowing, possibly with blades on the water during the recovery
2. More difficult	Same as 1, but with blades off the water
3. Challenge	Same as 2, but with eyes closed
4. Expert	Same as 3, but with squared blades
5. Top	Same as 2, 3 or 4, but with higher power and higher stroke rate

EXAMPLE B	
1. Easy	Rowers 1 and 2 in a four row while 3 and 4 stabilize the boat with the blades on the water. Then switch so 3 and 4 row and 1 and 2 stabilize (half boat rowing). Then 2 and 3 row and 1 and 4 stabilize etc.
2. More difficult	Same as 1, but with squared blades
3. Challenge	Ongoing change of two athletes rowing – 1 and 2 rowing; next stroke 2 and 3; next stroke 3 and 4; next stroke 1 and 4 etc.
4. Expert	Same as 1, 2, and 3, but the two rowers who are not rowing push the handles down into the boat, keeping the blades far off the water.
5. Top	Same as 3, but the two rowers who do not propel the boat carry out the rowing motion with the other two, but with the blades off the water (air strokes).

EXAMPLE C	
1. Easy	Rowing with pause after every third stroke – during the pause, the blades lay on the water and balance the boat
2. More difficult	Same as 1, but with blades off the water during the pause
3. Challenge	Same as 2, but performing a square and feather of the blades during the pause
4. Expert	Same as 3, but the rowers touch the top of the head with the palm of their hand (alternating right/left hand) after the square/feather
5. Top	Same as 4, but the rowers clap their hands during the pause (this must go fast, as the oars have to be released and caught again before the blades touch the water)

As the difficulty increases, every rower, every crew will notice on their own whether they can perform the drill proficiently. If not, go back one step (or more) and practice!

Chapter 5

BOAT RIGGING FOR THE MASTERS ROWER

Suitable rowing equipment, coupled with the right choice of rigging measurements, is not only the basis of tremendous enjoyment in rowing, but also prevents errors whose implications can adversely affect technique and sometimes even lead to physical discomfort or injury. The lack of preparation for an outing or the rushed desire to "get on the water fast" can quickly lead to big problems in a training session that threaten to overshadow a rowing experience that was supposed be amazing.

First, the proper boat needs to be selected for the specific crew. Experience, number and fitness of the rowers, weather conditions, club rules, as well as the stated goal of the session decide whether for example a pair or an eight is chosen. A crew, preparing let's say for the FISA Masters regatta, needs to do so in a suitable racing shell, while such a boat would be totally inappropriate for the same crew that plans to row on the ocean. Likewise, an eight crew with advanced-level technique, which regularly meets once a week for a session, should occasionally venture into smaller racing shells to promote balance and specific power applications. Nevertheless, environmental factors can put all other considerations on hold if driftwood, current or wind for example make it unsafe for singles or pairs, or if it would not be possible to keep inexperienced and experienced crews together when only one safety boat is available.

Above all, any rowing equipment must always be operative and in good working order. Safety first! Rowers and their coach must ensure that a boat can safely carry the crew, as well as withstand the loads generated while training or racing. All components, such as sliding seats, oarlocks and footstretchers must be in good working order, so that the rower can fully concentrate on their technique. They need to be checked thoroughly before putting the boat on the water. Broken parts or protruding sharp edges that can lead to injuries are unacceptable. Finally, special attention must be given to the correct rigging measurements for the crew, as well as the boat settings (footstretcher and slide positions).

5.1 WHAT IS THE PROPER EQUIPMENT FOR MASTERS ROWERS?

The development of boat materials has made rapid progress in recent years. Oars are a good example of this with innovations appearing almost annually. From a number of different grips to overall length adjustability to shaft material, weight and diameter to blade shape, today's rowers have a multitude of options. The principles outlined in this chapter apply to all aspects of rigging, both boats and oars, for masters rowers. Given the interconnectedness of each adjustment with all others, this chapter will also offer insight into the effects and mutual dependencies of rigging.

The right choice of boat is based on the particular purpose or goal of the rowing session. If the goal is to achieve a high boat speed (e.g. at regattas), racing boats are the first choice and ideally should be individually tailored to the crew. If a crew meets sporadically and in different combinations for rowing, an older, well-maintained racing shell or even a pleasure boat is quite sufficient, provided it is well rigged. Pleasure tour rowers and coastal rowers need specifically designed boats that can, for example, carry camping equipment or can be rowed in big open water waves. But even in this case, correct rigging is essential. Convenience and safe handling are paramount here, as even minor rigging errors can lead to very unpleasant overloading on long or rough outings.

If adult beginners are learning in a single, a wider boat should be chosen. This will reduce possible anxiety and can be better handled by an older person with limited mobility (e.g. extra weight, reduced flexibility etc.). Beginner training on waterways with environmental hazards is better done in larger crew boats so that novices feel safe in the learning situation. Of course, beginners also require a properly rigged boat, since it facilitates the learning of new movements (see chapter 3).

Basically all boats should be as light as possible. A lighter boat has less water resistance, gives the rower a better sense of motion and boat "feel", and increases the joy of rowing. Additionally, lighter boats are far easier to carry; a strong argument used my many older rowers.

The appeal of a newer boat over an older one is evident in the way that rowers of all ages seem universally drawn to new equipment. The prevailing assumption is that the newest equipment will guarantee the best row. This, however, is not always the case. Making a careful boat selection and, more importantly, proper rigging for the respective crew, have far greater impact on the comfort and enjoyment of athletes than choosing a boat simply based on its age. Ensuring that boats are well maintained and rigged is of vital importance for this reason and also because proper care increases equipment longevity and allows for quality rowing experiences for many years.

5.2 WHAT SHOULD BE CONSIDERED WHEN RIGGING A BOAT FOR MASTERS ROWERS?

The correct **rigging of each rowing station** (or "seat" in the broad sense of the section of the boat occupied by an individual rower) has a direct and combined impact on boat stability and comfort of the rower and crew. Improving balance skills is essential to rowing, and the ultimate sense of mastering rowing can only be achieved in an unstable boat. While methodical exercises (drills; see chapter 4) can mediate or train this feeling, a correctly rigged boat is the fundamental basis for learning good technique and improving boat feel.

Cardinal errors often found in an uncomfortably rigged boat are:

▸   loading is too heavy,
▸   footstretcher is too steep or too high,
▸   oarlock height are too low,
▸   not enough pitch on the blade, or
▸   slides are too short.

Overly **heavy loading** makes rowing laborious and cumbersome and can cause overload injuries.

The correct **footstretcher setting** has a huge impact on a rower's ability to stay relaxed on the recovery, attain a comfortable, proper catch position and ensure smooth blade entry at the catch.

An **oarlock** that is too low prevents the effective transfer of a rower's force, makes a clean recovery difficult and can lead to a feeling of tightness.

Too little **pitch on the blade** causes the oar to dive deep into the water with even the least amount of force, leading the rower to try desperately to hold the oar in its position, only adding to the boat's imbalance. This also impedes a clean release of the blade out of the water toward the finish.

Overly **short slides** cause the seat wheels to hit the front stops (or stern ends of the slides), often leading to a catch that is too short and choppy. Thus the run of the boat is severely limited. All these incorrect adjustments prevent the rowers from experiencing the easy run of the boat, which is the ultimate goal of every good rowing technique.

On the other hand, we should always keep in mind that masters rowers are especially happy when they improve their skills and stay fit. These are in many clubs a prerequisite to gaining permission to use the better boats in the boathouse, which adds to the satisfaction of exercising. These are, in no small part, reasons why many masters rowers also buy their own modern racing shell to make sure they can always enjoy a boat that is specifically rigged for them. Of course, this means that masters rowers need to investigate which boat is best for them, how to rig the boat and how to keep it in best working order.

5.3 HOW TO RIG A BOAT FOR MASTERS ROWERS

It is necessary to know all adjustable parts of the boat equipment:

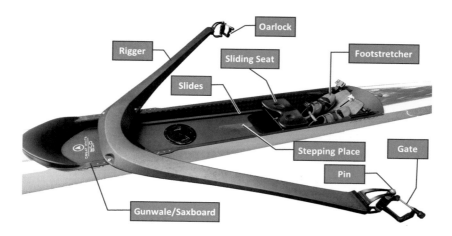

Fig. 31: The most important parts of the boat.

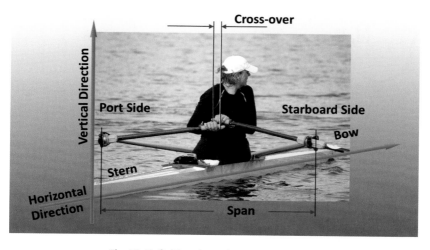

Fig. 32: Definitions in rowing.

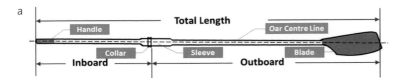

Fig. 33: Definitions of oar measurements:
a) Overall length, inboard and outboard;
b) Pitch on the blade.

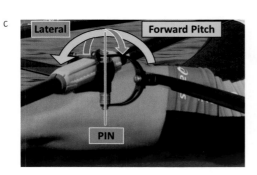

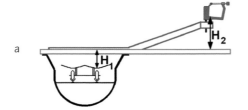

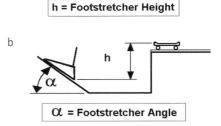

Fig. 34: Definitions of boat measurements:
a) Height of the oarlock;
b) Height and angle of the footstretcher;
c) Forward and lateral pitch on the pin.

5.3.1   Oar Design and Measurements

Sculls and oars, more than all other rowing equipment, have seen the biggest development in the last 20 years. Newer materials (especially higher quality carbon fiber) and modern procedures have allowed significant design changes. The weight of the oars was reduced. Blade shapes have been developed. A range of shaft stiffness is now available and shaft diameters have been reduced without compromising performance. Many materials, diameters and even contours are used to provide individualized handles for each rower. When it comes to adjustability, changing length for both outboard and inboard on all modern oars is a matter of a few simple steps.

Historically, the transition from wood to glass fibre to carbon fibre led to lighter equipment. New high module fibres now allow for the construction of such light oars that it can be difficult to handle them in all but ideal conditions and makes them vulnerable to breakage.

Blade design has been another subject of enthusiastic research. Presenting all possible variations of blades design would be overwhelming. As such we will limit our description to the three main different blade shapes (or styles) that have prevailed in recent years and are most widely used. We label each design style with the name by which they are marketed by their respective manufacturers, but it must be noted that many manufactures provide models of similar design with different names.

The three main blade designs are: "Slick" (also called: "Smoothie2 Plain Edge" and "Alpha"; the original first asymmetric blade shape with flat surface without the middle rib), "Smoothie2 Vortex Edge" (similar to the Slick shape, but with round edges at the end of the blade) and "Fat Blade" (similar to the Smoothie, but with a wider shape and larger surface).

Some oar manufacturers offer further blade designs featuring less commonly used shapes and surface areas and can therefore be considered as special types. Also, there are different edge (or blade tip) designs available (like the Vortex edge), as well as different blade thicknesses (although a minimum thickness is dictated by racing rules), and width and length dimensions for the same shape design. All manufacturers provide more detailed descriptions of their oars on their websites along with basic rigging dimensions and advice on how best to maintain their equipment.

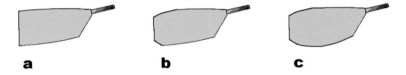

a   **b**   **c**

Fig. 35: The three different blade shapes, which have essentially prevailed in recent years. Depending on the manufacturer, they are called differently:

a)   *Slick, Smoothie2 Plain Edge, Alpha*
b)   *Smoothie2 Vortex Edge*
c)   *FatBlade*

Each blade shape has its own qualities, most of which are based on a rower's individual preferences. As long as the oars are rigged well, using the proper measurements relative to the blade shape, all blade shapes will allow proper rowing. The difference in efficiencies of the blade shapes only gains significance for the high performance rower who is seeking for every last bit of an advantage from their equipment. While the FatBlade seems to have the best mechanical efficiency, it is also the most difficult to row with because of being the shortest oar (balance) and having the largest width (entry and release). It is especially important for masters rowers to focus on setting the proper oar measurements rather than discussing design details.

The general rule:

The larger the blade area, the higher the mechanical efficiency of the oar, as long as the rower can properly handle the blades technically and conditionally.

The rower must be able to enter the blade properly into the water and release it without sacrificing stroke frequency and/or producing additional braking resistance. The blade shape, but above all the blade area associated with it, is the crucial factor in selecting the best oar rigging dimensions.

Thanks to the advanced carbon fibre material and modern manufacturing processes, oar shafts have achieved a greater consistency in quality, are lighter in weight and narrower in diameter. Of course, a lighter shaft makes it easier to reach a higher stroke rate, but it also makes balancing of the boat more difficult. A smaller diameter has of course decreased wind resistance, but requires a comparatively higher (and therefore more expensive) fibre material and a thicker shaft wall which makes the shaft heavier.

The **handle** of the oar is the contact point between rower and oar that puts a lot of strain on the palm and the fingers. Some rowers swear by certain materials, the thickness and even the contour of the handles. There is no immanent mechanical advantage to any of these parameters. The rower's individual preference is the deciding factor. If a selection is available, rowers should try the different handle types to find the best for themselves. The most significant factor is the handle diameters relative to the size of the rower's hands. Overly large handle diameters are not recommended for small hands and vice versa.

While it has always been possible to shorten an oar's overall length in the days before carbon fibre, sawing off the end of a wooden handle is not easily undone. The ability to repeatedly adjust the **length of an oar** to make it shorter or longer has had a significant impact on rigging. Oars can now easily be adjusted for rowing in different boat types or changing wind conditions at a regatta. It remains, however, extremely important when buying oars to choose an appropriate initial length with the current and future rowers in mind since there are physical limitations on how much shorter or longer an oar can be adjusted.

We highlight the average measurements in tables 20 and 21 with grey shading. These measurements are so to speak the normal **'starting point'** for rigging the equipment. Specific adaptations for individual rowers' needs will then be carried out in a logical manner. Such adaptation might include increasing the height of the oarlock for a rower with a long torso or decreasing the span and inboard for a rower who is smaller than their crewmembers.

Tab. 21: Measurements of the oars depending on the blade shape

SPAN/SPREAD AND OAR LENGTH

INCREASE LOAD (e.g. rowers younger, in tail wind or rowers less skilled) →

← DECREASE LOAD (e.g. rowers older, in head wind or rowers more skilled)

	BOAT	SPREAD (m)			OAR LENGTH (m)					
			NORMAL		SHORT		NORMAL		LONG	
SWEEP	2-:	0.88	0.86	0.84	3.69	3.63	3.72	3.65	3.75	3.68
	4-:	0.87	0.85	0.83	3.70	3.64	3.73	3.66	3.76	3.69
	4+:	0.88	0.86	0.84	3.69	3.63	3.72	3.65	3.75	3.68
	8+:	0.86	0.84	0.82	3.70	3.64	3.73	3.66	3.76	3.69
		SPAN (m)			SCULL LENGTH (m)					
SCULL	1x:	1.62	1.60	1.57	2.81	2.69	2.85	2.72	2.88	2.75
	2x:	1.62	1.60	1.57	2.81	2.69	2.85	2.72	2.88	2.75
	4x:	1.61	1.59	1.56	2.82	2.70	2.86	2.73	2.89	2.76

BLADE SHAPES: "SLICK" OR "SMOOTHIE"   "FAT BLADES"

OAR INBOARD

INBOARD SWEEP = SPREAD + 0.30 m

INBOARD SCULL = SPAN/2 + 0.08 m

EXAMPLE:

FOR SPREAD = 0.86m   INBOARD = 0.86 + 0.30 = 1.16m

FOR SPAN = 1.58m   INBOARD = 1.58/2 + 0.08 = 0.87m

We chose to identify the oars with the longest ("Slick", "Smoothie") and shortest ("FatBlade") measurements in Tab. 21. The oar measurements of all other blade shapes fall in between these two extremes. It is impossible to give for every rower and every possible blade shape the exact recommendation, since too many variables are involved. We therefore suggest to start with a "normal" measurement for the blade type used by the rower (highlighted with grey background in Tab. 21) and then conduct some testing, to find the individual best measurement (shorter or longer). This can be done for competitive rowers through time trialing over distances around half of the targeted race distance. Non-competitive rowers should find a measurement that fits their specific needs – comfort, easiness of handling etc.

5.3.2   Boat Measurements

While the selected blade shape will largely influence the best oar measurements, the **boat measurements** will be mainly tailored to the rower. The anthropometric measures and the rower's skill level significantly influence these settings: the **height of the oarlock**, **the pitch on pin and blade**, as well as **the footstretcher height and angle**. All the settings are measured and set on land, while the **position of the footstretcher in the longitudinal direction** of the boat and the **position of the slides** are adjusted on the water.

Tab. 22: Overview of recommended boat measurements

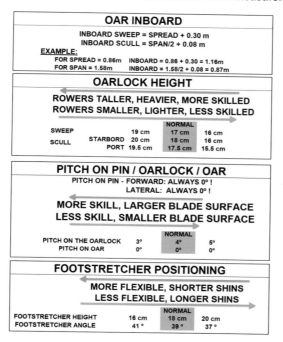

OAR INBOARD		
INBOARD SWEEP = SPREAD + 0.30 m		
INBOARD SCULL = SPAN/2 + 0.08 m		
EXAMPLE:		
FOR SPREAD = 0.86m	INBOARD = 0.86 + 0.30 = 1.16m	
FOR SPAN = 1.58m	INBOARD = 1.58/2 + 0.08 = 0.87m	

OARLOCK HEIGHT			
ROWERS TALLER, HEAVIER, MORE SKILLED			
ROWERS SMALLER, LIGHTER, LESS SKILLED			
		NORMAL	
SWEEP	19 cm	17 cm	16 cm
SCULL STARBORD	20 cm	18 cm	16 cm
PORT	19.5 cm	17.5 cm	15.5 cm

PITCH ON PIN / OARLOCK / OAR			
PITCH ON PIN - FORWARD: ALWAYS 0° !			
LATERAL: ALWAYS 0° !			
MORE SKILL, LARGER BLADE SURFACE			
LESS SKILL, SMALLER BLADE SURFACE			
		NORMAL	
PITCH ON THE OARLOCK	3°	4°	5°
PITCH ON OAR	0°	0°	0°

FOOTSTRETCHER POSITIONING			
MORE FLEXIBLE, SHORTER SHINS			
LESS FLEXIBLE, LONGER SHINS			
		NORMAL	
FOOTSTRETCHER HEIGHT	16 cm	18 cm	20 cm
FOOTSTRETCHER ANGLE	41°	39°	37°

The average initial or "normal" measurements are again highlighted in grey, while the indicated arrows in Tab. 22 point in the direction in which the dimensions should move, if the rowers have the respective characteristics. Thus the initial setting of 17 cm is the generally acceptable oarlock height for sweep rowers, with 0-degree pitch on the pin and blade, 4-degree pitch on the oarlock, a footstretcher height of 18 cm and a footstretcher angle of 39 degrees. For example, a smaller and/or less experienced rower should reduce the oarlock height a bit and could try to row with an oarlock pitch of 5 degrees.

These adjustments are to be measured precisely and carried out on shore. Basically, measurements are set the same for the entire boat and only exceptionally adapted separately for individual rowers, for example if their body measurements deviate significantly from the other rowers. Rigging with the same boat dimensions for all rowers guarantees better balance and equal torques on the boat. If, however, a rower is significantly larger than the rest of the crew, steps may need to be taken to ensure that this rower has optimal power delivery. The suggestions in Tab. 22, indicated by the arrows with the accompanying characteristics of the rowers, should be taken into account.

In contrast, the footstretcher and slides in the longitudinal direction of the boat must **always** be individually adapted to the rower. This is best done on the water at the beginning of the rowing session. The rowers check their respective footstretcher position. To do this, the rowers move into the finish position. The position of the hands relative to the body then indicates whether the footstretcher is set correctly, as presented in Fig. 36.

When the correct footstretcher position in the longitudinal direction is found, the slides can be adjusted if necessary. The slides can be moved in the longitudinal direction of the boat and should be adjusted so that in the catch position the front wheels of the rower's seat just touch the front ends of the slides, when the rowers perform their normal stroke movement. In this case, the front ends of the slides may be 5 cm to 15 cm sternwards from the face of the oarlock, depending on the leg dimensions and mobility of the rower. This measurement of the slides is called "workthrough". As long as the rower performs the correct technique (e.g. shins maximally perpendicular at the catch) and the rower does not touch the front ends of the slide with the seat, this measurement has no influence on the performance of the rower.

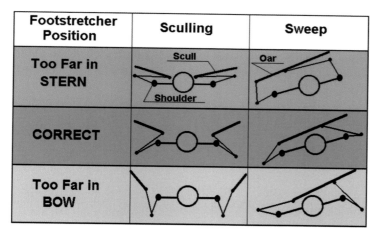

Footstretcher Position	Sculling	Sweep
Too Far in STERN		
CORRECT		
Too Far in BOW		

Fig. 36: Effect of the footstretcher position in the boat's longitudinal direction on the oars' position relative to the rower's body at the finish, here shown in bird's eye view. The rower is in the best position for a strong draw with the arms when the hands are pulling towards the shoulders and do not pass them (highlighted in green).

TOO MUCH SPACE – ROWERS PULL PAST THE BODY DURING THE RELEASE!

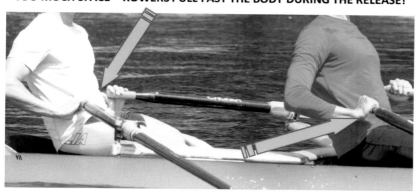

Fig. 37: Example of a footstretcher position in the boat's longitudinal direction where the stretcher is too far into the bow; the rower pulls past the body during the release.

If the slides are on the other hand moved too far towards the stern, the rower may touch the slides with their cafes and/or hit the back end of the slides with their seat in the finish position. This can lead to injuries and the inability to finish the drive properly, so that it is important to not set the slides further to the stern as just necessary for a proper catch position.

5.3.3   Tips for Adjusting the Boats

A poorly adjusted boat prevents the rower from rowing technically correct. It can even be argued that most technical errors are due to incorrectly set boats and oars. Or in other words:

A correctly adjusted rowing boat supports a good rowing technique!

A crew cannot effectively work on balance, for example, if the pitches on the pins are different from one side of the boat to the other. Likewise, it is impossible to slide in a controlled manner during the recovery, take a relaxed catch position or execute a smooth and quick entry if the footstretchers are set too high or too steep. In contrast, a well-rigged boat automatically assists the rower to do these movements properly.

Masters rowers should not be afraid to seek the advice and assistance of an expert to properly rig their boat and oars. However, they should also attempt to learn to do these measurements and adjustments on their own, which comes with practice.

On the other hand, it can be observed again and again that coaches and rowers spend enormous time rigging a boat for general use, but rowers then make smaller individual "adjustments" to their specific station on the water without re-setting them after the row. Such behavior means that, after a few training sessions, the boat is once again completely "misaligned" and has to be re-rigged. These unsystematic rectifications on the various rowing seats add up with each session and lead after a few sessions to a different and likely incorrect rig. Therefore, the general rule should be:

Set it right once and then keep your hands off!

Just as important as proper rigging is the proper care of the boat. This begins with always using professional tools to make the adjustments correctly to avoid unnecessary wear on all parts of the boat. It is also essential that the boat is regularly washed and wiped thoroughly, certain parts (oarlocks and sliding seats) oiled and the slides cleaned. This important daily maintenance becomes even more critical when rowing is done on salty water.

Even with the best care, a certain amount of wear and tear must be expected and worn parts should be replaced at certain intervals. It is more cost-effective in the long run to replace a broken part early with an original spare part, before major damage occurs. For example, worn out ball bearing components of the wheels on sliding seats should be replaced with new ones before any leaking rust has a chance to scratch the slides. The long life of a boat and the continued joy of rowing in it can only be ensured by such measures.

Proper maintenance of a boat starts with the purchase. Before a new boat is purchased, it should be carefully considered which boat best meets, and will continue to meet, the desired requirements. It should be analyzed exactly which type of boat is needed (high-tech racing boat, training boat or open water boat). Which boatbuilder guarantees the best quality, offers the best service and delivers spare parts in a timely fashion? The experiences of other rowers can be very helpful. A test row in a prospective boat should provide the final information about whether it really meets expectations.

Technical expertise is essential when selecting and buying a boat, which is always an expensive investment. Masters, much like any other crew, should therefore seek the expertise of an experienced coach and thus secure the short and long term benefits that come with a good coach and good equipment. A proper boat increases the learning experience considerably, provides significantly more enjoyment of our sport and helps to avoid injury. Ideally, support in selecting the most appropriate boat should be provided by the club. If this is not available, however, it is necessary to take the initiative.

Here a few general tips on how masters rowers invest their time most profitably:

▸ Choose the right boat for the crew, based on the level of physical fitness, the technical ability, the desired goal, but also the expected environmental conditions!

▸ Set the boat properly! Use the measures that are appropriate for the team and carry out this work with professionalism!

▸ Check if technical errors are due to incorrect rigging of the boat! Many technical errors are based on improper boat settings and experienced coaches can identify this quickly. Therefore, it is important to regularly use the services of an expert to increase the joy of rowing.

▸ Care for and maintain the boat regularly, so that the enjoyment of using good equipment lasts a long time and technical errors or even injuries and damage are avoided!

TRAINING FOR MASTERS ROWERS

6.1 GENERAL INFORMATION ON TRAINING FOR MASTERS ROWERS

The diversity of the individual goals and motivations in masters sport requires a rethink of what we mean when we talk about "training". When planning training for older adults, we must consider a broad range of questions regarding improvement, maintenance and restoration of physical performance. We must also be mindful of meaningful loading measures, as well as the risks for older participants in sport. Sport training means regular practice in order to maintain or improve performance levels of motor skills, but also to increase motivation and/or mental resilience.

The **training principles**, as they are formulated in training science, remain valid, but they must all be tailored depending on certain parameters that accompany aging: Degeneration of organs that get used less; reserves for adaptations and loading; changed regeneration times. For the most part, general training principles can be applied to an athlete of middle to older age with an above-average activity level. On the other hand, for older adults with little or no experience in competition or performance sport, a more sophisticated consideration of training principles must be developed (see Mechling, 1999, pp. 291f).

Also the training contents and methods must be individualized depending on a person's age. The call for older adults to perform weight training complements the need for training to maintain and improve movement coordination, motor learning, as well as physical mobility. It is important to avoid excessive demands and peer pressure when organizing training for older athletes and one must always account for the relative performance between athletes in a training group as well as individual abilities.

6.1.1   Physical Requirements for Rowing During Aging

The rowing motion is a dynamic movement sequence with the rhythmic use of force of large muscle groups under high general endurance demands. Practicing rowing – from recreational to competitive rowing – requires a minimum basis of agility, coordination and dynamic power, as well as local and general aerobic endurance. The sum of these physical skills together with personality characteristics, such as willpower and motivation, build the prerequisite for learning and practicing this sport. It should be noted that rowing-specific physical and psychological abilities are linked in a multi-layered fashion. Physical fitness abilities are not developed without a strong dedication and cannot be fully transferred into propulsion of the boat without the coordinative skills and a sufficient rowing technique.

6.1.2   Load and Strain

Training is characterized by systematic planning of physical exercises that manifests itself in an adequate change of loading and recovery that adhere to the training goals and the load handling capacity of the trainee. The overall load of the training leads to strain in the athlete that triggers the training gain. In healthy people - and this applies to humans of all ages - load handling capacity and performance go hand in hand. However, the likelihood is higher that older people will experience ailments to a higher degree and frequency. This means that compared to younger athletes, generally speaking, masters' performance capacity is relatively limited and can only handle a lower training load.

Unlike younger people, chronic diseases are more common in older people. Dickhuth and Berg (2007, p. 608) note that 75% of people over the age of 65 simultaneously suffer from at least three illnesses. The reduced adaptability of most organs in the average older person must be respected, as well as any side effects and interactions with medications an individual may require.

Consequences for the masters rower, who is ambitious to participate in competitive sport are clear: Modifications in the training load are primarily to be made quantitatively, less from a qualitative point of view; there is no type of sport that should be off-limits and improvements should not be confined to only one single form of motor stress, such as endurance or coordination. Masters athletes should choose a type of sport that satisfies the individual's expectations of health, experience and well-being, as well as strengthens the individuals' body to optimize natural functioning and everyday activities. This also implies learning new sports in old age.

Questions regarding "How often?", "How intense?" and "How long?" are frequently brought up.

A masters athlete should train at least three to four times per week to develop individual fitness skills. Two training sessions per week suffice to maintain general fitness. However, to optimize recovery, no more than four sessions of the same type and purpose should be performed per week.

Regarding the intensity of training, a distinction has to be made between the load – as an objective measure of the physical work – and the strain – as a measure of how the individual athlete experiences the overall demands. There is no doubt that masters rowers train – in absolute measures – at a lower intensity than elite rowers, but many find their training subjectively as exhausting as ever. This is a potential danger for overloading, damage to one's health and injuries.

In general, one can use the following guidelines for intensity in masters training:

▶ Strength training should be done with about 65-75% of the load that an athlete can move maximally for one repetition (65 – 75% of 1 RM).

▶ Endurance exercises should be performed with an intensity that the athlete assesses subjectively as stress between "still light" to "a bit exhausting" on the Borg scale (Corresponding information see chapter 6.3.3 in this book and Fig. 61).

▶ Competition-specific training corresponds to about 90 – 110% of the anticipated race speed.

▶ The question about the training volume can be answered generally in a similar way:

▶ The appropriate duration of a strength training session for masters is 30 – 45 min.

▶ Endurance training sessions in rowing, jogging and swimming should last between 45 – 75 min and 60 – 120 min in bicycling, depending on the training goal (prevention, health, long-distance races or sprints).

▶ The length of competition-specific training pieces should be 10 – 50% of the race distance.

6.1.3   Loading of the Musculoskeletal System

The load-bearing capacity of the musculoskeletal system is limited with age due to various factors. The articular cartilage is exposed to aging processes. It has also been shown that women lose some of their bone density and mass after the age of 40. However, proper and appropriate physical activity and training can protect muscle mass, bones, cartilage, and all joint mobility from premature degeneration. Bone mass can even be rebuilt through rowing.

All the more important is specific training that counteracts restrictions, acts as prevention and compensates losses. Although sports with a high aerobic endurance component are specifically recommended for older adults, regular strength training and skills training of the sensorimotor system (proprioceptive, coordinative skills) should accompany endurance exercises. This includes explicitly games and team sports, short training loads like sprint intervals, as well as technical exercises.

6.1.4   Principles for Old Age Sports

▶   With age, degenerative ailments increase, thereby limiting the exercise capacity.
▶   Due to delayed adaptation, it is necessary to increase loads at a slower rate during training and practice.
▶   Older athletes must prepare more carefully for physical stress (e.g. prolonged warm-up).
▶   Sports activities should take place in a fixed time frame and be firmly organized; just as essential are personal wellbeing and social inclusion.
▶   The idea of competing should be seen as less important, but not completely ruled out.

The length of regeneration after training depends on

▶   the fitness of the athlete;
▶   the type of the training stress (cardiovascular system, nervous system, musculoskeletal system);
▶   the intensity and duration of the training load;
▶   climatic and physical conditions (temperature, weather, humidity, altitude etc.); and
▶   hygiene and lifestyle during the recovery phase (sleep, luxury foods and beverages, nutrition etc.).

The regeneration process takes place differently in various phases (early and late phases, as well as supercompensation) and in different areas (see Tab. 23).

Tab. 23: Phases of regeneration

Phase	Recovery Process	Supporting Measures
Early phase End of training up to approximately six hours after exercise	▶ Normalization of heart rate/ respiratory rate ▶ Replenishing CP and ATP storages ▶ Removal of blood lactate ▶ Start refilling the glycogen storages	Taking in carbohydrates and fluid Beware: Increased risk of infection due to overloading or cooling-off after training
Late phase Ca. 6-36 hours after end of training	▶ Replenishing of glycogen storages ▶ Regeneration of structural proteins ▶ Regeneration of immune system to a large extent	Carbohydrate intake! Regenerative measures: Compensatory training, stretching
Phase of supercompensation Approx. 36 hours to several days	▶ Electrolyte compensation ▶ Compensation of the hormone balance ▶ Supercompensation of structural proteins ▶ Supercompensation of hormone and enzyme balance	Pay attention to longer term training planning! Especially after training camps or a series of competitions

Training can be started at almost any age, subject to a few basic rules and appropriate exercise progression. However, it should be noted that although the trainability of individual motor skills is possible into old age, the ability to exercise must be assessed in a detailed sports medical examination. This is especially true for newcomers to the sport from the age of 35 years and older that have certain pre-existing conditions such as high blood pressure, peripheral circulatory disorders, angina pectoris, after a heart attack, chronic bronchitis, diabetes mellitus, osteoarthritis, osteoporosis and gout.

The risk of overloading, excessive demands and insufficient recovery is equally high for newcomers, as it is for life-long rowers and former competitive rowers. Limited capacity, over-estimation of performance, excessive ambition, and social pressures can cause overloading that not only lead to accidents and injuries, but also results in a loss of performance beyond the age-related decline in function.

If masters athletes do not pay attention to appropriate regeneration phases which is a sign of incorrect training planning, especially when coupled with other performance-impairing factors, they can easily overextend their capacities. To avoid such overloading, the following measures should be taken into account:

▶ Careful structuring of training, loads and recuperation
▶ Limited use of forms of stress that are less favorable for masters, such as speed and power training, highly anaerobic training, exhaling against closed air passage (valsalva maneuver; e.g. due to trying to move excessive weight)
▶ Planning sufficient recovery periods after accidents and illnesses, even after seemingly light colds, throat infections, and intestinal infections
▶ Seeking consultation and advice from a physician, especially when experiencing unusual symptoms and regarding training when taking medication
▶ Choose appropriate training loads; do not push to the absolute maximum, keep instead always some "reserves" available

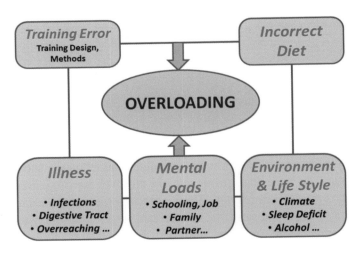

Fig. 38: Factors of overloading.

It is not reasonable and can even be dangerous for masters rowers and generally for all older athletes to simply copy training standards of high performance and elite athletes (duration and intensity). To the contrary, it is evident that lower training loads and age related exercises not only have positive health-related effects, but also lead to competition-specific improvements, if they are properly planned and performed over a longer period of time with the corresponding frequency.

The trainability of motor skills (strength, endurance, coordination, and flexibility) that are relevant for masters rowers also depends on mental factors, such as motivation to perform, willpower and resilience. It is important to promote these factors to guide masters rowers to independent and self-sufficient training.

6.2   TRAINING ROWING

Rowing training for adults can be divided into three basic categories:

1. Adult rowers train their physical abilities to achieve objectively measurable performances or to compare with other athletes. These rowers are **focused on competition**, their maximum development or as far as possible, the preservation of their performance. The orientation of their rowing training follows the structures of a high performance rower with corresponding objectives, but with some adaptations of the contents and programs. New training stimuli are planned and used based on the peak training gain reached during the recuperation phase.
2. Adult rowers use rowing as a means to **improve or maintain their physical fitness**. This objective also requires some knowledge about the "What?", "How?" and "With what?" at least in part knowledge of goal setting when rowing is used as physical training.
3. Adult rowers use **rowing for health reasons** and therefore, new training sessions will only be scheduled after a complete recovery from the last training. This is one main contrast to training focused on competition and performance-related aspects or the improvement of physical fitness.

These goals hold in common that all rowing is based on some kind of training program. However, the assembling of training sessions and the systematic layout of training planning will be different in each of the three categories. If you want to do justice to the different objectives that exist within masters rowing, **all training recommendations and rowing programs must observe the following principles:**

1. Athletes who are training in rowing must consider generic opportunities to improve and maintain performance, fitness and health that go beyond the sport of rowing
2. The selection of training content and programs must take into account the preconditions of the respective age and development stages of the masters rower in order to be effective
3. In addition to the goal of optimizing performance in competitive rowing of the masters, athletes must also aim for efficiency, which means they need to weigh effort and benefits
4. The design of competitive training program for masters puts specific demands on boat material and how to approach rowing technique
5. The greatest training effect in masters rowing is achieved through continuity and regularity of physical activity
6. Masters rowing thrives with the social integration of the athletes in the club – despite all the optimizing efforts, the aspect of social interaction and camaraderie must not fall victim to any stubborn training regime

Based on these principles, master's rowing training is divided into three areas:

1. On water rowing training
2. Supplementary training
3. Functional support training

6.2.1   On Water Rowing Training

Boat training or rather training on the water involves exercising specific requirements that are necessary to participate in rowing races of different lengths or in other meaningful rowing activities, like pleasure tours, rowing well in a crew boat, improving rowing endurance, etc. The following main principle applies to all of this:

If you want to get better in rowing, you have to row!

The training on the water consists – as it does in high-performance rowing – of training technique, of different types of endurance training and of rowing training under race conditions.

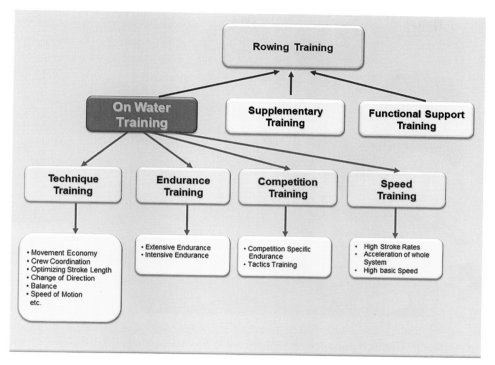

Fig. 39: Forms of rowing training: Here specifically on water training.

Many coaches argue, even in high-performance rowing, about the proper proportion of on water training in overall training. To get a better handle on this question regarding masters rowing, it is important to remember that an athlete requires a certain amount of complementary training to achieve age-appropriate fitness, since not all improvements of motor characteristics can be trained in the boat alone. That said, on water training offers a variety of loading modalities to train general physiological capacities. In addition to seasonal, injury and holiday reasons, there are other important motives to use equivalent forms and means of supplementary and functional support training for masters rowers. This, by the way, does not diminish on water rowing's role as the dominant form of training.

While indoor rowing is gaining popularity as a discipline of the sport in its own right, for many rowers, getting into a boat is the primary focus and for them the question remains: Why else would you want to row? Nevertheless, some athletes only want to exercise the sport of rowing indoors and the same rules of designing a proper training program apply for them except their main sport specific activity is rowing on the ergometer.

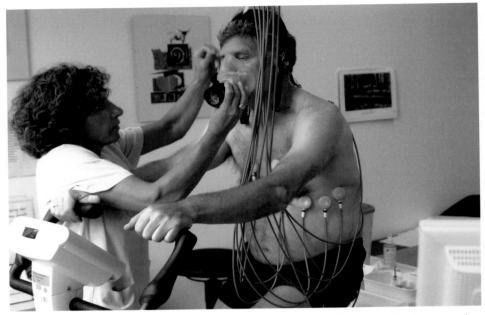

In old adulthood, endurance focused rowing training should pay particular attention to the age-related degenerative changes of the musculoskeletal and the cardiovascular systems, both regarding the choice of loading modalities and the prescribed amount of work. The content and methods of endurance training of older athletes must therefore primarily be based on age, health and fitness conditions, sport experience and individual resilience. It particularly makes sense to describe endurance training for competitive masters rowers through the following characteristics: loading intensity, duration of individual training pieces, overall extent of the work and design of recovery times.

OVERRIDING PRINCIPLE BEFORE STARTING PERFORMANCE TRAINING:
Medical examination and clearance certificate of health!

6.2.2 Training Areas and Intensities

The training on the water is based on proper rowing technique that needs to be practiced and maintained at all times. This technique training together with a smart selection of training pieces leads to specific training forms. The overall training load controls the development of fitness. Load is generally understood as the degree of physical work performed in training and we distinguish **external load** (objective description of the physical stress) and **internal load or strain** (subjective reaction to the physical stress). Remember that the same external training load can cause quite different internal strain on individual athletes!

Stress leads to a stimulus, which is the trigger of an action potential that then causes changes in the organism. Every physical activity is a stimulus. In order to achieve an effective training result, the intensity of the exercise must be set high enough that it exceeds a critical threshold, thus challenging the organism to react and adapt.

The threshold level of a stress stimulus depends not only on the objective intensity, but also largely on the actual performance capacity of the rowers and their subjectively experienced strain. A low and less specific stimulus will suffice for beginners or returnees compared to a very well trained masters rower. The load stimuli and specificity must of course be increased with improved performance capacity.

The identification of training intensities and methods is based on the actual boat speed a crew can achieve over 1,000 m and will be adapted to the different training goals. It seems to us that fixing heart rate or lactate levels are in general less helpful as guidance for masters rowers to set training intensities. Heart rates vary between individuals and are influenced by a number of effects besides the training intensity (temperature, nutrition, sleep, excitement levels etc.) and one needs specific measurement equipment to control lactate which is in most cases not available. With explicit knowledge of individual rowers, these physiological measurements may be helpful for these athletes, but one needs extra education in using them successfully. We will nonetheless provide some general guidelines later on, but caution against using them word for word and certainly not without first consulting a physician and undertaking a proper assessment of individual capacities.

In this context, we would like to differentiate four training intensity zones: **compensation/ regeneration, extensive endurance training, intensive endurance training, competition-specific training** presented in Tab. 24.

Tab 24: Training intensity zones for masters rowers

Zone	Compensation/Regeneration	Extensive Endurance
Objectives	▶ Recovery, compensation ▶ Economizing rowing technique ▶ Improvement of fat metabolism ▶ Economizing the cardiovascular system	▶ Development of (basic) aerobic endurance ▶ Training and stabilizing rowing technique at given boat speed ▶ Stabilizing and restoring endurance level
Intensity Heart rate as % of max HR	<60-65%	65-75%
Boat Speed/ Ergometer splits as % of expected race pace	<75%	75-85%
Subjective feeling, sense of stress	▶ Very pleasant ▶ Conversation is possible ▶ Breathing and heartbeat barely noticeable ▶ Enjoying the landscape and surroundings	▶ Breathing a bit accelerated ▶ Conversation still possible ▶ Increased concentration required ▶ Landscape and surroundings are still recognized
Subjective Stress Detector (SSP)* (see Fig. 61)	3-5	6-10
Suitable target group	▶ Competitive rowing ▶ Fitness ▶ Health ▶ Compensation	▶ Competitive Rowing ▶ Fitness ▶ Health ▶ Compensation

*SSP = Subjective stress perception after Borg (1985).

Intensive Endurance	Competition-Specific Endurance
▸ Improving organ strength ▸ VO2max ▸ Strength endurance ▸ Training of willpower ▸ Manifestation of rowing technique close to competition speed ▸ Improving crew- coordination	▸ Feeling for race pace ▸ Increase anaerobic capacity ▸ Tactics ▸ Technical economy under high loads and high speed ▸ Rowing race ▸ Training of will power
75-90%	>90%
85-90%	>90%
▸ Feeling of heavy stress ▸ Beginning shortness of breath ▸ Conversation is severely restricted ▸ Increased willpower and concentration required ▸ Average long-distance race pace	▸ Submaximal to maximum boat speed for respective race distance ▸ High motivation required ▸ Great willpower necessary ▸ Experience of reluctance to continue
11-14	15+
▸ Competitive Rowing ▸ Fitness ▸ (Health)	▸ Competitive Rowing

The correct training load is a fundamental prerequisite to achieve set personal goals. Training goals are often missed, because training loads do not reflect the rower's individual performance capacity and training level currently achieved. The methodical management of the training load is ideally carried out by means of sport-specific performance diagnostics. Indispensable in elite sports and increasingly used in fitness sports and even in masters rowing, laboratory or field tests are consulted to control the state of training adaptations. Those measures are, however, time consuming and costly.

Therefore, we have to find some more practical methods that will allow us to estimate the training zones presented in Tab. 24 for each individual athlete. One example of such a method is using the intensity percentages given in the Tab. 24 and Fig. 40. As long as one knows the speed of a crew at one of the training zones, the other zones' intensities can be calculated. To apply this method, we need adequate tests that reflect the intensity that is used in the respective zones. The following tests can for example be used to estimate the speed of crews at the four zones:

1. Compensation/regeneration:

Take the average speed of a continuous 60 min row. Choose the intensity so that you can maintain a conversation. Focus on good technique and try to achieve good run of the boat with moderate to light pressure on the blades. The stroke rate will usually be between 18 – 22 strokes/min.

2. Extensive endurance training:

Take the average speed of a continuous 60 min row maintaining solid pressure on the blades. Focus on good technique and try to maximize boat run while you still can talk in short sentences, but the flow of speech is interrupted by breathing. The stroke rate will usually be between 20 – 24 strokes/min.

3. Intensive endurance training:

Take the average speed of a 3 – 5 km long race piece. You can only communicate with single words or very short sentences, because of heavy breathing. The stroke rate will usually be between 24 – 28 strokes/min in a single and 26 – 32 strokes/min in an eight.

4. Competition-specific training:

Take the average speed of a 1 km race piece. Try to go as fast as possible. The stroke rate will usually be between 26 – 32 strokes/min in a single and 28 – 34 strokes/min in an eight.

*These instructions are for healthy athletes with at least good rowing experience between 40 – 60 years of age. Masters rowers with different qualifications and of different age need to adjust these measures accordingly. One should not hesitate to consult an experienced rower or coach for some input in the setup of these tests and the interpretation of the data.

Use the result of one of these tests to identify the intensity at the given training zone. You can then calculate the corresponding speed for the other training zones using Fig. 40. The respective speeds are of course only correct for the same boat class and environmental conditions that the test is run in.

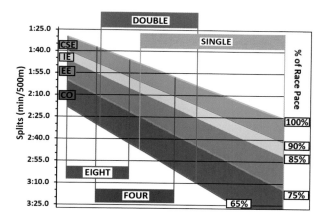

Fig. 40: Graphical display of the boat speed in split times per 500 m at different training zones depending on the individual performance level of the crew, the boat class and other conditions. The corresponding boat speeds at different training zones of a particular crew lie on a vertical line that goes through the point that is determined through a test or through prior experience.

Fig. 40 provides an aid in finding the corresponding boat speed at the intensity zones for different types of boats (Eights, Quads, Doubles and Singles) measured in time for 500 m which is often called "split time", which is also the measurement unit presented by rowing monitors like the Nielsen-Kellerman SpeedCoach or Coxmate GPS. The intensity ranges are indicated by the colored bands. Here is an example how to read the graph: Let us assume a masters double rowed a 1,000 m race piece under some headwind conditions and achieves a final time of 4:00 min, which gives an average split time of 2:00 min for 500 m. Mark the average split time at the 100% line (the top of the red bar crosses the 2:00 min/500 m horizontal line) and draw a vertical line through this cross point. The middle of the other colored bars on this line represent the estimated training splits for the respective training zones. The same rowers should then train in the same wind conditions at the following speeds:

- ▶ Intensive endurance training: Split times around 2: 13 min/500 m
- ▶ Extensive endurance training: Split times around 2: 22 min/500 m
- ▶ Compensation/recovery training: Split times slower than 2:40 min/500 m

Based on the race piece experience above (2:00 min/500 m splits in headwind) we can also estimate what this crew should be able to achieve and train in tailwind conditions. We assume that the crew can reach 90% of their maximal tailwind speed in headwind conditions. Again, we mark at first the average split time of 2:00 min/500 m at the 100% line and now draw a horizontal line to the 90% speed line. We then draw from this cross point a vertical line. Where this vertical line crosses the 100% speed line, we can get the speed (here ~ 1:47 min/500 m) that this double possibly can achieve in a tailwind 1,000 m race. The intensive endurance pace in tailwind would be about 2:00 m/500 m; the extensive endurance training splits would be about 2:08 min/500 m and about 2:25 min/500 m for recovery training.

Realize that these are not exact measurements, but very good estimates and orientations! Always keep health, recovery state, overall duration of the training in the respective zone and environmental conditions in mind when setting such training targets. Then adjust the targets accordingly. Rowers will get better with experience at setting personal speed targets for a given training zone. Training in groups helps learning to set proper targets and other athletes or coaches can give feedback by watching the crew in training. Also, be aware that this analysis actually gives you a range of speeds for the different training zones. Learn to use the whole range depending on the conditions and the specific training goal.

6.2.3 Training Methods – More Differentiated

We identified four distinct training intensities above. Three of these training forms, extensive, intensive and competition-specific endurance training, each can have a specific strength endurance or motor economics/rowing technique focus (see Fig. 41). While training in the lower intensity zones can more clearly be directed either towards strength endurance or motor economics/rowing technique, the athlete encounters increasingly overlapping training demands in the competition-specific zone. Of course, training must include competition-specific components, but should not and cannot only consist of competition-specific training intensities. It must rather shape effectively the basics and all individual components of the performance necessary for competition, as for example power, strength endurance, mobility or aerobic abilities.

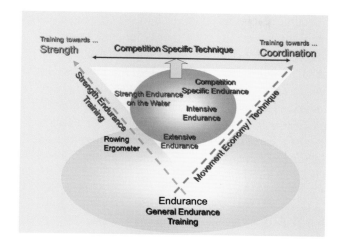

Fig. 41: Training of general and specific endurance abilities in rowing with different prioritizations.

Training methods help to achieve training goals and identified priorities through the smart combination of training sessions at different intensities and exciting exercise designs. For this, we can find a number of training methods that match the loading requirements of each intensity zone: **continuous, interval and competition methods**. We will present the different training methods graphically in their general form with respect to boat velocity.

The more intense a training load, the more important is the exact combination of work duration and intensity for each individual rower. Therefore, special care should be taken in the design of the training sessions in the intensive endurance and competition-specific endurance intensity zones. Due to decreasing anaerobic enzyme activity in late adulthood, the ability to build and break down lactate decreases. It is therefore too often the case that even "younger" masters rowers choose overly intensive workloads - even in their extensive endurance training. Additionally, we have to realize that the distribution of training intensities in the overall planning changes for the individual age groups for masters rowers (see Fig. 42).

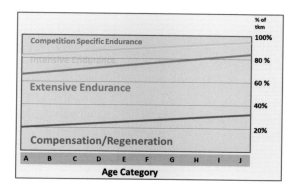

Fig. 42: Percentage of training kilometers in the different training zones for the FISA masters age groups.

Training of competitive-specific endurance loses its importance with increasing age. This means that the volume of training in this intensity zone shrinks for older rowers and a clear shift towards extensive and compensatory endurance training is advisable. Also, the identification of the 100% boat speed should move from the 1,000 m race pace to the long-distance race pace. However, newer research indicates that some vigorous exercise is advisable at any age. In this context, it is important to point out again how vital regular medical checks are, especially with increasing age; a physician should clear an athlete for high intensity exercises. Regardless of age and the ability to handle high intensity loading, training design can still be varied and one can find numerous forms of on water practices.

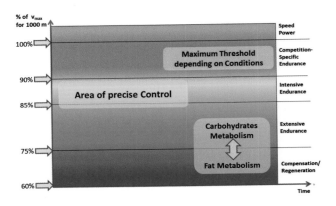

Fig. 43:
Schematic representation of the training intensity zones based on the percentage of the race boat speed.

It is important to point out that the transition area between extensive and intensive endurance training is quite small and therefore, needs precise assessment. "Too high" intensities and/or "too many" intense endurance training sessions can quickly lead to performance stagnation in masters rowers. A well-developed sense for the training load through frequent practical assessments (which intensities the individual rower truthfully can achieve) or even a regular performance diagnostic (e.g. spiroergometry) provides great service. We discussed this above in 6.2.2.

Extensive endurance training can be achieved within quite a range of boat speed. Depending on the training intensity, a higher proportion of fat (lower end of the intensity) or carbohydrate metabolism (higher end of the intensity) is involved in the energy production. The training intensity must be adjusted based on the corresponding training goal. Compensation training is primarily performed with a high portion of fat metabolism, while basic endurance-developing sessions require a little higher speed/intensity that leads to increased carbohydrate metabolism.

Steady state training methods

Steady state training methods are particularly suitable for extensive and intensive endurance training, as well as for regeneration. Thereby a certain distance or time is rowed without break. Interruptions occur only at turns, to ensure fluid intake or by unforeseen obstructions, like boating traffic. This method is central to improving basic endurance. Therefore, the intensity remains primarily at a level that energy supply is completely aerobic.

Even though this training method demands continuous work, stroke rates, concentration on specific technical details and drills can vary. Throughout these variations, however, the intended work intensity should be kept as constant as possible.

For this purpose, three main variants have emerged:

1. Continuous training
2. Fartlek training
3. Endurance training with systematically changing speeds

Continuous training is characterized by executing a consistent specific aerobic strain on the organism over a longer time reaching from 20 – 120 min and even more.

Fig. 44:
Schematic representation of continuous steady state training – here: Extensive endurance training.

Fartlek training

This training method was developed in Scandinavia and translates to English as "speed play". The fundamental idea of Fartlek training is that the athletes "play" with the intensity and the duration, changing the training load in an unsystematic way. Training load will however not leave the intended intensity zone and there are no rest times.

Fartlek Training was used in its original form in athletics and was run by a group of athletes trying to chase each other in different terrain. Depending on the terrain (e.g. hills, bends) or obstacles (e.g. trees in the forest, stones to skip) the load was constantly changing. Hills provide natural increases in intensity, trees serve as slalom poles, and grassy areas are used for push-ups. These changes were not exactly planned beforehand, but were based on the conditions encountered and the spontaneity of the athletes. Note that this kind of training not only provides physiological stimuli, but also trains agility, strength and reaction time.

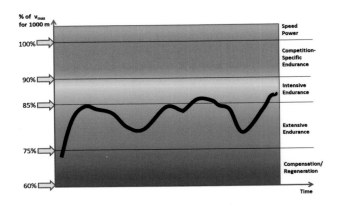

Fig. 45:
Schematic representation of a fartlek training at endurance pace –
here: Extensive endurance training with bordering to intensive endurance.

In rowing you have to be a bit more resourceful to use this method, since the water surface understandably does not offer such natural variations that you find in open terrain. Here are some examples how you can apply fartlek: **Headwinds** can be used to increase handle force; in **river bends** the crew can row with squared blades; at a **straightaway** the crew rows with very low stroke rate; **half-crew rowing** is used for specific strength training; **Tail wind** is rowed at higher stroke rates and with technical tasks. The ingenuity and the whims of the coach or the athletes knows no bounds.

However, it is advisable to set and maintain the intended training intensity (e.g. extensive endurance or competition-specific endurance) so that the fartlek training session stays within the overall training plan.

Steady state training with changing speed (Red Lining)

This kind of training is usually used for intensive endurance training. At the upper level of the athlete's aerobic endurance ability, stroke rate or force application is systematically varied over a longer period of time (10-30 min) with no rest and without leaving the training intensity zone. The basic idea of this form of training is to increase the organ power of the rowers, while at the same time a high flexibility in terms of stroke rate and power is to be achieved.

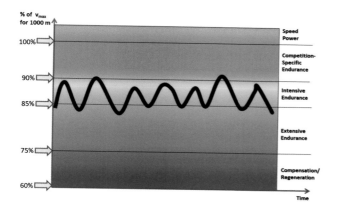

Fig. 46:
Schematic representation
of training with systematic
intensity changes (red lining) –
here: Intensive endurance
training.

This form of training requires the rower's full concentration and commitment. It therefore has not only excellent physical, but also enormous psychological training benefits.

Interval training

Interval training was developed in the 1960s and 70s and is closely associated with the name Karl Adam, the famous German coach who introduced this form of training into rowing. It has been very popular for a number of years, but was eventually replaced by a higher focus on long distance training. For some years now, this method has regained importance. Overall, intervals help to make training varied and more exciting. Also, this training method helps to keep concentration levels high.

The basic idea of this form of training is the repetitive change of loading at a higher intensity followed by periods of rest or recovery. Intensities, length of loading and times for recovery must be chosen depending on the health of the athletes and their physical and technical preparation for higher training intensities. A variety of training focuses can be achieved with this training method, for example peak power (very short work and long rest intervals), anaerobic lactic training (longer intensive work and shorter rest intervals) or aerobic training (increased number of longer work with relative short rest intervals).

Length of loading and rest is set by distance or time. Intensity of the exercise is given for both, loading and rest. These instructions provide endless possibilities for combinations and make interval training very exciting, but masters rowers must also be mindful of potential consequences. The excitement and high intensities can lead to injuries and overloading. Because of the possible high loading, athletes must first be prepared to take on such training, physically and mentally.

This training method also offers some variations:

1. Intensive interval training (higher intensity for shorter work periods),
2. Extensive interval training (lower intensity for longer work periods), and
3. Pyramid training (steady increase and then decrease of intensity/time/distance/ stroke rate for work periods).

Intensive interval training has grown in popularity in recent years under the name of high intensity interval training or **HITT**. This name indicates the explicit focus on the load, which is intended to be maximally applied for a very short time. The basic idea of intensive interval training is the repetitive nature of loading and rest at given durations. Very high loads of short duration of 10 seconds to 2 min alternate with comparatively long pauses 30 seconds to 5 min. The length of the load in relation to the recovery should be 1:2 to 1:3.

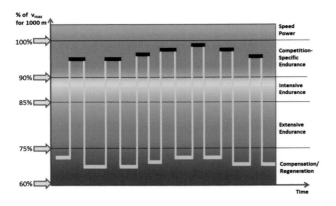

Fig. 47:
Schematic representation of intensive interval training.

Extensive interval training involves longer stretches of work pieces of 2-8 min with shorter breaks of 1-4 min duration. The intensity needs to be moderate and is at most in the range of intensive endurance training. The intervals are clearly structured and planned. Their lengths are determined by the training goal and the load intensity. The length of the load in relation to the recovery should be 2:1 to 3:1.

Fig. 48:
Schematic representation of extensive interval training.

The **pyramid training** combines both interval forms and special attention is paid to the speed variation. A given length of work load is repeated several times in interval form while the load intensity of each individual work piece is increased and then reduced. An example for this kind of training is when five 30-stroke work pieces alternate with 2 min of rest, but stroke rate varies from 24 to 28 to 32 and back to 28 and 24 strokes/ min for each piece. Variations can be used in that the load duration can be changed in a pyramidal fashion (e.g.: 1, 2, 3, 2, 1 min work with 2 min rest) or the load intensity varies with the duration of the load (e.g.: 5 min @ SR 22; 3 min @ SR 26; 1 min @ SR 30, etc.). This training method is an excellent way to develop the feeling for speed and pacing, as well as to combine different speed levels.

Competitive methods

Competition methods are mainly used for two reasons: first to improve competition-specific endurance and, secondly, to maintain the current performance level. We distinguish the following three forms for masters rowing:

1. Pace training,
2. Race simulation, and
3. Sprint training.

Through using **pace training**, the rower learns to experience the effort and stroke rate that is needed to reach a certain speed (pace) and maintain it as efficiently as possible. Any speed can in general be chosen as pace and the main goal is to not change it, but to row at it and feel the effort necessary to maintain it. However, in many cases, the targeted pace in training will be the speed that the crew plans to achieve in the middle of their race. Although this is not the highest speed the crew can possibly reach, the intensity is relatively high, especially at the beginning of the competitive season. Rowers, therefore, must begin by pacing shorter distances and increase the length of the training piece gradually. If for example a crew strives to row through the middle section of their 1,000 m race at 30 strokes per min, it makes sense that they try to maintain this stroke rate as efficiently and effectively as possible. For this purpose, one could start rowing at the target stroke rate first for five times 200 m. The next step might then be to increase the training session up to 10 times 200 m and the final goal could be to lengthen the pieces up to two times 750 m.

Of course, if pace training is intended for a long-distance race, the length of the pieces and the pace have to be chosen accordingly. Otherwise, the same criteria are used as for the shorter races. An example of pace training for a long distance race where the crew plans to row at 26 strokes per min would be rowing five times 500 m and then increase over time to up to two times 2,500 m.

The goal of the training method is to concentrate on the given stroke rate while at the same time trying to reach and maintain the highest possible boat speed for the chosen distance. Since the training distance is shorter than the race distance, this should be well in reach of the crew, so that the athletes can focus on rowing as economically as possible. The rest periods between pieces could be relatively long and should be selected, so that the speed goal of the following piece can be achieved again. Depending on the athletes' level of performance, there are individual design options with regard to the stroke rate (e.g. if the planned race rate is 30 strokes per min, one could train at 28 or at 32), the load duration (200 – 750m) and the length of rest intervals (2-5 min).

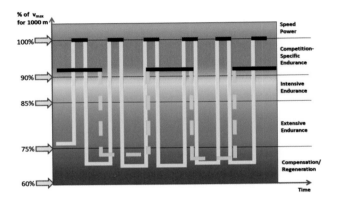

Fig. 49:
Schematic representation of a pace training session for a 1,000 m and a long-distance race.

In race simulation, parts of the race are rowed just as planned later on in competition. This can be done by dividing for example the 1,000 m race distance into the following training pieces:

▶ 250 m: Start and transition strokes just like the first 250 m in the race; start of the piece from a standstill.
▶ 500 m: Row the piece with the same stroke rates that are intended between 250-750 m of a race; bring up stroke rate and speed about 10 strokes before the start line of the piece, so that you begin the piece with exactly the same intensity as you ended the prior 250 m piece and follow through with the 500 m planned for the middle of the race.
▶ 250 m: Final sprint like the last 250 m in the race; bring up stroke rate and speed over about 10 strokes, so that you begin the piece with exactly the same intensity as you ended the prior 500 m piece and then increase intensity and stroke rate every 7 strokes. Go for the line!

Rest time between the pieces should be such that the athletes recover reasonable well, so that each piece is rowed with high concentration. 2 – 4 min rest is a practical rest time, since each individual piece is not performed at maximum effort.

The three pieces strung together make up the complete 1,000 m race. Therefore, the sum of the achieved times for these pieces can serve as an indication of the time the crew can achieve for a planned race, given the environmental circumstances. It is important that the race is actually simulated and not with each interval rowed as a sprint at maximal effort. Firstly, this would not correspond to the desired goal of the training and, secondly, would not give a good estimation of the crew's abilities for the pending race.

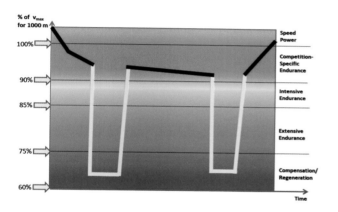

Fig. 50:
Schematic representation
of a race simulation.

Another form of race simulation is training against one or more crews. In this case, the other crews create a competitive situation that leads to increased adrenaline production and higher motivation within the rowers. Moreover, such side-by-side racing also requires tactical behavior and steering as in a real competition. If the crews row different boat classes or belong to different performance levels, these differences can be compensated for by handicaps. For example, a four, which is about 10 seconds slower than an eight over 1,000 m, could be started 3 seconds earlier for a 500 m piece. The four will then try to keep their lead as long as possible, while the eighth will only overtake the lead at the end of the piece if they row according to their ability.

This form of training needs to be reserved only for well-trained masters rowers maximally once per week during the racing season and should not be used too often especially if crews participate frequently in competition.

Sprint training

It is important for any competitive training group to find out what the highest stroke rate is that they can achieve and still be technically effective, but it is even more fun for recreational rowers simply to feel the sensation of moving fast or just being curious of "how much we can increase the stroke rate". Also, in order to effectively maintain a certain stroke rate over a longer distance, frequencies above such a rate must be mastered for short periods. Therefore, competitive crews must incorporate high stroke rates bursts into their training and recreational rowers can do the same, but of course less frequently. It is sprint training that is used in these circumstances.

You need strength, speed, agility and very good coordination skills for high stroke rates. These abilities need be taken into account in the overall training planning. If a crew for example wants to row at a stroke rate of 34 strokes per min over a certain distance, rowers must be able to generate the required force on the handle to move the blade quickly enough through the water and skilled enough to perform entry, release and recovery fast to reach this stroke rate. They must therefore include strength and coordination exercises in the preparatory training. Additionally, they must include exercises in their on-water training where stroke rates are increased step by step. A good example for such sprint training is 10-15 stroke intervals at increasing stroke rates with 20 – 30 strokes rest (in the number of strokes per interval are 3 – 5 strokes included at high effort, to bring the stroke rate up to the intended level). The stroke rate could be raised by 2 starting at 24 strokes per minute up to a frequency where the movement can still be executed safely. If a stroke rate is reached that the crew cannot master technically well any more, the crew should take a longer rest and start the progression again. Other examples of sprint trainings are:

▶   Starts of 10 – 20 strokes from a standstill to reach maximal speed
▶   Races over 100 m
▶   Trying to reach the highest speed on your boat monitor from a running start – You will quickly learn that you need to reach the highest speed within about 10 strokes after which boat speed decreases inevitably; so, you really need to focus on the very first strokes of the piece

Sprint training is generally done with large breaks. The lengths of the training pieces, number of strokes or duration of the intervals are short, for example from 10 strokes, 100 m or 10-30 seconds to a maximum length of a sprint piece of about 250 m, 30 strokes or 1 min. The intensity is very high to maximal and along with the number of repetitions of the pieces causes a major strain for a masters rower. This form of training should be done relatively seldom in masters rowing and demands a high level of technical skills.

6.2.4   Training Programs

"Let's train today a little longer and less hard!"

Training programs are more detailed instructions for individual training sessions and therefore the attempt to achieve special goals systematically and with high probability. Good rowing examples for such goals include "specific endurance", "development of race pace" etc. Ideally, training programs should not only involve instructions for physiological workloads that athletes have to perform, but also need directions with regards to skill development. Coaches and rowers therefore need to skillfully choose sequences of exercises to develop training programs, that not only support the desired physiological training effect, but at the same time meet the high coordinative demands of rowing technique. If for example rowing with squared blades is included during a continuous extensive endurance session, the athletes not only achieve some development of their aerobic capacities, but are forced automatically to improve their releases and balance to maintain clean rowing strokes. Similarly, if rowers focus on quick catches during pace training, they are focused on one important part of a proper stroke motion that will help them to maintain effectively a high boat speed at a given stroke rate.

A training program needs to entail certain parameters to achieve the specific training goals, but also to prevent overloading and provide variety. The following basic conditions must be observed for effective training planning:

- ▸ Goal of the training
- ▸ Training experience of the rowers
- ▸ Fitness of the rowers
- ▸ Integration in the medium- and long-term planning
- ▸ Weather conditions
- ▸ Existing training options (size of training group, available equipment, training area etc.)
- ▸ Personal emotions/feeling (desire – lethargy, willingness to perform)

Additionally, load specifics (intensity, duration, density of load and rests, as well as the overall frequency of training) are used to describe training in more detail.

Looking more specifically at all these conditions and details, they open up an array of possible variations to define the detailed content of training. This can be used for masters rowing in order to make training targeted, systematic and exciting. In particular, training methods offer a large number of variants.

Using the described training methods and forms, the following examples will serve masters rowers as basic ideas for programs at different training intensities. These examples encourage readers – we hope – to invent further variations that are tailored to individual and personal circumstances.

Be aware that the specified stroke rates (SR) in the individual programs can sometimes only be achieved if the power input per stroke is reduced and adjusted. For example, to maintain a stroke rate of 22/min at a compensation intensity level continuously for 30 min, fitness rowers need to keep their movements light and fluent without exerting high power. As a guide to meet a certain intensity serves again the specified range of boat speed in relation to the aimed long distance (LDP) or 1,000 m race pace (RP) presented in Fig. 40.

Tab. 25: Training programs – Compensation

Training intensity	Competitive rowers/ Returners	Advanced /Fitness Rowers first time in racing shells	Health/Fun also in pleasure boats
Compensation	Total training time: 30-70 min ▶ Steady state: • SR 18-21 ▶ Interval training: 4-10 intervals: • 1 min SR 20/ 4 min SR 18 • 500 m SR 23/250 m SR 19 • 5 mins SR 22/ 5 min SR 18 ▶ Fartlek training: • SR 18-22 variable	Total training time: 30-60 min ▶ Steady state: • SR 18-22 ▶ Interval training: 4-10 intervals: • 1 min SR 20/ 4 min. SR 18 • 400 m SR 22/ 200 m SR 19 • 3 min SR 21/ 5 min SR 18 ▶ Fartlek training: • SR 18-22 variable	Total training time: 20-60 min ▶ Steady state: • SR 18-22 ▶ Interval training: • 4-10 intervals: • 30 sec SR 22/ 4 min SR 20 • 100 m SR 22/ 500 m SR 19 • 1 min SR 21/ 5 min SR 18 ▶ Fartlek training: • SR 18-22 variable

Special exercises:
▶ Include special tasks for about 250 m; for example: rowing with squared blades, pause every three strokes to balance, row inside hand only in sweep, row with a wide grip, air stroke every five strokes.
▶ Vary stroke rate while maintaining the training intensity and boat speed.
▶ Rowing next to another crew with the same stroke rate and intensity, but trying to increase speed only by rowing technically better not working harder.

Tab. 26: Training programs – Extensive endurance

Training intensity	Competitive rowers/ Returners	Advanced /Fitness Rowers first time in racing shells	Health/Fun also in pleasure boats
	Total training time: 30-75 min ▶ Steady state: • SR 18-23 ▶ Interval training: • (4-10) x (1 min SR 24/4 min SR 20; no rest) • 4 x (2 km SR 21-24/2-6 min rest) • (3-5) x (4/3/2/1 min at SR 20/22/24/26; 3 min rest) ▶ Fartlek training: • SR 18-24 variable	Total training time: 20-60 min ▶ Steady state: • SR 18-23 ▶ Interval training: • (4-10) x (1 min SR 23/4 min SR 20; no rest) • 4 x (1 km SR 21-23; 2-6 min rest) • (2-4) x (3/2/1/2/3 min at SR 21/23/24/23/21; 3 min rest) ▶ Fartlek training: SR 18-23 variable	Total training time: 20-40 min ▶ Steady state: • SR 18-24 ▶ Interval training: • (3-5) x (30 sec SR 23/4 min SR 20; no rest) • 4 x (500 m SR 21-23; 2-6 min rest) • (1-3) x (4/3/2/1 min SR 18/20/22/24; 3 min rest) ▶ Fartlek training: • SR 18-23 variable

Special exercises:
▶ Include special tasks; for example: 1 min rowing with squared blades while maintaining intensity and stroke rate; stroke rate changes while maintaining intensity; rowing 20 strokes with half slide every 4 min etc.
▶ Rowing alongside another crew, where technique changes can be checked for effectiveness.
▶ Rowing with different (longer or shorter) outboard length.

Extensive Endurance

Tab. 27: Training programs – Intensive endurance

Training intensity	Competitive rowers/ Returners	Advanced /Fitness Rowers First time in racing shells	Health/Fun also in pleasure boats
	▶ Steady state: • 4 - 10 km just below long-distance race pace (LDP) • 2 x 2.5 to 5 km just below LDP; 10 min rest ▶ Interval training: • 4 x (2 km SR 24-28; 4 min rest) • (2-5) x (4/3/2/1 min at SR 22/24/26/28; 3 min rest) • 5/2.5/1 km SR 24-28; 4 min rest ▶ Pace training with 4 min rests: • 1-3 x 7 min just below LDP • (2-4) x 1,000 m LDP • 10 x 500 m LDP • 2/1/0.5 km SR 26-30 ▶ Fartlek training: • SR 18-30 variable	▶ Steady state: • 10km about 2-4 strokes/min below LDP stroke rate ▶ Interval training: • 4 x (2 km SR 23-26; 5 min rest) • (2-5) x (4/3/2/1 min SR 21/23/25/27; 5 min rest) • 5/2.5/1 km SR 24-26; 5 min rest ▶ Fartlek training: • SR 18-28 variable	▶ Steady state: • 5km at increased pace ~ SR 23 ▶ Interval training: • 2 x (2 km SR 22-24; 6 min rest) • (2-4) x (4/3/2/1 min SR 20/21/22/22/23; 4 min rest) • 2/1/0.5 km SR 22-24; 4 min rest ▶ Fartlek training: • SR 18-23 variable

Special exercises:
▶ Include several times 20 strokes at long distance pace (LDP) with different stroke rates to find the most effective one.
▶ Installing special tasks: For example, row 1 min with squared blades while maintaining intensity and stroke rate.
▶ Rowing with adjusted (longer or shorter) outboard lengths.

Intensive Endurance

Tab. 28: Training programs at the aerobic–anaerobic threshold

Training intensity	Competitive rowers/ Returners	Advanced /Fitness Rowers First time in racing shells	Health/Fun also in pleasure boats
Threshold Training	▶ Steady state: • 5km time trial/race ▶ Interval training: • (2-4) x (2,000 m SR 16-18 with maximum force application; 2 min rest) • (2-5 x) (3/2/1 min SR 26/30/34; 3 min rest) • 2/1/0.5 km SR 28-34; 4 min rest ▶ Pace training in each case 4 min rests: • 1-3 x 5 min SR 28-32 • 2-4 x 1,000 m S 28-32 • 2/1/0,5 km SR 26/29/32 ▶ "Red Lining": • (5-15) x (1min SR 30/1 min SR 26; no rest) • (5-15) x (1min SR 22/1 min SR 18 with maximum force application; no rest)	▶ Steady state: • 5km time trial/race ▶ Interval training: • (1-3) x 2,000 m SR 20-22 with maximum force application; 4 min rest) • (2-5x) (3/2/1 min SR 26/28/30; 4 min rest) • 2/1/0.5 km SR 26-32; 4 min rest ▶ "Red Lining": • (3-10) x (1min SR 26/1 min SR 24; no rest) • (3-10) x (1min SR 22/1min SR 18 with maximum force application; no rest)	This training intensity is not advisable

Special exercises:
▶ Rowing with bungees around the boat or dragging a can.
▶ Half boat rowing.
▶ Rowing with longer outboards.

Tab. 29: Training programs – Competition-specific

Training intensity	Competitive rowers/Returners	Advanced /Fitness Rowers First time in racing shells	Health/Fun also in pleasure boats

Competition Specific Endurance	▶ Steady state:
	  • 1,000 m time trial/race
	▶ Interval training:
	  • (2-4) x 1,000 m at two strokes below race stroke rate; 5 min rest
	  • (4-6) x 500 m with start; 3 min rest
	  • (2-5x) x (2/1/0.5 min SR 30/34/38; 3 min rest)
	  • 30/30/40/40/50/40/30 strokes; SR varying between 30-36 every 10 strokes; 2 min rest
	▶ Pace training in each case 4 min rest:
	  • 2/1/0.5 km SR 28-34
	  • 3 x 7 min SR 30/32/34
	  • 4 x 500 m race pace
	▶ Speed training:
	  • 1 x 500 m best time
	  • (4-8) x (250 m best time; 4 min rest)
	  • 2 x (6 x [30 sec start/30 sec rest])
	  • (4-6) x (45 sec maximum effort; 2 min rest)
	  • 10 x (100 m sprint; 2 min rest)
	  • 15 x (10 strokes at maximum SR; 2 min rest)
		▶ Steady state:
		  • 500-1000 m time trial/race
		▶ Interval training:
		  • (6-8) x (250 m at RP; 4 min rest)
		  • (2-4) x (500 m with start; 5 min rest)
		  • (1-3 x) x (2/1/0.5 min SR 28/30/32; 3 min rest)
		  • 30/30/40/40/50/40/30 strokes; SR varying between 28-34 every 10 strokes; 2 min rest
		▶ Pace training in each case 5 min rests:
		  • (2-4) x 500 m race pace
		  • 1/0.75/0.5 km SR 26-32
		  • (1-2) x 7 min SR 26-30
		▶ Speed training:
		  • (2-4) x (250 m best time; 4 min rest)
		  • (2-4) x (30 sec maximum effort; 2 min rest)
		  • 5 x (100 m sprint; 2 min rest)
		  • 10 x (10 strokes maximum SR; 2min rest)
			▶ Steady state:
			  • 250-500 m time trial/race
			▶ Interval training:
			  • (1-3x) x (60/45/30 sec SR 28/30/32; 3 min rest)
			  • 30/30/40/40/50/40/30 strokes; SR varying between 24-30 every 10 strokes; 2 min rest
			▶ Pace training in each case 5 min rests:
			  • (1-2) x 500 m "race pace"
			  • (1-2) x 3 min SR 26-30
			▶ Speed training:
			  • (2-4) x (15 sec maximum effort; 2 min rest)
			  • 3 x (100 m sprint; 2 min rest)
			  • 5 x (10 strokes maximum SR; 2 min rest)

Special exercises:
▶ Start exercises – progression 1/2/3/…15 strokes from standstill.
▶ Rowing with dragging a can or bungees around the boat.
▶ Half boat row.
▶ Rowing with changed (longer or shorter) outboards.

6.3 GENERAL FITNESS AND SUPPLEMENTARY TRAINING FOR MASTERS ROWERS

In addition to on water training, masters rowers should use programs to improve general endurance, strength, agility and coordination skills. Similar to junior rowers and elite teams, the improvement and maintenance of rowing performance is not only achieved through on-water training. Masters rowers must use a variety of training means that need to be meaningfully coordinated and integrated into a long-term training plan.

An athletic beginner initially needs a moderate training in all of the aforementioned motor areas. In doing so, consideration must be given to the individual needs, interests and demands. Training must also fit the personal lifestyle. Training with like-minded athletes is highly recommended. Common goals and experiences, social interaction and fun within the sports program are essential prerequisites for adults and older people to enter successfully into a new sport. Learning new movements and improving individual technical skills − especially in rowing − are easier to achieve in groups and crews. This is particularly true if you add some feedback from an experienced facilitator or coach, something more easily organized for larger groups of athletes.

Experienced masters rowers need to pay attention to the general benefits of training outside of rowing for their long-term improvements and overall health, and also to underdeveloped physical abilities that may lead to injuries. The following is an example of well-rounded fitness and health training for older people in the areas of endurance, strength, flexibility and coordination:

Tab. 30: Recommendations for fitness and health training for the elderly

	Endurance	Strength	Agility	Coordination
Potential training frequency per week? All training forms included*	4-7x	2x	2-3x	2-3x
Intensity	"Easy" to "Little strenuous" (see Fig 61)	50 - 60% of max. Force	Stretching with light effort or until noticeable resistance	Increase difficulty over time and with experience
Duration	At least 20-40 min: Use different training forms	Max. 45 min: 2-3 sets of 10-15 repetitions with a total of 6-10 exercises for upper and lower body	Approximately 20 min: Max. 3 times 10-30 sec stretching of main muscle groups	Approximately 20 min: 4-10 different exercises
Special information on possible progression	Increase duration; possibly increase force application	Modify exercises; increase loads moderately	Incorporate into everyday life; proprioceptive neuromuscular facilitation (PNF) stretching technique	Integrate into everyday life; increase complexity; more difficult tasks

*Some of these training goals (e.g. agility and strength, or endurance and coordination) can be achieved together in one training session, so that the number of overall training sessions per week do not exceed the recommendations from Tab. 10.

Such training outside the actual rowing motion is called "supplementary training" and is important for the overall development of an athlete. Not only is with such training a larger variety introduced in the rowing program, they help to prevent injuries, provide larger variety in the overall training and lay the basis for long-term sustainable improvements. Fig. 51 shows how this training fits within the overall program.

Supplementary Training

▸ Is partly the prerequisite of physical conditioning and coordination to perform rowing persistently, powerfully or economically
▸ Helps increase rowing performance
▸ Prevents (training) monotony, provides variety and fun
▸ Can avoid muscular imbalances and thus prevents overly specific rowing stress
▸ Can reduce the overall stress on the musculoskeletal system
▸ Develops all types of muscle fibers and can thus contribute to faster regeneration after rowing workloads and generally in all sports
▸ Presents training and movement alternatives, e.g. at home, after injuries, on vacation, on business trips, if bad conditions prevent rowing

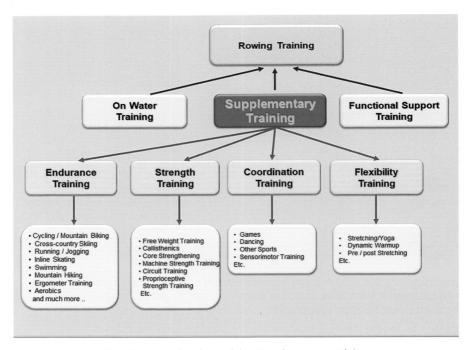

Fig. 51: Forms of rowing training: Supplementary training.

Incorporating other sports and means of training – in addition to actual rowing – into their workout system can be productive not only for competitive rowers, but also those focusing on health, fitness and recreation. By developing technically sufficient movement execution in a range of exercises, athletes increase overall health benefits, avoid injuries

due to incorrect loads and are able to safely increase training intensity if intended. The different coordinative and fitness demands also help to prevent, or at least slow down, age-related losses. Similarly, it is highly recommended to learn sports that have not yet been practiced or only rarely practiced until older age, like for example cross-country skiing, pickleball or different swimming strokes.

In general, it should be noted that the intensity and extent of unusual endurance exercises must be slowly increased, so that the organism and the muscles can adapt to the new stresses.

Masters rowers need to fit the selection and design of supplementary training in their overall training planning. It is of course important whether complementary sports or supplementary training is performed to increase performance, or to compensate for lopsided rowing loads. It is necessary to compare the mutual and different demands of these sports with rowing in terms of movement economy, coordination, endurance and strength development, as well as the load they place on the body's various systems to fit them best in the overall training plan.

There is currently not much research into the influence of different training aids and supplementary sports on rowing performance. It is an area where we still have much to learn. It is relatively easy to understand that supplemental training is performed in the off season, as many competitive masters rowers already do, thereby it should be practiced parallel to rowing throughout the year, especially to counteract the one-sided loads that inevitably result from on water training.

The quality of the rowing technique is very closely linked to movement economy, that optimizes to a certain degree with the number of kilometers rowed and over the years of training in the sport. The idea of using all available time for in-boat training however must be put into perspective for all rowers, not only masters. Cycling, running or cross-country skiing can be useful training tools for masters rowers even on a limited time budget. The positive effects of these sports lie in the fact that they stress the body physically in similar ways to rowing, while providing a break for the rowing-specific supporting apparatus and movement systems and encourage varied intramuscular coordination. These different activities create new muscular and coordinative training stimuli. On the one hand, this relieves some muscles that experience lopsided stress during the rowing movement, and on the other hand helps to develop underutilized muscle groups.

It is strongly recommended that adult rowers perform complementary training - regardless of the objectives, the motivation, the training effort and the time available - throughout the year. Doing so can increase the quality of their rowing abilities, bring variety in their sporting activities, provide relief for the movement and support apparatus and slow down the age-related performance degradation.

6.3.1 Additional Strength Training for Rowers Over 40

Why additional strength training for rowers over 40?

Strength endurance along with maximum strength declines with increasing age in trained as well as untrained humans (see Fig. 52). Due to the length of the race and thus the shortened race time (1,000 m compared to 2,000 m of junior and elite rowers), the proportion of strength in the overall performance is naturally greater in masters' sprint races, although endurance remains the determining factor.

In addition, there are age-related transitions in the nervous system, which are responsible for the information transfer and activation of the muscles. This explains why simple and complicated movements can only be performed more slowly with increasing age. By contrast, physically active older people are only slightly slower than young, active people.

Loss of strength and changes in the nervous system not only affect competitive performance, but also affect more simple tasks. How many older rowers for example experience large difficulties getting in and out of a boat?

Strength is important for rowers! Strength training is even more important for masters rowers!

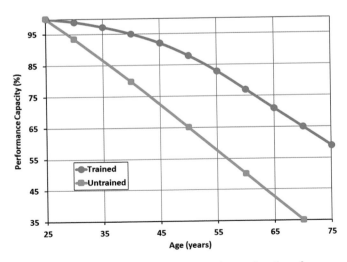

Fig. 52: Decrease in leg extensor muscle as a function of physical activity in men (after Schmidtbleicher, 1994, p. 150).

Women show based on the difference of their hormonal balance a somewhat lower trainability of strength than men, whereas this ability levels out with age (see Fig. 10). Although trainability of strength decreases in both women and men from the age of 25 on average, it is important to note that strength can always be trained and improved well into old age.

Is strength training important for older rowers who have no competitive ambitions?

The recreational, health and fitness-oriented rowers also benefit from a well-developed musculature. Strength training is among other things a safe investment against the loss of muscle functions and the deterioration of muscle structures as people get older. It also has a positive influence on the endurance performance, normalizes the blood pressure and increases reduction of body fat.

With relatively little effort, muscle loss can be significantly reduced. This has, in addition to the positive results for performance in sport, also improving effects on the overall quality of everyday life. Climbing stairs and carrying loads require strength, and being stronger makes daily tasks easier and help to prevent injuries like falling.

Complementary strength training is an integral part of the training process in almost every sport, even in endurance sports. Discussions of whether endurance athletes should undergo strength training at all, because this might limit endurance capacity or influence skills, are obsolete, provided that certain methodological principles are followed. Studying any endurance exercises, you find that they all also require strength. Stronger athletes need less of their maximum strength to perform the respective endurance movement and are therefore better prepared for any work over a long period of time.

In the following, we want to understand strength as an ability to move a mass, like your own body or a boat, as well as to overcome a resistance through muscle work. Strength and force are interchangeable terms, where strength is used here for the force that a human can generate. The scientific unit for force is N for Newton. In North America the pound or lb is still in common use as a unit of weight and force. Most other countries use kgF, which means the force that is needed to hold 1 kg mass off the ground. In the middle of a race, a high performance rower generates a peak force of more than 90 kgF (or 200 lbs) during the drive on the handle. A masters woman generates a peak force of about 45 – 55 kgF (or 100 – 120 lbs) in her 1,000 m race and a masters men about 65 –75 kgF (or 150 – 170 lbs). Even a recreational rower still has to pull with a peak force of perhaps 20 – 30 kgF (40 – 70 lbs), but this is continuously over an hour or more.

Which goals are important to masters rowers in their strength training?

In general, strength training has two basic goals (also see Fig 53):

1. Improvement of the innervation capability of the musculature (nervous system) and
2. Expansion of the energy capability of the musculature (muscle cells)

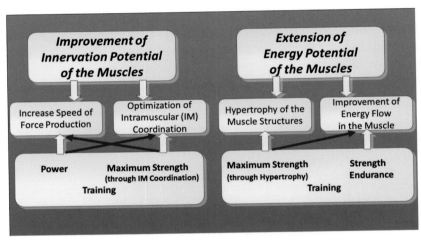

Fig. 53: Relationships between goals and methods of strength training
(mod. after Martin, Carl & Lehnertz, 2001).

Strength and performance capacities of the musculature can be increased in several ways:

▸ The **speed** at which force can be increased is optimized by special stimuli of the stretch-shortening cycle (reactive training)
▸ Optimization of **inter- and intramuscular coordination**
▸ Intramuscular: Improvement of the interaction of muscle fibers of one muscle
▸ Intermuscular: Contribution of a number of different muscles in one movement, which leads to an improved movement coupling and is therefore very important in rowing, as well as in all weight training for rowing
▸ Increasing **muscle mass** through the enlargement of the muscle cross section leads to improvements of maximum strength
▸ **Energy flow** improvement is achieved through strength endurance training and helps with the ability to maintain a relatively large force production over longer times

The authors believe that the main focus for rowers from the age of 40 on should be improving muscle energy flow together with the optimization of intramuscular coordination. We realize of course the protective effect of all around well-developed muscles and believe that all these goals can be best achieved with circuit and station training.

A key distinctive feature for strength training relates to the selection of exercises and workloads (see Fig. 54). Thus, we need to separate **general** and **specific** strength training. **General strength training** is used to improve and maintain physical performance and the necessary resilience of the postural, musculoskeletal system. All muscle groups are trained regardless of whether the musculature is performance-related for the sport being practiced. This strengthening can take place with or without equipment and be carried out as circuit training, station training and also in the form of sensorimotor training.

Specific strength training serves to build up power in the respective sport and should in our case develop muscle groups used as well as those neglected in the rowing motion for the specific demands of (competitive) rowing. In particular, station training on land and strength-endurance training in the boat or on the ergometer are suitable for this goal. It needs to be pointed out that brisk rowing sufficiently achieves this goal for recreational rowers.

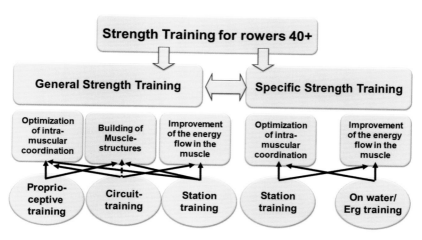

Fig. 54: Strength training for rowers 40+.

Both forms of strength training influence each other. This means that specific strength training for rowers of course also includes some general strengthening and vice versa. Of course, this is due to the large number of muscle groups used in rowing, the development of which always includes some general strengthening. Regardless of whether competitive ambitions exist, strength training increases the efficiency of rowing technique and movement economy for all masters rowers. Especially in rowing, movement-related demands (e.g. the use of the shoulders and arms in the final pull or the postural stability to execute the movement over a longer period of time) are not possible without well-developed core musculature that allows the best transfer of the rowers' leg strength throughout the entire rowing cycle. Apart from that, weight training is a preventative measure against injuries and harm, and serves well in rehabilitation after injuries, illnesses or surgeries.

Rowing strength should therefore never be considered as something apart from the rest of training, but always in connection with coordinative, technical challenges, even with endurance and movement economy. Fig. 55 attempts to clarify the relationships between various training goals and organizational forms of strength training in rowing. This model describes the main goals and their priorities: strength endurance, muscle building and optimization of intramuscular coordination.

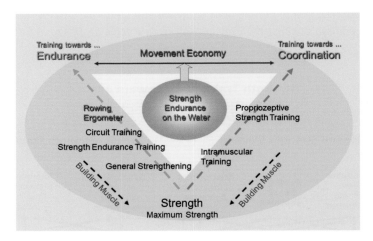

Fig. 55: Training of general and specific strength abilities in rowing with different prioritizations.

If masters rowers primarily want to improve their strength endurance/energy flow in the musculature, they should choose a general form of training like circuit training. The rowing ergometer is also a good option to emphasize more rowing specific strength training. If athletes want an even more specific strength training, it makes sense to select strength endurance training in the boat, i.e. rowing with artificial breaking systems (bungee, cans etc.) or half crew rowing.

If general coordination with the optimization of intramuscular coordination is the main focus, sensorimotor-accentuated strength training or specific intramuscular coordination training will prove beneficial.

How can strength training be designed for masters rowers?

The following principles should be used for the selection and the design of strength training and a general strengthening for older athletes:

1. Supplementary weight training in rowing should not focus on increasing muscle mass, but rather to improve the capacity of the muscles in terms of rowing performance
2. Supplementary strength training should be designed effectively and economically, which means that two approximately 40 min training sessions per week are enough, even for competitive rowers
3. Priority should be given to the trunk and shoulder muscles
4. For each muscle group, rowers should know a number of different exercises with and without additional equipment available to keep this training exciting and activate different combinations of muscles fibres of the same region

Tab. 31 provides an overview of the possibilities for general and specific strength training and for the use in different masters groups: competitive/race oriented (R), fitness (F), health (H) and compensation (C) rowers. Examples of exercises for the different strength training forms are in the following pictures.

Tab. 31: Training forms and exercise selection for general and special strength training in rowing

Training Means	Loading Recommendation	Masters Target Group				Comments
		R	F	H	C	
General Strengthening	20-45 min Maximum 2x per week	X	X	X	X	Versatile and comprehensive exercises, especially to strengthen the core muscles!

(continued)

(Tab. 31, continued)

Training Means	Loading Recommendation	Masters Target Group				Comments
		R	F	H	C	
Circuit Training	2-4 circuits, approx. 8-10 general stations of 15-30 sec work, 50% of 1RM	X	X	(X)		General strengthening should be carried out regularly year-round at any age
Station Training	Approximately 6-8 exercises, 3-5 sets with approx. 8-15 reps. and 50-65% of 1RM	X	X	X		
Rowing Specific Strength Training	20-45 min Maximum of 2 x per week	X				Rowing specific strength training should be reserved for competitive masters rowers and replaced by general strength training at an older age
Station Training	3-5 sets of 4-6 rowing specific stations with 10-20 reps., rest approx. 30 sec, approx. 50-60% of 1RM	X				
Sensorimotor-focused Strength Training	20-30 min 1-3x per week	X	X	X	X	This kind of training is an absolute must for masters rowers of all target groups. Can be carried out without problems at home.
Agility, Callisthenics	10-30 min 2-4x per week	X	X	X	X	For all target groups a meaningful supplement after all sports activities. Can be carried out everywhere.

Circuit training is a popular technique for improving fitness. It is mainly used to improve strength endurance, but also for general strengthening. The trainee goes through several stations with different exercises in a certain order before repeating the circuit. Care must be taken to ensure that there is a systematic loading of major muscle groups: For example, arms then legs then abdominals then shoulders then legs again and then back muscles.

The most important component in strength training is the **intensity** of the stress. For simplification, for a particular exercise we use the maximum achievable load in kg, which is called one repetition maximum (1RM) that an athlete can move/lift only once, as 100% intensity. With this number, training loads can be graded as percentages of the maximum intensity (e.g. if 1RM=100 kg then 80% of 1RM=80 kg). This definition is particularly helpful when it comes to objectives that serve to expand the energy potential of the muscles.

The **volume** of the work is calculated by multiplying the number of sets by the sum of all repetitions of the movement multiplied by the load in kg that is moved, if anything beyond simple bodyweight is being used. The **load density** includes the length of the rests between each movement repetition and between the sets and is a measure of the overall intensity of the workout. The load density is mainly dependent on the design of the rest periods between each repetition and the series. Load density is significant for achieving certain strength training goals. For example, strength endurance training repetitions should be performed almost without rest which represents a high density. To improve the muscle cross-sectional area, each repetition needs to be performed in a more deliberate fashion even with a short rest of 1 to 3 sec. Optimizing intermuscular coordination requires even more time for each repetition, leading leads to a lower density. Rests between sets usually have a length of 1-3 min.

For the sake of simplicity, we will only compare the strength-endurance focused training with the muscle-building focused version (Tab. 32) for the strength training of the health-oriented fitness athlete (Boeck-Behrens & Buskies, 2002). Training for these athletes is aimed at body shaping and fat reduction in addition to the development of strength endurance and building muscle mass. Due to the lower repetition numbers, the muscle-building-oriented version uses higher intensities (resistances, weight loads) and lower density.

Tab. 32: Health-oriented fitness strength training

Loading	Strength-endurance focused Improving energy flow	Hypertrophy Muscle building
Repetitions (# reps just achievable); Intensity	▸ 15-20 reps; 30 – 50 % of 1RM	▸ 8-10 reps; 50 – 70% of 1RM
Sets/Volume	▸ Beginner: approx. 1-3 Advanced: approx. 3-5 ▸ Rest: about 1-2 min between sets	▸ Beginner: approx. 2-3 Advanced: approx. 3-4 ▸ Rest: about 1-3 min between sets
Exercise/ Force Application	▸ Technically correct ▸ Continuously and deliberate ▸ Regular breathing	▸ Technically correct ▸ Continuously and deliberate ▸ Regular breathing
Training frequency	▸ Beginner: at least 1x per week ▸ Advanced: 2x per week	▸ Beginner: at least 1-2x per week ▸ Advanced: 2x per week
Training effects	▸ Improvement of energy capacity ▸ Some fat loss ▸ Body shaping ▸ Small side effect: Increase in muscle mass ▸ Small side effect: Improving maximum strength	▸ Increasing muscle mass (long term) ▸ Improvement of maximum strength ▸ Body shaping ▸ Some fat loss ▸ Side effect: Improving strength endurance

Strength training machines or free weights?

Strength training on machines is quite popular nowadays. Many rowing clubs and specifically all fitness centers are very well equipped in this regard. These machines of course guarantee a certain technical determination for a specific movement execution and with it some safety, but since the movement path is largely predetermined, it also means that there is little or no stabilizing muscle work to do during the motion. Thus, training of many small muscles is neglected. These small muscles contribute to balance and stability in the boat, and consequently also to the coordination of the rowing motion that influences technique.

It is quite understandable that these strength training machines are gladly supplied and used in many places, since it means that strength training can be performed relatively safely with little supervision. In addition, intensity can be set quite accurately while the risk of injury during this kind of strength training is relatively low.

Training with free weights and dumbbells on the other hand is more effective in many ways. This kind of strength training provides simultaneous improvement in balance and athleticism. If properly executed, it is also a better preparation to reduce the risk of injury later on in the boat, but it takes more effort to learn the correct technique and often an experienced person to supervise and support.

It is important to note that when organizing strength training, we must account for more than simple external circumstances (e.g. space, security, exercise selection), but must also take into consideration content-related aspects and certain objectives. This is especially important when creating a distinction between general and specific strength training phases. The following selection of instructions for strength training with equipment may be helpful. Exercises are mainly focused on effective and time-limited training for older rowers (based on Hottenrott and Zülch, 1998):

1. Always train with a partner
2. Consider the actual capacity of how much load the athlete can **safely** handle (do not always focus on best performance!)
3. Perform a general warm-up and core exercises **before** every strength training session
4. Stretch the exercised muscle groups specifically **after** strength training
5. Prefer exercises where the movement is executed in the axes of the joints
6. Pay attention to relaxed and steady breathing during execution
7. Avoid maximum bending of the joints
8. Avoid extremes of flexion and extension in back (e.g. slouching or exaggerated erect posture)
9. Avoid muscular imbalances
10. No strength training after exhausting endurance training
11. Support effective impact of strength training: Strength-training stimulus is strongest when a phase of passive regeneration follows. Therefore, masters should avoid any further strenuous activities after strength training, such as an ergometer session, and certainly not any more intensive work. The rowing-specific coordination/rowing technique, which may have been influenced by the strength stimulus, can be maintained by performing a very short and light session in the boat.

Tab. 33: Organizational forms of strength training in rowing for masters

Organizational Form	Characteristics	Specifically Suitable for	Examples
Station Training	5-10 stations; 1-4 sets each; finish all sets before moving to the next station	▶ General Strength ▶ General strength endurance	5-10 stations 1-4 x
Circuit Training	8-10 stations; 2-3 circuits; finishing all stations before moving to the next circuit	▶ General Strength ▶ General strength endurance	8-10 stations 2-3 x
Sensorimotor Training (e.g. Balance)	4-10 exercises; performing for 15 – 120 sec; special tasks possible	▶ Muscle growth ▶ Coordination ▶ Functional joint stability ▶ Neuromuscular responsiveness	See images below
Boat / Ergometer	▶ 10 – 20 – 30 – 20 -10 strokes at SR 16-20 ▶ 10 x 30 sec highest power application SR ~ 20 ▶ 30 – 90 sec SR 24 with dragging a can 15 strokes half crew at max effort; alternating half of the crew	▶ Specific strength endurance	

Sensorimotor training

Sensorimotor training was originally used as a method in rehabilitation as a gentle method to restore coordination skills and strength after surgery and injury. Top athletes in many sports have also adopted sensorimotor training in its numerous variants to achieve a positive interaction of coordination with strength and endurance. Using unstable surfaces (Pezzi balls®, wobble boards, Airex pads®, soft floor mats, etc.) for balancing or strengthening exercises, it is possible to build muscle without being exposed to weights or conventional strength training equipment. This kind of training develops enormously important coordination and balance abilities while at the same time improves body sensation, something so important for rowing and definitely for older athletes. The relatively low equipment costs make this form of training simple enough to be performed at home or while traveling.

Sensorimotor training is particularly suitable for developing functional joint stability as an important protective mechanism for foot and knee joints. This improves body control in daily life and when learning new movement patterns. The improvement of neuromuscular reactivity as a protective mechanism is particularly important in sports for older adults and contributes significantly to injury prophylaxis, has muscle-building effects and economizes the use of force in everyday tasks and athletic exercises.

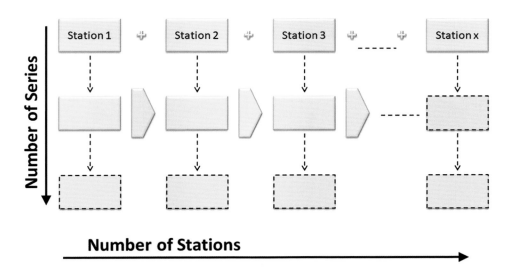

Fig. 56: Exercise examples of sensorimotor training.

Examples of strength training for masters rowers

The following overview describes different objectives and methods of general strength training for masters rowers. It is assumed that the fitness level of the athletes is good to very good. The weights have to be chosen so that even the last repetitions of each set can be completed without jeopardizing technique.

Tab. 34: Overview of general strength training for masters rowers

	Strength Development	Strength Endurance	Strength Coordination
Aim	Developing Muscle Structures	Improving Energy Flow	General Strengthening
Possible forms of training	Station training	▶ Circuit training ▶ Station training	▶ Sensorimotor strength training
Stations (Exercises)	6-8	8-10	8-12
Sets / Rest between sets	2-3 / R: 90-120 sec	2-3 / R:15-30 sec	2-3 / R:30-60 sec
Repetitions	6-8	15-20	8-12

Here are illustrations with exercises:

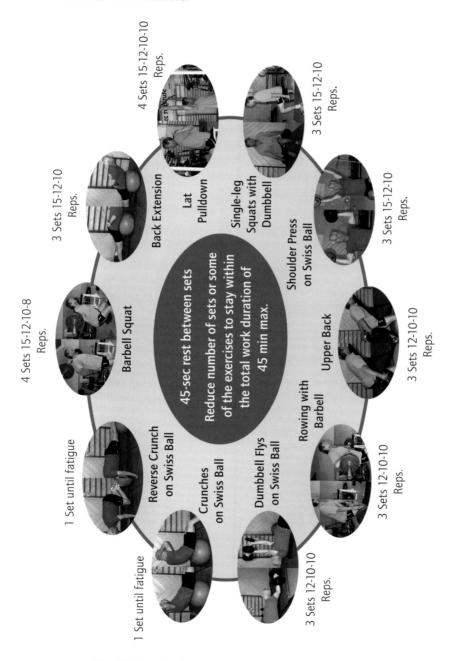

Fig. 57: Example of a general strength training program.

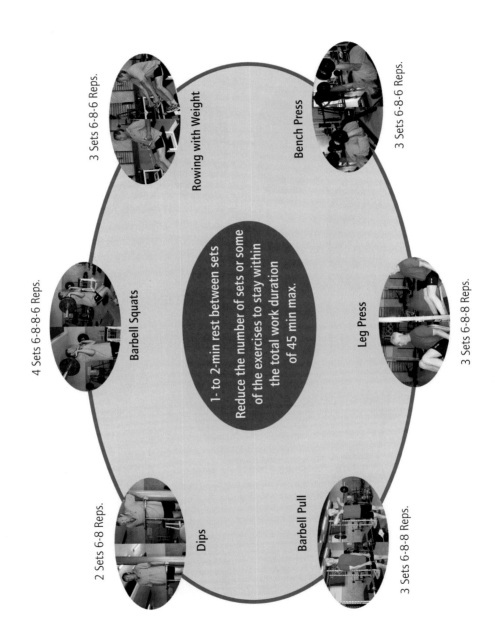

Rowing with Weight
3 Sets 6-8-6 Reps.

Bench Press
3 Sets 6-8-6 Reps.

Barbell Squats
4 Sets 6-8-8-6 Reps.

Leg Press
3 Sets 6-8-8 Reps.

1- to 2-min rest between sets Reduce the number of sets or some of the exercises to stay within the total work duration of 45 min max.

Dips
2 Sets 6-8 Reps.

Barbell Pull
3 Sets 6-8-8 Reps.

Fig. 58: Example of a general muscle developing training program.

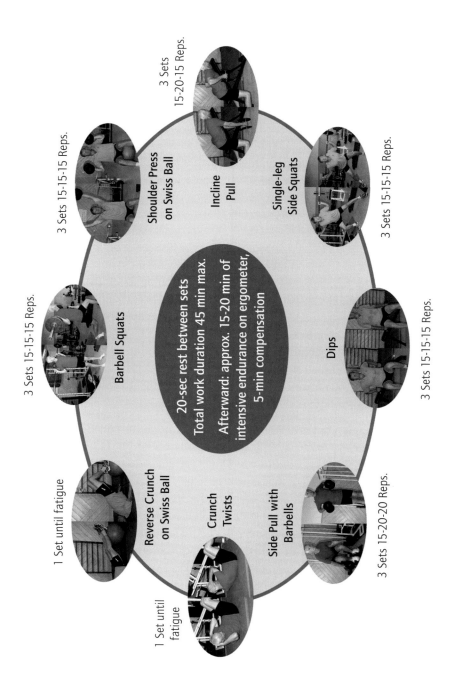

3 Sets 15-20-15 Reps.

3 Sets 15-15-15 Reps.

3 Sets 15-15-15 Reps.

3 Sets 15-15-15 Reps.

3 Sets 15-15-15 Reps.

1 Set until fatigue

1 Set until fatigue

3 Sets 15-20-20 Reps.

Shoulder Press on Swiss Ball

Incline Pull

Single-leg Side Squats

Barbell Squats

20-sec rest between sets
Total work duration 45 min max.
Afterward: approx. 15-20 min of
intensive endurance on ergometer,
5-min compensation

Dips

Reverse Crunch on Swiss Ball

Crunch Twists

Side Pull with Barbells

Fig. 59: Example of a general strength endurance training program.

For beginners or less well-trained masters rowers, the exercises need to be varied and both the number of sets and repetitions need to be adapted to athletes' individual abilities.

Specific strength training in the boat and on the rowing ergometer

A specific strength training program in rowing should have the following characteristics:

▸ The kinematic and dynamic parameters should match the rowing movement
▸ The force to be applied by the rower should have a training effect on strength-endurance

The latter requirement can be met by increasing the resistance on the braking system of the rowing ergometer (opening the vent on the widely used ergometer models; for more details, see chapter 6.3.2) or by increasing resistance on the boat (for example: usage of oars with a larger blade size, inboard/outboard adjustments, bungees around the boat, part-boat rowing, dragging a towel/cloth/can behind the boat). It should be noted that the number of strokes per piece and the stroke rate need to be adjusted depending on the individual goals of the **specific strength endurance training**. This means that not more than 10 – 20 strokes at race stroke rates should be taken when strength development is the aim, while 20 – 40 strokes can be performed at lower stroke rates around 20 – 24 strokes per min for strength endurance.

It needs to be pointed out that all types of specific strength training on the ergometer or in the boat tend to cause a large load on the back of the athletes. It is therefore essential that everyone pays attention to proper technique to minimize the risk of injury. Athletes with back problems or rowers who struggle to maintain proper technique when fatigued should not engage in such training. If rowers feel any discomfort through the extra load, this kind of training should be abandoned. Also, it is important that masters rowers progress gradually into full strength endurance training. This means that strokes are taken with controlled effort at first and strength efforts increase only step by step. At the same time, the overall number of hard strokes with higher resistance needs to be limited in the beginning to 5 x 10 = 50 strokes and then gradually increased.

Explosive strength training in the boat can be performed without additional resistance through strokes at highest speed in combination with competition-specific rowing technique. This training is important to improve the quality of start and sprint strokes, as well as the execution of excellent technique at race stroke rates and under fatigue. Examples for such a training are race starts of 10 strokes with maximum effort at race frequency and above or intervals of 5-8 strokes from a running start at full stroke length with maximum effort – maximum force application and stroke rate – to reach maximum boat speed.

Part-crew rowing means that only a part of the crew rows while the other rowers sit still and balance the boat with their blades flat in the water. This exercise is recommended for the training of ambitious masters rowers. This kind of rowing of course means that the boats are moving more slowly, which increases the loads on the blades. This kind of training has several organisational advantages, since the overall movement is slowed down and rowers have more time to focus on specific parts of their stroke. This means that part crew rowing with light to normal effort can also be used as a form of technique training. The technical difficulty can then be increased by having the rowers who sit still push their handles down towards the gunwales, so that their blades are off the water and the boat needs to be balanced by those rowing. This exercise adds a high demand on balance in addition to the strength training effect.

One aspect of rowing with only part of the crew deserves special attention in that only a limited number of strokes should be performed by each part of the crew! First, the rowers who do not work will cool down and/or get bored. Secondly, by spending too much time on this exercise, the crew loses out on valuable time that could be spent on learning to row well together as a complete unit.

Often it is precisely the combination of a strength-driven movement with high coordination requirements, offered by the above-mentioned forms of training, that achieves special effects (see sensorimotor training). For this reason, many rowers and coaches are convinced that focused **high-quality coordination training** in the boat is sufficient as specific strength endurance training and thus primarily only general strength training should be necessary on land. This means that it often suffices especially for the older competitive rowers to concentrate on developing general strength training on land, which helps managing their overall time constrains for training and recuperation.

Strength training goals for masters rowers

McNeely (2005) developed charts for masters rowers of different age groups by converting ideal strength performances of young rowers to adequate strength training goals for older athletes. Those numbers provide approximate guidelines for ambitious masters rowers as to whether increased strength training is required or whether other performance factors like coordination, technique or endurance should be focused on.

The use of the table is pretty simple:

A rower's body weight is multiplied by an achievement factor specific for the athlete's age group to receive the 1RM "performance target" for the respective exercise. This number represents the theoretical target load for an athlete to move one time at the specified exercise. The actual 1RM of an athlete is then compared with this target and one can then evaluate what kind of training is necessary. If athletes reach or exceed the target, it is more important to engage with strength endurance training. In the case that athletes do not reach the target, it would be advisable to focus more on strength development.

Here is the calculation:

> **If you have your body weight in kg:**
>
> **Body weight x achievement factor = 1RM (target)**
>
> **If you have your body weight in lbs:**
>
> **Body weight x 0.454 x achievement factor = 1RM (target)**

Tab. 35: Achievement factor for weight training goals for masters rowers – Strength to Body Weight Factors for Masters (McNeely, 2005)

WOMEN								
Age	35-39	40-44	45-49	50-54	55-59	60-64	65-69	70+
Squat	1.22	1.16	1.08	1.00	0.91	0.80	0.72	0.50
Deadlift	1.22	1.16	1.08	1.00	0.91	0.80	0.72	0.50
Bench Pull	0.93	0.88	0.82	0.76	0.69	0.60	0.55	0.38

MEN								
Age	35-39	40-44	45-49	50-54	55-59	60-64	65-69	70+
Squat	1.37	1.30	1.2	1.15	1.03	0.95	0.82	0.60
Deadlift	1.37	1.3	1.2	1.15	1.03	0.95	0.82	0.60
Bench Pull	1.02	0.98	0.94	0.88	0.78	0.71	0.62	0.45

Examples:

How much weight should a 46-year-old 63 kg female masters rower use as a maximum 1RM reference load for bench pull? The achievement factor for this athlete is 0.82, which leads to

> **63 kg x 0.82 = approx. 52 kg = approx. 115 lbs**

How much weight should a 174 lbs masters rower of 59 years use for his 1RM squats? The achievement factor for this athlete is factor 1.03

> **174 lbs x 0.454 x 1.03 = approx. 81.4 kg = approx. 180 lbs**

Masters rowers should carry out strength training throughout the year. The recommendation is not just for those masters who want to improve their race performances and win. Even recreational and health motivated rowers benefit from sustained weight training even once a week. Masters rowers, who have systematically and regularly increased their strength over the winter months, lose those laboriously acquired capacities within months if they return to exclusively on-water training. One or two strength training sessions per week, possibly with a reduced volume, are enough to maintain the acquired and existing strength level.

Principles for conducting strength training with older athletes

Execution
▸ Warm up, familiarize with the exercises used later on
▸ Select exercises according to technical abilities
▸ Include exercises for agonists and antagonists to avoid muscular imbalances
▸ Choose loads appropriate for actual strength capacity
▸ Avoid maximum joint positions
▸ Maintain relaxed breathing and avoid exhalation against closed air passages (valsalva maneuver)
▸ No round or hollow back – keep core tightened
▸ Stretch after training

General rules
▶   Strength training always with partner – even better with a group of athletes
▶   Optimal training frequency: 2x per week
▶   All year round training for all performance groups; make it a main focus for competitive rowers
▶   Maximum 30 – 45 min per unit (not included is the time for warming up and stretching afterwards)
▶   No strength training after exhausting endurance training

6.3.2   Training on the Rowing Ergometer

Training on the rowing ergometer is often misunderstood and not used optimally. On the one hand, it is praised as a fantastic training tool, with the help of which even rowing technique can be improved, because it is "easier" and a coach can "engage" and "correct" immediately. On the other hand, it is often described as a "torture device" on which one cannot last for more than 20 minutes.

Rowing ergometers have their origins in the beginnings of the modern sport. On the one hand a replica of a seat in a rowing boat was sought, on which beginners could more easily learn the rowing movement in relative safety. On the other hand, it was used as a training device, which should mimic the rowing movement as closely as possible and use the same muscle groups. The first functional devices consisted of hydraulic resistors, each connected to an oar-handle kind of lever, which could be moved similar to sweep rowing or sculling with one resistor on each side. Such devices were for example installed in the training room of the famous Atlantic liner "Titanic", which could be seen briefly in the eponymous Hollywood movie. It was firmly believed that you could learn proper rowing technique on such devices.

Further developments simulated the rowing movement ever better and also enabled "objective" performance measurements. These ergometers were at first still too expensive, needed a lot of space and required constant maintenance.

It took until the end of the 1980s, when the Dreissigacker brothers from the small village of Morrisville in Vermont did away with many of the previous disadvantages. They stimulated a development that had a lasting effect on rowing. As a final thesis of their university studies, the brothers had to present a business idea, a "concept". As oarsmen, they chose a theme from their sport and designed an idea for a rowing equipment manufacturing company. The brothers' vision was to make rowing accessible to more people, through the development of rowing equipment, and ensuring that it was affordable for everyone. This was only possible if the devices were simple, robust, affordable and could be manufactured in large numbers.

After successful completion of their studies, the brothers founded a company that they named after their final thesis: Concept2. One of the devices they developed based on this business idea was their rowing ergometer that was supposed to simulate movement and resistance of the rowing stroke as close as possible, be robust and almost maintenance-free. In addition, the new ergometer would provide feedback on training time, stroke rate and performance, and above all be very reasonably priced. Today, Concept2 is the market leader and their ergometers are used all over the world. The mechanism allows to a great extent the simulation of the rowing motion, and the resistance mechanism is designed to match the force curve in the boat. This makes it possible by and large to imitate any boat training, including any race training.

Of course, over the years, other types of ergometers have come onto the market, some with additional features. The most famous developments are dynamic ergometers that reduce the movement of the rower's centre of mass and some electronically controlled breaking systems. It is claimed by some that the dynamic ergometer provides a better simulation of the rowing movement as experienced in the boat. Research shows that dynamic ergometers expose rowers to lower peak loading than stationary models, leading some to suggest that they could provide more protection against back and rib injuries. All these claims are disputed in science and no final assessment can be provided. The electronically controlled ergometers allow for more game-type visual effects that help to make training on the machine more entertaining.

Overall, it is left to the individual athlete to have their preferred ergometer type, but since ergometers are so widely accessible, there is no reason for any rower, including the masters, to do without specific rowing training on land. It can be safely assumed that every rowing club and fitness club in the world has available some rowing ergometers of some type for indoor training. Neither high water nor winter storms, tropical heat or just the absence of a rowing boat can prevent rowers today from performing specific training with the best possible control measures.

Most modern ergometers now have electronic monitors that measure and display a number of rowing performance factors. These systems are so good and reliable that different rowers can be compared accurately. Therefore, it is possible to set up internationally recognized leaderboards and so it is not surprising that even national and international ergometer championships are organized. This also means that one can accurately control individual training, which allows for an effective year-round training process. It is no wonder that the development of these rowing machines has made a significant contribution to the performance increase in our sport and also in masters rowing.

The rowing ergometer plays a central role in the training of many masters. Here are some reasons for this:

- The rowing ergometer makes it possible to practice our sport at any time, in any weather and when there is no possibility of rowing on the water
- The rowing ergometer is an ideal piece of training equipment for Para-athletes
- The rowing ergometer is easy to operate and to use - you can learn the functions of the device (monitor, vent etc.) and even the 'rowing' motion in a matter of minutes
- As long as the rower maintains a proper posture (a solid neutral spine), the resistance setting is low (e.g. vent is mainly closed) and the length of the workout is adapted to the rowers' physical ability, training is quite safe and the risk of injury on the rowing ergometer is extremely low
- Anyone can use the rowing ergometer, regardless of height and weight. Even joint alterations that restrict the range of motion, allow a meaningful use of the training device
- Anyone, even an inexperienced rower, can complete training sessions of any intensity; from endurance to high intensity racing loads, from easy rowing to strength training, from continuous to interval training, any form of training and intensity can be performed, which is important for athletes who have not yet mastered rowing on the water to be able to achieve the desired training intensity in the boat
- You can become physically fit on the ergometer, so that you then can enjoy rowing on the water more
- The training on the rowing ergometer is highly time-effective – there is no additional work required before training (bringing the boat to the water, setting footstretcher or oarlock height etc.) or after (bringing the boat back to the boathouse, clean it etc.). Every available minute can be used for training; in addition, at any time one can choose training forms that generate the maximum training stimulus in the shortest amount of time
- You can effectively train alone, as well as in a group – it is even possible to connect multiple devices electronically or even virtually and project the results of all connected ergometers on a monitor or a screen, so that collaborative, controlled training sessions or races are possible; such setups are highly motivating
- Likewise, "slides" can be used or parts of ergometers can be locked together, so that several ergometers are connected to each other and rowers have to coordinate their movements similar to the boat

Overall, the rowing ergometer is a highly effective and enormously important training device for rowers of all ages! Of course, training on the rowing ergometer also has limits and disadvantages: Ergometer training can be experienced as boring or demotivating, if stimuli of varying workouts or engaging environments are missing. Exercising of our sport outdoors, on the water and in a crew is much more appealing and demands much greater coordination and adaptation. Above all, the challenge of handling the balance of a single scull or the experience of perfect teamwork in a four or eight cannot be replaced by this training device.

Yet a positive attitude to indoor rowing helps to make this kind of training very relaxed, rewarding and often even interesting. It helps a lot to implement many training variations, to keep training demands with respect to volume reasonable, to organize team workouts and to set appealing technical or performance related challenges.

Here are some tips:

▶ **Look forward to training – have a positive attitude!** Those who use the ergometer correctly can make tremendous progress in training and enjoy their performance. A positive attitude makes ergometer training less intimidating and athletes can enjoy the benefits.

▶ **Choose an adequate workout duration!** Masters rowers who are in a training phase of building up their fitness should limit themselves to 15-20 min; well-trained athletes can row for 60 minutes (or more) on the ergometer.

▶ **Vary the training!** It is not for everyone to row non-stop for 45 min or more on the ergometer. The total time can be apportioned in smaller intervals (see training suggestions). Other variations are: changing stroke length, grip, force; rowing with feet out of the straps; team training in which for example two rowers on a single machine alternate or one rower on an ergometer in front of all other ergometers takes the "stroke" position and all other athletes copy stroke rates and intensities; technical variations, e.g. pause at the finish, accentuated pull and slow recovery, "Russian catch" = rowing only with leg movement without arms and back motion.

▶ **Choose the right intensity!** Numerous masters rowers tend to "turn up" the intensity too high. If you plan to row for 20 min and start with a relatively high power output, the minutes on the machine will feel longer and you may even be forced to reduce power more than intended over the training piece. The decreasing numbers on the monitor will inevitably discourage the rower and make the experience unpleasant. The intensity must fit the individual's fitness. Long training sessions should be started light and relaxed, so that the feedback from the monitor is encouraging. If you want to "put your foot down" and see fast splits, you should choose short intervals with appropriate breaks.

▸ **Train in a group!** It is more motivating to do an ergometer session as part of a group. For each interval, let another rower choose the specific training focus. One by one the athletes propose the task for the next interval: specify the stroke rate, damper setting, technique task, and intensity. All participants are involved in the training design, many variations are possible and other objectives addressed. For example, for a group of five rowers you plan to do 5x10 min intervals with 2 min rest; athlete A chooses 4-3-2-1 min at stroke rates 20-22-24-26 and during the rest rower B proposes to change the stroke rate between 20-24 every 2 min etc.

▸ **Also, integrate racing into the training!** For this purpose, the length or duration of the race needs to be set properly: perform for example 5 km or 20 min races to control endurance; for race preparation, 1 min intervals can be set. If there are big performance differences in a training group, handicaps can be built in. So for example, one rower sets their race distance to 1,000 m, while the stronger rower might set their monitor to 1,100 m.

Of course, the maximum power - even that of the best masters rower – decreases over the years. There is nothing wrong with this and there is no need to end up in despair. Older athletes should enjoy realizing that they can keep an age related high level of performance while preserving their health. Of course, masters athletes who train properly can achieve improvements for example in their technique and even sometimes in their performance, but one should not expect new personal bests on a daily basis.

Any "skill" training on the ergometer can be limited to movement corrections that **teach the basic on-water technique** features (e.g. proper gripping of the handle with a flat wrist during the drive and relaxed fingers during the recovery), that emphasize the correct sequence of the joint movements and that prevent injuries. Trying to teach more details of the on-water technique is mostly inefficient and could lead to frustration of the coach and the athlete, since the rower will not be able to transfer them to the boat. In the same way, it does not make sense to unnecessarily waste time and efforts exercising movements that are not used in on-water rowing, for example extreme "pulling up at the finish and pushing-down of the hands to start the recovery". Although this movement is possible to execute on the ergometer, it is not on the water. On the other hand, it would be wrong if the handle is returned at a higher level during the recovery than during the drive. The rowing technique on the ergometer should be simple and healthy.

Note!
It is not possible to learn the rowing technique used in the boat on the ergometer. While a good approximation, rowing on the ergometer is fundamentally a different skill than rowing on the water. It lacks the balance, the handling of the oars and the adaptation to wind and waves.

The determination of the training intensity is facilitated by the monitor. On most of the ergometers, one can choose between the display of the average power per stroke in Watts, the work per stroke in Calories and a calculated speed in 500 m splits. The most common indicator, which also connects to rowing on the water, is the "500 m split time". This monitor unit is modeled on what is often used with speed measuring devices in boats and the display shows about how fast athletes would cover 500 m in a straight four, if they worked with the respective intensity. Many rowers have developed a feeling for this measurement unit and it is therefore motivating to row with this information on the ergometer.

Controlling training intensities on the ergometer is relatively simple. Not only do rowers get feedback about how hard they work immediately after every stroke, it is possible to identify each rower's individual intensity level. Split times for the specific training intensities are quite closely related for every athlete independent of the performance level of the rower. Of course, the stronger athlete will row at faster split times for each workout intensity, but the differences of the split times measured in seconds are somewhat similar for each rower. In general, the differences in split times for certain training intensities are shown in Tab. 36 and work for every athlete.

This means that a rower only needs to know the actual splits for one of their individual intensity levels to be able to calculate the splits to be used at all other intensities. Since one can design specific tests for each training intensity, as indicated in Tab. 36, it is sufficient that an athlete performs one of these tests to be able to then calculate splits for all other training intensities. Of course, in order to improve the accuracy of the determination of the training splits for each intensity level, one should repeat the test or perform tests for other training intensities. This admittedly rough calculation of the individual training speeds for all training intensities presents for any athlete quite good and sufficient "numbers" to identify proper training intensities.

If an athlete for example rows for 45 min continuously at an intensity where a conversation is still possible which would identify the extensive endurance level for this athlete, the average splits for this training piece can be taken as the starting point. The same rower would then have to row at splits held 11 seconds faster for a training intensity at the anaerobic threshold or would row at a split time 23 seconds faster over a 1,000 m race piece. Or, if an athlete performs a 2,000 m race, the average splits for this piece can be taken as a starting point and the same athlete would have to row with splits held 13 seconds slower for their intensive endurance training or 21+ split seconds slower for a recovery row.

Training Intensity	500m Split time difference in sec compared to splits for Extensive Endurance	Test to find 500 m split time for the respective training intensity
1.000 m Race Pace	-23 sec	1.000 m Race
2.000 m Race Pace	-19 sec	2.000 m Race
Anaerobic Threshold	-11 sec	10.000 m Race or 40min Time Trial
Intensive Endurance	-6 sec	15.000 m Race or 60 min Time Trial
Extensive Endurance	0 sec = Starting Point	Intensity of 30+ min at which conversation is still possible
Compensation	+ 2 sec and more	Light rowing with easy conversation – not applicable for testing, since splits can vary too much

Tab. 36:
Relationship of the split times for the individual training intensities and the necessary tests to determine the individual performance level

Example 1: A masters rower achieves 4:04 min for 1,000 m at maximum intensity. The average split time displayed on the monitor is 2:02 min/500 m. If this rower then plans interval training at race pace, like 6 x 250 m intervals, one should aim for splits of 2:02 min/500 m. In a continuous extensive endurance training over 45-60 min, the same rower should aim for 2:25 min/500 m splits (2:02 min + 23 sec = 2:25 min).

Example 2: The same rower now wants to verify the training splits, chooses to perform a 10,000 m test which represents the anaerobic threshold level and reaches the total time of 45:20 min so that the monitor shows an average split time of 2:16 min/500 m. The calculation for an extensive endurance workout produces the following result: 2:16 min + 11 sec = 2:27 min which of course is somewhat different from the previous test. This can have the following reasons: The athlete did not perform on their maximal level at the 10,000 m test, is less efficient at longer exercises or is more of a sprinter type. In any case, the rower should adjust the actual training intensity for extensive endurance to 2:26 m/500 m splits and observe over a period of one to two weeks, if the new intensity scale fits their training better.

Tab. 37 gives actual numbers for these relationships. Each row of the table provides split times of each specific training intensities for athletes 1 to 9 of different performance levels. For example, an athlete (here rower 5) who can row a 2,000 m race at an average split of 1:56 min/500 m will find their individual training speeds for each intensity in the same column where the 1:56 min/500 m appears.

Training Intensity	PERFROMANCE LEVELS (500 m Split Times)								
	Rowers								
	1	2	3	4	5	6	7	8	9
1.000 m Race Split	2:12	2:07	2:02	1:57	1:52	1:47	1:42	1:37	1:32
2.000 m Race Split	2:16	2:11	2:06	2:01	1:56	1:51	1:46	1:41	1:36
Anaerobic Threshold	2:24	2:19	2:14	2:09	2:04	1:59	1:54	1:49	1:44
Intensive Endurance	2:29	2:24	2:19	2:14	2:09	2:04	1:59	1:54	1:49
Extensive Endurance	2:35	2:30	2:25	2:20	2:15	2:10	2:05	2:00	1:55
Compensation	2:37+	2:32+	2:27+	2:22+	2:17+	2:12+	2:07+	2:02+	1.57+

Tab. 37:
Split times of individual training intensities (rows) for rowers of different performance levels (columns)

The specified split times are useful approximations, but no absolute norms. Small variances are possible – and normally occurring – depending on the athlete's form of the day which is affected for example by sleep, temperature, food intake etc. Every masters rower needs to develop a "feel" for their individual situation, especially to avoid overloading. If for example a 2:10 min/500 m split time was found as an individual measure of a specific intensity for this athlete, it may be that after a stressful day you are better off training at a level of 2:12 min/500 m splits. Similarly, it is also important to ensure that training improvement are achieved. After a few weeks of effective training, the training splits of the same athlete may need to be increased to 2:09 min/500 m to achieve the same training effect.

The damper setting regulates the airflow through the flywheel housing and can be varied on the Concept2 ergometer from setting 1-10. The amount of air that gets moved through the flywheel generates the resistance of the ergometer. Position 1 corresponds to the lowest airflow and thus produces the lowest resistance, while position 10 means the highest resistance. Position 2-3 corresponds approximately to a normal load experienced in on-water rowing and should therefore be the setting for a normal ergometer training session. Position 10 can be compared to a strength endurance training session with a can pulled behind the boat or rowing with "half crew".

The resistance that the flywheel generates can be affected by dust covering the air holes that accumulates in the housing and restricts the airflow. Therefore, the ergometer should be cleaned once every so often by removing the outer housing part and then vacuuming the inside. Depending on the degree of dust, the damper position could indicate a different resistance that actually exists. Conversely, it is important to know that the accuracy of the split and power measurement is not affected by this, because the computer monitor calculates the actual and correct resistance of the flywheel for each stroke.

For regularly maintained and cleaned ergometers, the damper setting between ergometers is comparable. The resistance can be determined for an exact comparison between ergometers with the function "Drag Factor" on the monitor - see the manufacturer's instructions for use. During each recovery, the monitor calculates the actual drag factor and accurately calculates the rower's power output. Drag factors between 115-130 indicate the resistance that resembles a normal boat setting, which should be used for normal training or racing. If masters rowers want to reduce the load on their backs, they should set the drag factor to 90-110. If one needs to use a damper setting of 5 or more to generate a drag factor of 120, the flywheel housing needs to be cleaned.

In summary, here are some ideas for training sessions on the ergometer:

Tab. 38: Effective, entertaining and healthy exercising on the rowing ergometer

Training goal	Ideas for training variations	Things to take care of

Basic Endurance and Compensation	▶ Continuous training of any length between 15 min and 120 min and more
	  • Constant stroke rate
	  • Variations of stroke rates
	  • Variation in damper settings
	▶ 2-4 x 20 min with 2 min rest
	▶ 1-4 x (4/3/2/1/2/3/4 [=19] min at stroke rate 20/22/24/26/24/22/20) with 5 min rest
	▶ 2-6 x (4/3/2/1 min with 2 min rest and different stroke rates)
	▶ 4-20 x 5 min with 1 min rest
		▶ Prefer damper settings between 1-4
		▶ Stick to the respective split time at any stroke rate
		▶ Rowers should be able to maintain a conversation
		▶ Start with shorter units and pay attention to "healthy" technique
		▶ Stay hydrated during longer sessions

Intensive Endurance	▶ Continuous training of any length between 10 to 60 min or 2.5-15 km
	  • Constant stroke rate
	  • Variation in stroke rates
	  • Variation in damper settings
	▶ 20/15/10/5 min with 5 min rest
	▶ 1-3 x (4/3/2/1/2/3 min with 5 min rest and different stroke rates)
	▶ 2-4 x (3/2/1/2/3 min with 4 min rest and different stroke rates)
	▶ 4-10 x 5 min with 1 min rest
		▶ Prefer damper settings 1-4
		▶ Stick to the respective split time at any stroke rate
		▶ At low frequencies you have to pay attention to good force application and healthy technique
		▶ Stay relaxed at higher frequencies
		▶ Training should feel easy in the beginning of the training session, but gets more exhausting towards the end

Anaerobic Threshold	▶ Time trial between 3 km and 10 km ▶ Red lining: 40 min nonstop – alternating 3 min at 3 sec split slower and 2 min at 1 s split faster than individual split at anaerobic threshold ▶ 2-5 x 2 km* with 4 min rest ▶ 15/10/5 min* with a 3 min rest ▶ 2-4 x 7 min* with 4 min rest ▶ 10 x 3* min with 2 min rest ▶ Constant splits at anaerobic threshold	▶ Prefer damper positions 1-4 ▶ Maintain intensity of individual split time at anaerobic threshold ▶ Training is exhausting and you have to be motivated ▶ Training in a group helps
Training goal	Ideas for training variations	Things to take care of

Strength Endurance	▶ 5-10 x 10 strokes maximum effort at stroke rate 20 with 3 min rest ▶ 5-10 x 100 m best time with 3 min rest ▶ 1-3 x continuous 20 min at basic endurance pace with 10 strokes maximum effort at various stroke rates every 2-4 min ▶ 1-10 min maximum effort at stroke rate 18 ▶ 5 km time trial at stroke rate 19 ▶ 5-10 x 1 min without legs = no slide (so only trunk and arms)	▶ Special attention to proper technique and posture! ▶ Air damper can be set up to 10 ▶ Use preferably low stroke rates ▶ Full relaxation during recovery and maximum effort during drive
Long Distance Races	▶ 42.195 km = Marathon ▶ 20 km ▶ 10 km ▶ 5 km	▶ Prefer damper settings 1-4 ▶ Relaxed rowing and keep stroke rates high ▶ Rowing with as constant intensity as possible ▶ Stay hydrated in tests over 60 min ▶ Work in a group helps
1,000 m Race	▶ 1,000 m maximum effort - Race profile should be similar to an on-water race: Strong start and transition at the beginning, splits may drop slightly in the middle and trying to sprint for the last 200 m	▶ Preferred damper settings: 1-4 ▶ Proper warm-up ▶ Full concentration and motivation

Safety and wellbeing is also the first consideration during ergometer training.

Before the training session:
▶ Wear comfortable, somewhat tight-fitting clothing – make sure no part of the clothes hangs over the seat that could be caught in the wheels of the seat
▶ Wearing clean sport shoes with narrower soles is recommended; if rowing without shoes, make sure you get used to the back straps on your heels
▶ Adjust foot mount according to shoe size, leg proportions and ankle mobility
▶ Check the handle, seat, rail and footboards for cleanliness
▶ Set the damper to the desired position – you may want to check the drag factor on the monitor
▶ Set the monitor to the desired training
▶ Tighten foot straps

During training:
▶ Do not let handle suddenly go
▶ Do not twist the chain
▶ Always row with both hands

After training:
▶ Set the handle back close to the vent – release tension in the pull-back mechanism
▶ Wipe seats, handle, monitor, footstretcher and rail

6.3.3   General and Supplementary Endurance Training for Masters Rowers

The importance of taking part in additional sports and general forms of training beyond rowing has already been emphasized for the various target groups of master rowers. Besides additional strength training, supplementary endurance training not only has a positive transfer effect on overall rowing performance, executing other sports also extends the range of types of movements. In addition, it offers alternatives that can be used when time is sparse, can help to recover from specific injuries or muscular overuse, can be used in different climatic as well as geographical conditions and can be integrated into holiday and vacation planning.

Endurance is also referred to as resistance against fatigue during activities that involve large muscle groups. Endurance training aims to ensure that efforts can be sustained over the longest possible period of time without signs of fatigue. Performance improves after only a few endurance training sessions and physical well-being increases.

Maximum oxygen uptake per minute (VO2max/min) is the main measure of endurance performance. Even though an individual's potential capacity for endurance will inevitably decrease in the second half of life, for example as a result of the changes in the cardiovascular, vascular and respiratory system, one should strive through athletic activity to maintain one's personal level of endurance as long as possible. Endurance can be trained throughout the whole life span and relative improvements – especially for those who are new to regular exercise – are still possible even at advanced age.

Similar to the classification in strength training, endurance training can be divided into **general** and **specific endurance** in terms of importance for respective sport performance. General endurance training in competitive rowing is considered the wide-ranging basic capacity of performance, while specific endurance relates to endurance capacity that is adapted to the load structure explicit to rowing, which means for example the development of base endurance or competition-specific endurance in the boat.

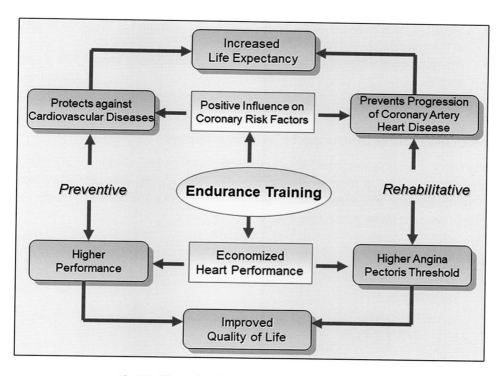

Fig. 60: Effects of endurance training (mod. Feldt, 1999).

Endurance training increases - whether in rowing or in any other sport - life expectancy, as well as quality of life. It initiates changes in the autonomic nervous system, which has economical and protective consequences for the cardiovascular system (see Fig. 60). Prerequisite for this is endurance training at our extensive endurance level where all energy is supplied by oxygen, also called aerobic endurance training, with a minimum duration of 15-20 minutes and the use of at least half of the body's muscles. The reasons for the economisation of the cardiovascular system are to be found in the adaptation responses of the trained musculature (Feldt, 1999):

▸ Enlargement and increase of mitochondria, the so-called "power plants" of the muscle cell, in which oxygen is used to produce ATP, the actual energy supply for muscle fibres
▸ Improved replenishment of glycogen depots in muscles and liver
▸ Increased fat oxidation for energy supply, which increases the overall available amount of energy and thus saves and protects the sugar metabolism
▸ Increased number of capillaries, resulting in better utilization of the blood oxygen in the muscle
▸ Optimization of blood distribution between active and passive musculature during exercise

Which sports can be used for aerobic endurance training?

The range of possible sports and activities to improve the aerobic endurance of masters rowers is enormous. In general, all sport activities in which the musculature performs recurring (cyclical) movements can be used for this training. The following sports are specifically suitable for masters rowers:

▸ Fast walking
▸ Hiking
▸ Running
▸ Swimming
▸ Biking and Cycling
▸ Cross-country skiing

Other alternatives for endurance training of masters rowers are: mountain biking, spinning on a stationary bike, endurance circuits or mountain tours. These sports are more intensive and include more power components, which is why the chances of producing lactate are relatively high, especially for beginners. Care should be taken here that training intensity is not increasing to such levels, since this could cause health concerns especially when performed in high altitude conditions.

Tab. 39: Suitable sports for supplementary endurance training for masters rowers – competitive/race oriented (R), fitness (F), health (H) and compensation (C)

Sport	Exercise recommen-dation	Target Group				Advantages
		R	F	H	C	
Rowing Ergometer	20-60 min; all intensity levels possible	X	X	X	X	▶ Accurate intensity dosage ▶ Almost like rowing ▶ Regardless of weather conditions ▶ Good comparisons possible ▶ Contests/tests possible ▶ Full body training
Running	20-80 min; extensive and intensive endurance	X	X	X	X	▶ Anytime and almost anywhere feasible ▶ Independent of sport equipment ▶ Simple motion
(Trekking) Hiking	60-300 min; extensive (and intensive) endurance	X	X	X	X	▶ Simple motion ▶ Nature experience ▶ Group experience ▶ Long durations possible
Nordic Walking	45-90 min; regenerative and extensive endurance		X	X	X	▶ Very gentle full-body workout at a low intensity level ▶ Simple motion ▶ Nature and communication
Swimming	20-60 min; regener-ative, extensive and intensive endurance	X	X	X	X	▶ Strengthening of the trunk and shoulder muscles ▶ Gentle on joints ▶ Physical stimuli through water and temperature ▶ Inurement of the body
Aqua-Jogging	20-40 min; extensive and intensive endurance	X	X	X		▶ Gentle to joints ▶ Relief of load on spine ▶ Active relaxation of the muscles ▶ Physical stimuli ▶ Low technical requirements ▶ Alternative to swimming ▶ Easy to learn

Disadvantages	Notes
▶ Danger of boredom ▶ Some space/equipment needed ▶ Can negatively affect rowing technique	▶ Possible until late adulthood ▶ As an alternative if on water training is not possible ▶ Home training (no gym or boathouse needed) ▶ Time efficient
▶ Overloading of joints, especially for heavier athletes	▶ Careful: Possible overloading for overweight athletes ▶ Slow progression of duration necessary at beginning of training ▶ Proper running shoes necessary!
▶ Potentially long travel to destination necessary ▶ Weather dependent ▶ Load on joints	▶ Meaningful and possible for all ages ▶ Careful at high altitudes
▶ Technique to some extent difficult ▶ Muscles may get fatigued quickly ▶ Infection risk ▶ Overcrowded pools	▶ Until late adulthood possible ▶ Should be an integral part of supplementary training (e.g. 1x per week)
▶ Place in the swimming pool ▶ Organization	

(continued)

(Tab. 39, continued)

Sport	Exercise recommen-dation	Target Group				Advantages
		R	F	H	C	
Road Bike & Mountain Bike (MTB) Cycling	30-360 min; Regener-ative, extensive and intensive endurance	X	X	X	X	▸ Gentle to joints ▸ Large volume possible ▸ Leg strength development ▸ Road bike particularly suitable for consistent load ▸ MTB independent of roads, increased coordinative demands improves attraction; cycling in nature and scenic, maybe challenging terrain
Spin Bike & Bicycle Ergometer	20-120 min extensive and intensive endurance		X	X	X	▸ Weather independent, ▸ Simple and excellent individual power control
Inline Skating	15-100 min Regenerative and extensive endurance	X	X	X	X	▸ Gentle stress for muscles and joints ▸ Balance training ▸ Rhythm training ▸ Longer distances possible
Cross-Country Skiing - Classic & Skating	45-300 min Regener-ative, extensive and intensive endurance	X	X	X	X	▸ Full body training ▸ Offsets muscular imbalances ▸ Use similar muscle groups as rowing ▸ Balance training ▸ Controlled force application ▸ Gentle on the joints ▸ Training during winter (holidays) ▸ Competitions available for all levels of competitiveness ▸ Off-road activity – Nature experience ▸ Long distances possible ▸ Individual load dosing

Advantages	Notes
▸ Traffic ▸ Risk of accident ▸ Partly expensive equipment ▸ Weather permitting ▸ High coordinative demands ▸ Danger of falling ▸ Danger of excessive risks through terrain	▸ Road bikes may not be suitable for older athletes (~60+) especially in busy traffic ▸ Long climbs with MTB in challenging terrain especially in high altitude maybe dangerous
▸ Risk of overloading ▸ Boredom	
▸ Risk of falling and injury ▸ Not everywhere to perform ▸ Equipment necessary	▸ Older athletes should abstain due to the risk of falls and accidents
▸ Snow and trails required ▸ Potentially long travel to destination necessary ▸ Equipment ▸ Weather dependent ▸ Increased Coordination Requirements - Movement must be learned	▸ Ideal supplementary sport for any age ▸ Snow walking up to cross-country ski racing possible with appropriate technique instructions

Criteria for choosing a supplementary endurance sport beyond rowing are:

1. Preference and fun
2. Technical ability – can the masters rower perform the sport well enough to benefit from practicing it without getting injured?
3. Integration in a training group
4. Favorable circumstances, availability
5. Training volume and control options are possible to reach planned training goal

How can endurance be increased in old age?

The best training effects are achieved if the endurance activities involve large muscle groups. At the same time, continuous training sessions of at least 15-20 min must be achieved, which can often be lengthened and even extend up to several hours. The longer the duration of the training, the lower the training intensity must be chosen. From a health perspective, a distinction is made between a minimal and an optimal training program (see Boeck-Behrens and Buskies, 2002).

A minimum program must be performed, if significant positive health effects are to be achieved. Untrained athletes will increase their performance at the beginning even with a relatively modest training volume, which must be increased after corresponding adaptations. An optimal program requires individual design. In particular, the extent to which training intensity and volume needs to be increased to achieve performance gains without jeopardizing health improvements is important to observe.

Tab. 40: Minimal and optimal health training programs in endurance sports

	Minimal Health Program	Optimal Health Program
Training Volume	80 min per week, e.g. 9-12 km running or 20-25 km cycling Additional calorie consumption approx. 500-1,000 Kcal	180 (120-240) min per week, e.g. 35-40 km running or 50-175 km cycling Additional calorie consumption approx. 2,000-3,000 Kcal
Exercise Intensity	Ca. 50% of VO2max Heart rate: 160 – age	70-80% of VO2max Heart rate: 160 – 1/2 age
Number and Duration of Training Sessions	3 x 20 – 30 min or 4 x 20 min	3 x 60 min or 6 x 30 min or 5 x 40 min

Possibilities of intensity control in health and fitness-oriented endurance training

The intensity of endurance training for older athletes should not only be controlled by using heart rates that are derived from simple formulas. Individual biological variabilities and numerous influencing factors, such as the type of endurance sport being practiced, temperature or food intake, can affect heart rate in different ways. Such factors may well cause the heart rate to appear too high or too low in relation to the training goal. It is appropriate to combine heart rate with other control variables, such as **subjective stress perception** (SSP).

SSP actually provides a suitable control option, even more if the athlete's own body perception and real self-assessment becomes more reliable. To estimate subjective stress, Borg (1985) -proposes an 18-point scale (Fig. 61).

The advantage of SSP as a control variable is that the scale can be used continuously during training without any measurements and gives an immediate individual sensation of the actual stress situation (Buskies, 2001, p. 41).

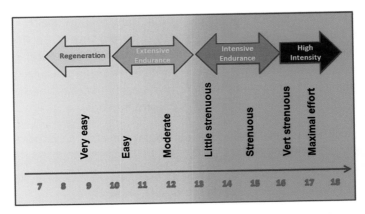

Fig 61: Subjective stress perception scale (mod. after Borg, 1985).

Beginners and less trained athletes particularly should do their endurance training on the level of the subjective feeling of "Easy" to "Moderate". The corresponding lactate values are then usually in the desired and effective range. Caution is required for some sports regarding the variances that different age groups experience performing them. Older recreational athletes for example seem to run at a too high speed, if they use the same SSP values as younger athletes. On the other hand, women's blood lactate measurements tend to correspond with slightly lower SSP intensities. An athlete's experience and technical ability in the respective sport seems to also have an influence on the subjective stress perception. For example, skilled cross-country skiers hit the proper intensities more adequately than technically less experienced cross-country skiers (see Melges and Fritsch, 1999).

Breathing can also serve to control the individual and desired training intensity. Buskies (2001, p. 41) proposes the four-step breathing rhythm for less-trained and older runners, which means that one complete exhalation and inhalation cycle involves eight running steps, for example four footfalls for inhaling and four footfalls for exhaling or three footfalls for inhaling and five footfalls for exhaling, whichever fits the individual runner best. Younger and more highly trained runners can shorten the breathing sequence to seven or even six steps.

Above all, the phrase "run without huffing and puffing" still provides a good criterion for finding the proper extensive endurance training intensity. This can of course also be transferred to other endurance sports. The load is to be chosen so that a coherent conversation with a training partner is possible. Another simple method to control intensity to extensive endurance training is only breathing through the nose. If breathing through the nose becomes no longer sufficient, the exercise intensity is too high.

Another method to control intensity is through the heart rate using the so-called Karvonen formula, which calculates the training heart rate based on the resting and maximum heart rate like this:

> **Training heart rate =**
> **Resting heart rate + [(maximum heart rate - resting heart rate) x intensity]**
> **± 3 beats [1/min]**
>
> **"Intensity" is set as percentage of maximum**

The resting heart rate is determined after a 10-minute rest while lying down or in the morning still lying down 5 minutes after waking up. If one does not know their maximum heart rate on the rowing ergometer, one can estimate it according to the formula: 220 - age.

Example: An untrained 50-year-old with the resting heart rate of 65 beats/min would like to start rowing-ergometer training, but does not know her maximum heart rate. So, she estimates her maximum heart rate to 220 − 50 = 170. A good starting point for her training would then be:

> **Training heart rate = 65 + [(170 - 65) x 60%] ± 3 beats = 128 ± 3 beats [1/min]**

Tab. 41: Overview of possibilities to monitor exercise intensity for endurance training of fitness-oriented older athletes (Mod. after Boeck-Behrens and Buskies, 2002)

Control Parameters	Example for: Running	Example for: Cycling	Other Endurance Sports
Lactate	Up to 3-4 mmol/l		
Heart rate	▶ Karvonen formula with 60-75% intensity depending on age and fitness ▶ Training heart rate =190/195 - Age +/- 5	▶ Karvonen formula with 60-70% intensity depending on age and fitness ▶ Training heart rate = 180 - age +/- 3	▶ Karvonen formula with 60-75% intensity depending on sport, age and fitness

(continued)

(Tab. 41, continued)

Control Parameters	Example for: Running	Example for: Cycling	Other Endurance Sports
Stress Perception	▶ Easy – still just easy ▶ Still just easy – medium effort	▶ Easy – medium effort ▶ Medium effort ▶ Medium effort – a bit strenuous	▶ Easy – still just easy ▶ Still just easy – medium effort ▶ Medium effort
Respiratory	Nasal breathing		
Theme	"Train without huffing and puffing" "Talk test"		
Well-being	"Feeling good"		

Tips for endurance training

▶ Have a physician check you over before you begin and then continue with regular check-ups
▶ Consult with your physician regarding the planned activities and intensities
▶ Consult with your physician regarding training when sick, especially with feverish infections
▶ Exercise endurance sports regularly
▶ Look for partners to train together
▶ Pay attention to all criteria for choosing a sport
▶ Change up sports and activities
▶ Avoid breaks from training
▶ Forgo endurance training outdoors under severe environmental influences (like: lightning, storms, pollution, smog, heat, ozone, etc.)
▶ Wear proper clothing
▶ First increase duration then intensity, if you plan to build up your training
▶ Train in a way that you always have fun

6.3.4 General Coordination Training for Masters

The importance of general coordination training for masters rowers

Coordination training becomes one of the most important pillars of fitness and health training as we get older, and thus for the complementary training for masters rowers. The term coordination is a collective term for a range of abilities. These govern all movements under the control function of the central nervous system, the brain and spinal cord, in cooperation with the skeletal musculature. The interaction occurs on the level of individual muscle fibers (intramuscular coordination) and on the other hand on the level of individual muscle groups (intermuscular coordination).

Coordination cannot be overstated; it is arguably the most underrated fundamental motor function of many masters rowers. High levels of general and rowing-specific coordination abilities are equally important with increasing age as well as in fitness and health training and manifest themselves in:

a) Economization of movement sequences means
- ▸ less fatigue in everyday life and in training,
- ▸ conservation of energy reserves,
- ▸ reduction of the risk of injury (fall prevention, reduction of accidents in everyday life) and
- ▸ reduction of forces necessary in everyday movements.

b) Increased capacity to focus: "Coordination training sharpens the senses"

c) All this fosters enjoyment of physical activity

In detail, coordinative abilities are (Hohmann et al., 2003, p. 103):

- ▸ Responsiveness
- ▸ Rhythm ability
- ▸ Balance ability
- ▸ Spatial orientation ability
- ▸ Kinesthetic differentiation ability
- ▸ Coupling ability
- ▸ Ability to adjust

Sports-specific terminologies are often developed, especially in competitive sports which describe specific skills. Some good rowing examples include: "boat feel", "suspension" or "catching the water during the last part of the recovery" etc. Such terminology helps to describe complex movements and can help the rower to get some direction for their practical technique training. This is especially significant for older athletes where coordination training has practical implications for real world mobility. As such, we support the idea of a continuum between the sport-specific coordination skills of rowing technique and the coordination that goes beyond all sports and movements (see Fig. 62).

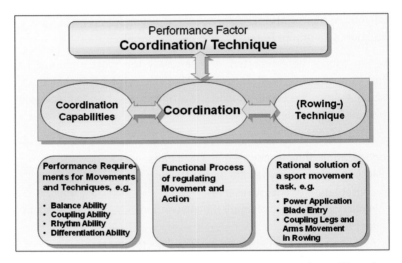

Fig. 62: Relationship between general coordinative abilities and the specific rowing technique (mod., Schmidt, 2003, p. 188).

Coordination helps in the learning, controlling and adjusting of movements. The central nervous system requires many environmental inputs to execute precise control and adaptation.

Important sensor systems in the head to control movement:

▸ Optical system: Control of the position of the head in space and feedback about position of certain parts of the sport system
▸ Equilibrium organ: Acceleration of the head that helps sense motion, but also with the orientation of the body's positioning in the given space
▸ Hearing: Acoustic mapping and special spatial perception

Important sensor systems for motion control positioned in the musculoskeletal system:

▶ Muscle Spindles: Measuring muscle length and tension (tension=pulling force)
▶ Tendon organs: Registering tendon tension
▶ Joint Receptors: Detecting joint position
▶ Skin receptors: Registering touch, pressure, pain

A well-coordinated or successful movement depends on internal factors and processes involved in the necessary coordination of muscular actions, as well as an athletes' developmental state and level of motor abilities and skills:

▶ Awareness and observation: Acquisition and selection of information from the environment
▶ Motion design: Programming of the movement and mental anticipation of expected force patterns and sensory feedback of the event including some input from motor memory
▶ Control impulses to the musculature
▶ Movement execution by the movement organs
▶ Ongoing feedback on the progress of the movement
▶ Appropriate correction pulses

Deficits or obstacles even in a single aspect of this complex structure can hinder or prevent well-coordinated movements.

Improving general coordination also results in increased movement economy. Thus, Hollmann et al. (1976) demonstrated a 12% improvement in oxygen consumption as a result of simply improving coordination (see Fig. 63).

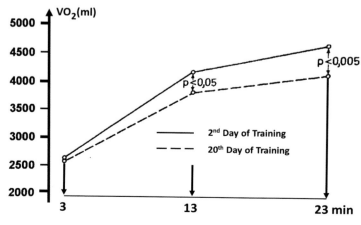

Fig. 63:
Oxygen savings for a given running performance on the treadmill through improved coordination (after Hollmann et al., 1976, p. 145).

The authors' own spirometry investigations in the boat with highly qualified national team level rowers confirm the results of Hollmann et al. Field tests with pairs doing step tests of identical volume and intensity provided further clues on how better coordination of movements (rowing technique) influenced higher motion economy in competitive rowing (Nilius 2009).

Problems with movement coordination occur mainly during motor learning processes, movements under unfamiliar conditions or new situations, after prolonged breaks and as a consequence of biological aging processes (Schaller & Wernz, 2008, p. 12).

Motor learning abilities must be practiced throughout life. Everyday accidents occur more frequently in old age, since the interaction between the central nervous system and the skeletal muscles no longer functions optimally due to a lack of exercise or a general activity reduction.

The following causes are responsible in various degrees and combinations for the age-related decline of coordinative abilities (Schaller & Wernz, 2008, p. 32):

- Weakening of the sensory organs
- Power loss
- Weakening of and changes in the joints (e.g. flexibility)
- Changes in the neuronal network
- Changes in the metabolic system
- Lack of physical activity in childhood and adolescence

How do you train general coordinative skills?

To train general coordinative skills, exercises should be chosen in such a way that "the trainee is pushed to the limit ... of their information processing in order to induce self-organization processes that lead to an improvement in the quality of motion control" (Hohmann et al., 2003, p. 111). This means general coordination exercises must be difficult and challenging; ideally they should include a lot of new and unknown movements.

Although rowing as a sport provides a range of coordinative skills, these do not develop in a well-balanced way and certainly not sufficiently to cover general coordination. Only those programs, which contain a large reservoir of new, unfamiliar and complex exercises that are upgraded by variations, combinations and spontaneous modifications present older athletes with decisive impulses for the preservation and promotion of general and rowing specific coordinative abilities. Sport in general offers a wealth of unfamiliar or complicated tasks, which can be adapted to the ability level of the target groups, as well as to both the general coordination training and the rowing-specific technique training (Schaller & Wernz, 2008, p. 40).

General coordination training of course offers immediate advantages for rowing technique. However, in our attempt at successful aging through sport training, we should also have an eye on coping with everyday situations that come with increasing age. Engaging in complementary general coordination training is therefore important in addition to the continuous work on rowing techniques. Our sport is most fun when the movement is executed well whether you row on your own or in a crew. The quality of coordinative skills not only plays an important role during the learning process of rowing, but also in the application and economization of physical capabilities, as well as when skilled rowers adapt to any situation like wind and waves.

Many aging related losses in coordinative abilities are due to a lack of activity. Rowing alone cannot fully compensate for the loss. On the other hand, above-average quality of movement coordination generally can be maintained into old age through adequate activities and appropriate exercise selection. Depending on an individual's baseline levels of coordinative ability, regular practice can lead to improvement, slow pre-existing degenerative symptoms, or even delay involution processes (Schaller & Wernz, 2008, p. 37).

Movements that have already become automated no longer contribute to the improvement of coordinative abilities. So, the best way to improve coordination skills is to learn new sports!

Over the course of a lifetime, activity levels will usually go down with age; decline of coordination follows suit. While the onset of this trend is not universally set, maintaining or increasing your levels of physical activity can be difficult all on your own. Group exercise, on the other hand, can make staying active longer in life a lot more fun by joining the lead of others or under the guidance of a coach. It makes sense to execute only a limited number of repetitions, but expand on many different exercises and a large variety of changing exercise conditions. At the same time, difficult exercises should be performed at the beginning of the training session, since fatigue will negatively impact the quality of execution and with this the training effect of the exercise.

The following principles can help to systemize the enormous amount of possible exercises. Thus, one exercise incorporating various principles can address a range of coordinative demands (see Hohmann et al., 2003, pp. 112-113):

▶ **Change of external conditions:** surroundings, equipment, necessity to react to activities of a partner or an opponent
▶ **Targeted principles:** Revised information intake and adaptation of one's own movement
▶ **Variation of movement execution:** amplitude, speed, frequency
▶ **Targeted principle:** Differentiation of motion control
▶ **Combination of different skills**
▶ **Practicing under time pressure:** Competitive situations, timing, number of athletes per team
▶ **Variation of information intake:** Turning off of optical, acoustic, tactile, kinesthetic and/or vestibular information
▶ **Practicing under physical stress:** Increase difficulty by fatiguing the rower
▶ **Practicing under psychological stress:** Competitive situation, demonstration of the movement in front of group, spectators, as well as emotionally charged situations and adverse conditions (more sensitive sports equipment, height above ground, etc.)

 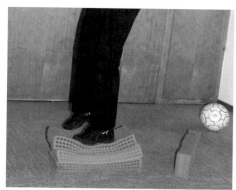

6.3.5   Flexibility

Flexibility or limberness is the ability to perform movements with a large range of motion in a joint or a number of joints. This capability is crucial for the transfer of an athlete's mechanical energy and needs to be consistently and sufficiently trained independent of the training goal of an athlete. Flexibility depends on abilities that a person can influence and properties one can hardly change, as well as exogenous factors (like time of day or outside temperature) and external forces (like a partner, gravity or inertia).

Flexibility varies greatly due to the different mechanical build of athletes. One can influence the elongation of the antagonistic muscles through relaxation and to a lesser degree the elasticity of tendons, ligaments and joint capsules. It is possible, although incredibly difficult to influence the mechanical mobility or the structure of a joint.

The importance of mobility lies in the optimization of the qualitative and quantitative movement execution and in the prevention of accidents and injuries for older adults. It is therefore an essential part of performance, fitness and health training for masters rowers.

Increased or sufficiently good mobility:

▶ Leads to an optimization of the movement flow and the movement harmony
▶ Extends the range of sport-specific technique
▶ Speeds up the motor learning process
▶ Makes an important contribution to the load compatibility and injury prophylaxis
▶ Allows to achieve an higher power application

The development of flexibility is influenced relatively early in life by the aging process. Humans reach their best flexibility as early as the transition from childhood to adolescence after which point this ability decreases continuously and steadily. Women are in general more flexible than men and the decline of flexibility is faster in males than females.

The flexor muscles of the locomotor and supportive systems generally tend to shorten with age and with less practise flexibility decreases quickly to a low level. Nonetheless, flexibility can up to about the age of 80 years not only be maintained through appropriate exercises, but even improved.

Typical "warm-up" procedures that are used in many sports hardly contribute to sustainable flexibility improvements. Above all, neuromuscular conditions are of great importance for elasticity of the musculoskeletal system (Hohmann et al., 2003, p. 97). This means that relaxation is necessary to achieve flexibility gains. Ballistic stretching, especially performed in a fast swinging manner, was a common warm-up procedure in the past, but has shown negative effects and is no longer used. Such exercises provoke proprioceptive reflexes (myotatic reflex), which are responsible for an immediate contraction of the musculature and thus achieve the opposite of a muscle stretch (Hohmann et al., 2003, p. 100).

Properly applied, stretching exercises of the muscles are useful to maintain or improve flexibility and to accelerate regeneration.

The actual flexibility of a masters rower (check out: muscle function tests) determines the choice of exercises. Stretching too much can lead to health problems, so does incorrect stretching or stretching of the wrong muscles. If you stretch using the wrong method at the wrong time, e.g. with the classic long-lasting stretches before a competition or a workout, both the performance can be reduced and the risk of injury can be increased. If you stretch too much before a competition, performance is inhibited since the muscles lose their ability to absorb kinetic energy.

How do I improve my flexibility?

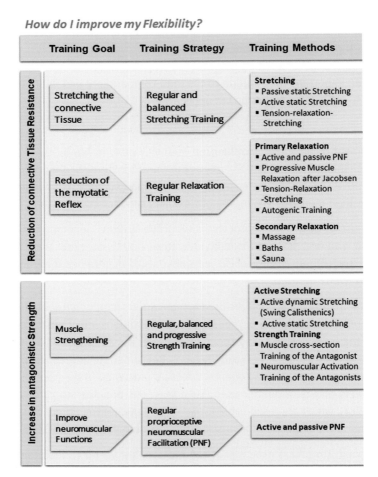

Fig. 64: Objectives, strategies and methods of flexibility training
(mod. After Hohmann et al., 2003).

One can achieve an increase in flexibility through reducing the resistance of the connective tissue and on the other hand through strengthening the antagonistic muscles (see Fig. 64). One can reduce the resistance of the connective tissue for example by using methods to stretch the connective tissue, or by relaxing the myotatic reflex and strengthen the antagonistic muscles with appropriate strength training, or through improvements of neuromuscular functions.

Stretching exercises are believed to produce the best results to increase flexibility, but there is no scientific agreement on a "best" method. Our best current understanding is that musculature should be stretched slowly until you feel tension. Then breathe deeply, relax and hold this position for about 15-30 seconds. If you feel pain, you went too far with the stretch, however you should try to reach a little further with every repetition of the stretch. The tension that one feels during the stretch should subside through relaxation which allows muscle to be stretched a little further the next time. Stretching exercises should be repeated 2-4 times.

The required force to stretch a muscle is passively applied by the contraction of the antagonistic musculature, by gravity using one's own body weight or with the help of a training partner. If a training partner is used, the stretching force has to be increased very slowly and carefully, and immediately reduced when pain is experienced.

One other effective stretching method is called **proprioceptive neuromuscular facilitation (PNF) stretching**, also called tension-relaxation-stretching. For this, you put the muscle in a lightly stretched position for about 10-20 seconds, then contract the muscle against resistance for 1-6 seconds, release the tension without changing position, and then move the muscle in a slightly larger stretch, usually with the assistance of a partner who "pushes" the stretch. While PNF can be very effective, it can also be dangerous if done improperly. Pursue it only under the supervision of a physical therapist or trainer.

In contrast to the strategy of relaxation, one can also **strengthen the antagonists** (Hohmann et al., 2003, p. 101). This strategy will allow the athlete to execute a larger range of motion with the help of the strengthened musculature.

Stretching needs to be learned properly and ideally with some expert advice until the athlete knows which exercises should be executed and in which way. Athletes need to know the stretching exercises that are appropriate for them, how to prepare for stretching and how far stretching should go. Stretching should either be performed after a workout or as a stand-alone training session. Athletes have to be relaxed and not be rushed to achieve positive results.

Suitable stretching for rowing

Stretching should generally be exercised only in a warmed up state. There are a few exceptions to this rule in physiotherapy and also in rowing, for example if an athlete has moderate back problems. In this case, it may make sense for such a rower to "loosen up" the abdominal muscles and the lower back through very light stretching before a training session and especially before a workout on the water. This takes place before the actual warm-up. The actual warm-up should then include some exercises that lightly strengthen and mobilize.

Stretching before training

It was believed for a long time that stretching before training would help to prevent injuries and improve performance. However, since stretching is only done properly when the athlete relaxes the muscles and gets into a "slower" state, the ability of the muscles to contract quickly and powerfully is actually reduced, which affects especially intensive training. Stretching still has its place in the warm-up of athletes with severe limitations of their mobility or for sports that include movements that require large ranges of joint radii. In these two cases, it is necessary to prepare the body for larger ranges of movements but it should always be left to the athletes, if indeed warm-up stretching provides them with positive feedback.

▸ Only stretch muscles that have to perform a large range of motion in training
▸ Each position is executed for 10 seconds
▸ An intense sense of stretch is generated
▸ The working method is dynamic or intermittent

Nowadays, we prefer so-called active-dynamic stretching for warm up before speed and strength loads or to strengthen the antagonists. This means that athletes go actively through movements that are closely related to the sport they want to train in, at first slowly and gently and then a little more dynamically. This type of warm up should not be confused with ballistic stretching which intends to expand movement beyond the range of motion, while active-dynamic stretching involves controlled and gentle leg and arm swings that only cover the natural range of motion.

Stretching after training

Stretching after training is considered more important as a positive measure. It not only helps to maintain flexibility, but also improves regeneration.

▶ The stretching exercises are selected according to the needs of the rower – it can be supplemented by stretching and mobilization exercises for the lower back

▶ Athletes should not rush through the exercises, but use a mindful approach and each stretching position should be held for 15-30 seconds – remember that stretching gains are mainly achieved through relaxing the nervous system

▶ The more intense the preceding training, the more carefully should athletes perform their stretching to avoid injury

▶ Performing stretching together in a group helps to keep athletes motivated, focused on the exercises and keep the variety of exercises up

The following exercise examples should help masters rowers to select their favorite exercises for a stretching program:

For many masters rowers, the improvement in flexibility mainly relates to the requirements of the rowing movement. Nevertheless, stretching and strengthening exercises should also be carried out for general health reasons. They should be used as compensatory exercises to correct shortening of the musculature due to one-dimensional rowing and training processes and thus help to prevent long-term restrictions in the passive and active musculoskeletal system.

Flexibility training is always associated with strengthening: The stronger a muscle or muscle group is, the more it needs to be stretched and loosened right after training.

6.4   FUNCTIONAL SUPPORT TRAINING

Functional support training should be understood as regular and short training sessions that correct existing muscular, coordinative and conditional imbalances. Masters rowers using this type of training should be less concerned with improving performance directly, rather than correcting one-sided physical ailments, such as back and knees problems, muscle shortenings, insufficiencies and the elimination of coordinative deficits. Performed regularly, functional support training serves not only therapeutic purposes, but helps also to prevent many complaints of older rowers.

Functional support training includes specific strengthening, improved mobility, relaxation techniques and coordination training.

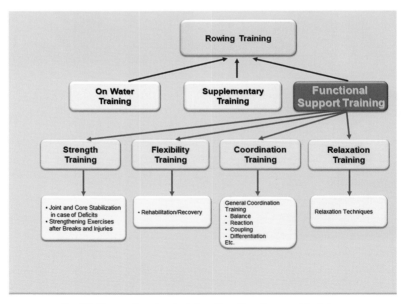

Fig. 65: Forms of rowing training: Functional support training.

The ideal goal of every rower should be to develop and maintain an optimally trained and balanced musculature that not only allows them to perform a certain amount of training, but is also the basic prerequisite for maintaining and developing physical fitness at any age. Many complaints, such as thoracic and lumbar spine complications, knee and tendon problems, as well as rib stress fractures are due to muscular imbalances, shortenings and insufficiencies and coordinative deficits. Performing rowing-specific and individually tailored functional calisthenics, in which strength, coordination and flexibility are regularly addressed and developed, can help prevent most negative health symptoms (Reifschneider, 2000).

Rotational forces and torsion of the spine are amplified to control boat stability in weather conditions such as wind or high waves. These extra movements of the boat in unfavorable rowing conditions can cause blockages of spinal segments. Cold temperatures can put extra stress on different body systems like hands or feet that may influence technique. Reifschneider (2000) describes the following factors, which mainly occur generally speaking within the rowing training process:

▶   Shortened hamstring muscles – often, this shortening is associated with the rowers' inability to fully rotate the hip around the lateral axis in the seated position which puts strain on the lumbar spine
▶   Shortened quadriceps muscles
▶   Relatively frequent attenuation of the oblique abdominal muscles that can inhibit proper lateral movements of the trunk
▶   It is common for humans to have legs of different lengths that ideally should be compensated for on the footstretcher; a lack of such compensation can cause a non-physiological twist of the pelvis that leads to functional overloading of the lower lumbar spine
▶   Waves require additional balancing of the boat and extra movement in the lumbar spine; if such lumbar movement occurs during the drive, the rower loses core stability which can lead to injuries of the spine or the hip
▶   Unfavorable rainy or cold weather can put extra strain on the musculature and also stiffen hands that could influence the grip and the technique of the rower which in turn can put extra stress for example on forearms or knees

In many cases, rowing training itself is not directly responsible for the extra loads on rowers' bodies that may lead to injuries. For example, running and strength training that is mainly used during the times a rower cannot go on the water often causes knee problems. Also, the rowing-specific exercise "leg press" performed with large range of motion represents a high load on the knee joint. Poor technical execution of exercises like deadlift and snatches can be the initiating strain on the back of a rower that could lead to back pain. Similarly, typical rowing-specific strength endurance trainings with several sets and numerous repetitions, as well as using excessively heavy weights accumulate to extreme overall stress.

Some sport-specific imbalances are often found in adults after just a few months of beginner training. These complaints arise despite performing "correct" rowing technique. This can be due to an overall activity overload, monotonous, one-sided loading, lack of regeneration and neglected stretching or strengthening of muscles. Therefore, it is necessary to implement preventive measures regarding muscular imbalances from the beginning of regular rowing sessions and at the latest with the start of performance training.

The core muscles are often not well prepared for the higher loads they will encounter in rowing. Above all, the lumbar spine is an especially weak point. The following muscle groups are often prone to weakening and shortening. For more information on shortened or attenuated musculature, refer to some simple test procedures (see Page, Frank & Lardner, 2010; Reese & Bandy 2002).

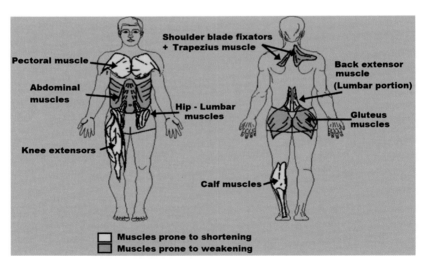

Fig. 66: Illustration of the muscles prone to shortening and weakening (Fritsch 2005 p. 69).

Tab. 42: Muscle groups that tend to weaken and shorten

Musculature tending to attenuate	▶ Abdominal muscles
	▶ Gluteal muscles
	▶ Scapular stabilizers
	▶ Back muscles in the area of the thoracic spine
Muscles tending to shorten	▶ Chest muscles
	▶ Back muscles in the area of the lumbar spine
	▶ Hip-lumbar muscles
	▶ Thigh muscles (front and back)
	▶ Calf muscles

COMPETITION FOR MASTERS ROWERS

Competitions for masters rowers enjoy increasing popularity. This form of rowing offers a variety of exciting opportunities for all ages and race distances, given that the athletes are healthy and prepared for such events in a systematic way.

However, it seems to us that it is particularly important to find the right attitude towards competitions and to put their significance in the proper context, especially in relation to the individual stages of masters rowers' lives. A competition is about measuring, experiencing and displaying one's own abilities, but also respecting at the same time the other competitors who help to achieve one's best performance. Races where the result comes down to the line, where the winning crew has succeeded only through great effort and skill, where each crew is pushing the entire course, these are the ones that provide the most satisfaction to all competitors and are remembered with the most pride.

Of course, it is a primary goal of each competitor to win. While every participant in a race should strive to do so, it is essential to set your own realistic goals in addition to winning and then experience the effort to achieve these goals or even surpass them. Each athlete knows how much effort they put into the preparation for a race and what they have been able to achieve in training. A race, therefore, provides the opportunity to showcase one's own abilities and measure them against the competition. Sticking to the race plan, reaching the targeted stroke rates while maintaining the best possible technique and even initiating a strong finishing sprint despite the fatigue of racing are the real measures that an athlete should use to validate their performance. Competition is merely an aid in unleashing one's best performance and provides a comparison to other rowers of the same age or ability.

The major gains of a competition are found primarily in learning experiences one takes from the race. Did you choose the best race tactics? Were you able to keep up your best technique even in the heat of the moment and the strain of the race? Did you choose the proper rigging for the weather conditions and the length of the race, so you could maintain your highest possible speed over the whole course of the race? What implications for future training or racing can you draw from the experience? In contrast to elite sports, the personal commitment of masters rowers should be optimized and not maximized.

Among the positive and captivating experiences are the excitement of race day (arrival at the regatta, boat rigging, gathering as a crew to prepare for the efforts to come, warm-up for the race, etc.) and the joy of competing. Also important are the social interactions with the own team members, opponents, other rowing friends, officials and spectators.

There are probably two forms of competition, that are most widespread: the official and internationally agreed upon masters rowing race distance of 1,000 m and long distance races of 3 to 10 km (2 to 6 mi) in length.

Sprint Races for Masters

Races over 1,000 m demand a high amount of power, especially in the start phase, a high endurance level and staying power over the entire race distance. Long distance races necessitate a high level of endurance, good technique and frequently steering abilities. The different demands for the respective race distances require careful preparation not only to reach a high level of performance, but also prevent health problems, as well as to enable positive competitive experiences and successes.

In a 1,000 m race, the rower exerts great forces during the start strokes and the ensuing sprint, which can lead to overloading of the skeletal system and joints of an underprepared athlete. Older rowers are frequently burdened with back or knee problems; start or sprint strokes can easily magnify these issues, especially in an unbalanced boat. Therefore, methodical introduction to such loads with targeted strength training is important, which requires long-term training over several months. Likewise, the higher stroke frequencies at the start represent a technical and coordinative challenge. A planned and focused progression towards these start strokes is therefore indispensable.

Completing the entire race successfully requires a combination of well-developed specific endurance and solidly established rowing technique. In the final sprint to the line, the rower must be able to enter high lactic acidosis. This ability takes a relatively shorter

time to be developed, compared to endurance and strength. The anaerobic training is therefore best planned for inclusion in the weeks leading up to the regatta. An older person needs a little more time to achieve such anaerobic adaptations, progressively building up the frequency and duration of this high intensity training is warranted. About 4 – 6 weeks of specific and highly concentrated workouts are necessary.

In addition to general health, psychological aspects also are an essential factor in the long-term preparation for races. Masters rowers must learn to persevere under stress and stay motivated to perform at a high level. It is important that rowers can recognize and enjoy the progress that they achieve during this preparation phase, but at the same time gain information that enables them to realistically assess their performance level to set proper targets for both training and racing.

Long Distance Races for Masters

Long distance races in particular require economical rowing on a high level, solid rowing technique, excellent endurance capacity and tactical awareness to act most appropriately in situations where a crew needs to be overtaken or a competitor tries to overtake. Additionally, some of the long distance races run over challenging courses with turns and obstacles, like bridges, so that strong steering abilities are necessary.

Such races historically take place in the fall, but can also be used as a specific form of training, for example as preparation for the sprint season. Long distance races offer rowers of almost every performance level the opportunity to experience a competitive atmosphere. Prerequisite for a long distance race is maintaining a healthy body and a sound technique under increased physical fatigue. The length of the race ensures that the intensity and physical demands during the competition stay below maximal, anaerobic efforts.

Regardless of competition length, gaining the necessary fitness in a healthy way requires several months of systematic, longer-term training. The most appropriate competition goals should be determined individually, as well as within the crew.

Other Forms of Competition

For masters athletes who enjoy racing, the planning of competitions must not be limited to rowing regattas. They can be supplemented by ergometer competitions, running or cross-country ski races and other competitive sporting activities. By adding such competitions to the rowing schedule, athletes can build new goals into their training program and perform at a high physiological level while taking the psychological stress in a different direction and possibly giving the body some rest from rowing specific strains.

In particular, ergometer competitions are gaining more and more popularity. These are of course similar to rowing races but require less technical skills, are easier to organize, don't need transportation of equipment and can be carried out at any time and in any weather. Results can be very well compared, since in general only one type of ergometer is used, namely the Concept2 rowing ergometer. This simplifies the organization of competitions from informal ergometer competitions within a club up to the official World Rowing Indoor Championships that are now held at a venue that moves to a new country each year. There are now even virtual races in which competitors connect via the internet from any place in the world.

In preparation of any competition, masters should ask themselves and come up with specific answers for the following main questions:

1. What are realistic speed levels for the planned races based on the pace that I achieve in my training?
2. What is the stroke rate, step frequency etc. that I need to achieve a certain speed, but at the same time be able to maintain good technique for the whole race distance?
3. How do I develop a sense of speed and feel for technique that puts me in the position to design a smart race plan for optimal race execution?
4. If competing in a team, what is the best approach to support the whole crew to perform well and maintain a competitive spirit?
5. How can I develop challenging, but also realistic goals against which I can assess performance during the race, so that I can have a positive learning experience regardless of the finishing position? Such goals could be: perform all race preparations in time and with precision; focus on the clean execution of the start; stick to the race plan; keep my focus (e.g. in the boat); have a solid finish sprint; improve on the previous race etc.

7.1 ANNUAL PLANNING FOR MASTERS ROWERS

The following annual plan can be considered a starting point for drawing up an individual plan:

Tab. 43: Possible annual plan with test and competition objectives for a masters rower who wants to participate in competitions of different lengths (LD – Long-distance race)

Month	Nov	Dec	Jan	Feb	Mar	Apr	May	Jun	Jul	Aug	Sep	Oct
Periodi-sation	Trans-ition		Preparation					Competition 1			Competition 2	
Ergometer Tests			60 min	10km	5km	2km	1km					
Races						LD	LD	1000 m	1000m	1000m	LD	LD
Number of Races						1	2	4	4	4	2	1

The number of tests and races must of course reflect the main training goal and at the same time the rower's individual situation, so that the figures given in Tab. 43 can only be examples, but are somewhat ideal recommendations. At this point, we would caution that while the desire to train and compete at a high level can be a powerful motivator, masters rowers should set reasonable goals to avoid extreme stresses. Obsessive racing, especially as masters grow older, can have severe negative medical, social and psychological consequences.

Masters rowing and training should never get out of hand with regards to sacrificing health, time and money. Of course, each person needs to decide for themselves how far to pursue their competitive ambitions, but the moment health is jeopardized, other people (like family or friends) are negatively affected, fun is lost and unnecessary financial investments are made, things are going beyond what is appropriate for masters rowing.

We propose, therefore, a reasonable target of one or two regattas or competitions per month and that the emphasis be placed on quality over quantity when it comes to number of races entered at any given regatta. For example, racing one long distance event or two 1,000 meter races on each day of a regatta is a challenging but achievable plan. At some regattas there is already a limit on number of races a master may enter. Tab. 43 gives an overview of the total number of races per training year that seem to be appropriate for masters rowers.

7.2 TRAINING PLANNING

Everything goes better with a plan! You need to think and decide on personal and crew goals, overall training volume necessary, time available for training and of course also money that needs to be spent on entry fees, accommodations and traveling, etc. Once a plan is designed, it will keep you focused and you are more likely to stick to the intended training efforts. Rowers should set up their training in such a way that their body, technique and psyche are increasingly aligned and prepared to successfully handle all stresses of the intended competitions. This means that the appropriate basics such as endurance, strength and technique, but also the mental aspects, are trained and controlled.

The following weekly training schedules serve as examples of how the annual training schedule from Tab. 43 could be implemented. These examples can only be general ideas of more detailed plans and need to be adjusted to the individual circumstances. Four training sessions per week are sufficient to prepare for some successful participation in competitions in their own age category. Experienced athletes with higher aspirations can add training days with compensation or extensive endurance training sessions that should be focused on regeneration, basic endurance or technique. We distinguish between weeks where rowing on the water is possible and those where it is not, as well as weeks leading to a regatta and those without a regatta.

After the example weekly training plans, we will give some hints how such plans can be individualized, reduced or expanded. We will not mention specifically any health related sessions, like stretching or proprioceptive training, but we highly recommend taking time either directly after a training session, as a morning routine or as a specific additional training session to add such supplementary training to the overall regime.

Tab. 44: Example of a weekly training plan based on the yearly plan in
Tab. 43: **Preparation Period**

	Monday	Wednesday	Friday	Saturday
	STRENGTH TRAINING	ANAEROBIC THRESHOLD	STRENGTH TRAINING	EXTENSIVE ENDURANCE
Rowing is possible	**Warm-up:** Jog 10 min **Intensity:** Maximum strength **Duration:** 40 min 4 exercises (e.g. cleans, leg press, bench pull, bench press) 3 series with 5 repetitions and about 60 – 80% 1RM load **Cool-down:** Ergometer Intensity: extensive endurance or compensation Duration: 30 min 3 x (4/3/2/1 min Sf: 18/20/22/24)	**Warm-up:** Dynamic stretching 10 min **Intensity:** Threshold training **Duration:** 45 min Rowing 2 x (5/4/3/2/1/2/3/4 min – SR: 20/23/26/29/26/23/20) Or 5 – 10 km time trial **Cool-down:** 10 min jog + 15 min stretching	**Warm-up:** Jog 10 min **Intensity:** Maximum strength **Duration:** 40 min 4 exercises (e.g. cleans, leg press, bench pull, bench press) 3 series with 5 repetitions and about 60 – 80% 1RM load **Cool-down:** Ergometer Intensity: extensive endurance or compensation Duration: 30 min 3 x (4/3/2/1 min Sf: 18/20/22/24)	**Warm-up:** Dynamic stretching 10 min **Intensity:** Extensive endurance **Duration:** 60-80 min Rowing Continuous SR 20 or Interval or Fartlek variations at SR 18 – 22 including technique drills **Cool-down:** 15 min stretching

Monday	Wednesday	Friday	Saturday
STRENGTH TRAINING	ANAEROBIC THRESHOLD	STRENGTH TRAINING	EXTENSIVE ENDURANCE
Warm-up: Jog 10 min	**Warm-up:** Dynamic stretching 10 min	**Warm-up:** Jog 10 min	**Warm-up:** Dynamic stretching 10 min
Intensity: Max strength	**Intensity:** Threshold training	**Intensity:** Max strength	**Intensity:** Extensive endurance
Duration: 30 min 4 exercises (e.g. cleans, leg press, bench pull, bench press) 3 series with 5 repetitions and about 60 – 80% 1 RM load	**Duration:** 45 min Ergometer 2 x (5/4/3/2/1/2/3/4 min – SR: 20/23/26/29/26/23/20) Or 5 – 10 km time trial	**Duration:** 30 min 4 exercises (e.g., cleans, leg press, bench pull, bench press) 3 series with 5 repetitions and about 60 – 80% 1 RM load	**Duration:** 60-80 min Ergometer Continuous SR 20 or Interval or Fartlek variations at SR 18 - 22 including some technique focus; e.g. proper sequencing
Cool-down: Ergometer Intensity: Extensive endurance or compensation Duration: 30 min 3 x (4/3/2/1 min Sf: 18/20/22/24)	**Cool-down:** 10 min jog + 15 min stretching	**Cool-down:** Ergometer Intensity: Extensive endurance or compensation Duration: 30 min 3 x (4/3/2/1 min Sf: 18/20/22/24)	**Cool down:** 15 min stretching

Rowing is NOT possible

279

Tab. 45: Example of weekly training schedule based on the yearly plan in
Tab. 43: **Competition Period 1**

	Monday	Wednesday	Thursday	Saturday
Week without Regatta	Warm-up: Row 15 min Intensity: Specific strength endurance in boat Duration: 40 min 2x {4x (30 strokes with bungee/can/half boat SR 24; Rest: 2 min)} Cool-down: Row 10 min Focus: Technique	Warm-up: Row 10 min Intensity: Extensive endurance Duration: 50 min Rowing – ontinuous long distance Cool-down: Row 10 min	Warm-up: Row 10 min Intensity: Intensive endurance Duration: 30 min Rowing – 2 x 2 km Sf: 24/26/28/30 Sf increase every 500 m; Rest: 10 min Cool-down: Row 10 min	Warm-up: Row 10 min Intensity: Competition-specific/HIIT Duration: 45 min Rowing – 2x { 6-8x (30 sec start or sprint; 1:30min easy); Rest: 5 min} Cool-down: Row 10 min
Week with Regatta	Warm-up: Jog 10 min Intensity: General strength endurance Duration: 40 min 6 exercises 3 series with 15 repetitions Cool-down: Ergometer Intensity: Endurance Duration: 30 min Focus: Technique	Warm-up: Row 20 min with 10/10/20 sprint strokes and 2 x 10 stroke starts Intensity: Competition-Specific Endurance Duration: 30 min Rowing – 250/500/250 m Start/mid race/Sprint Race simulation Rest: 5 min Cool-down: Rowing 10 min easy	Intensity: Regeneration Duration: 50 min Rowing – Continuously With: 5 x 10 strokes starts Cool-down: Rowing 10 min easy	1,000 m REGATTA

Tab. 46: Example of a weekly training plan based on the yearly plan in
Tab. 43: **Competition Period 2**

	Monday	Wednesday	Thursday	Saturday
Week without a Regatta	Warm-up: Jog 10 min Intensity: General strength endurance Duration: 40 min 6-8 exercises 3 series with 15 repetitions Cool-down: Ergometer Intensity: endurance Duration: 20 min Focus: Technique	Warm-up: Row 10 min Intensity: Extensive endurance Duration: 50 min Rowing – continuously SR 20-24 Focus: Technique Cool-down: Row 10 min	Warm-up: Row 20 min incl. 5 x 10 strokes around LD Race Pace Intensity: Threshold training Duration: 30 min Race distance time trial at SR 1-2 below Long Distance Race Pace Cool-down: Row 10 min Focus: Technique	Warm-up: Row 10 min Intensity: Extensive endurance Duration: 60 min Rowing – continuously SR 20-24 Focus: Technique Cool-down: Row 10 min
Week with Regatta	Warm-up: Row 15 min Intensity: Specific strength endurance in boat Duration: 40 min 2x {4x (30 strokes with bungee/can/half boat SR 24; Rest: 2 min)} Cool-down: Row 10 min Focus: Technique	Warm-up: Row 10 min incl. 3 x 10 strokes around LD Race Pace Intensity: Threshold training Duration: 35 min Rowing – 5x4 min at Long Distance Race Pace; Rest: 3 min Cool-down: Row 10 min easy	Warm-up: Row 15 min Intensity: Compensation Duration: 50 min Rowing continuous SR 20 with: 5 x 15 strokes at Long Distance Race Pace Cool-down: Row 10 min Focus: Technique	LONG DISTANCE (LD) REGATTA

Tab. 47: Example of weekly training plan based on the yearly plan in
Tab. 43: **Transition Period**

	Monday	Wednesday	Friday	Saturday
Every workout with fun	40 min swimming Intensity: Compensation	30 min jog & 30 min health strength training Intensity: Compensation	60 min calisthenics & stretching Intensity: Compensation	60 min playing soccer/basketball or tennis Intensity: Having fun

The training days in the week and the sequencing of the training intensities were chosen to give masters athlete's time for proper recovery. Ideally, an extra endurance training session should always follow days with higher intensity training and higher intensity training sessions should not directly follow each other.

Training plans can be individualized as following:

▸ **Reducing training volume/load** for family or work reasons to maintain time for recuperation or if there is not enough opportunity for recovery to get over an illness: Either take one day of higher intensity training off the plan or switch a session of higher intensity to a lower intensity over a two-week period, or reduce training time, number of sets or length of each set.

▸ **Increasing training volume/load**, if more time is available or athletes strive for higher training goals: One can always add another extensive endurance training session, if an athlete has more time available and they can take on an additional training load. One can also increase the volume of each training session. These actions can be taken, if there is also enough time for recovery measures, like extra napping, but, one should first consider to increase the quality of training, for example by putting a little more effort in each stroke, maintaining a certain pace by reducing the stroke rate, rowing with a little bit more stroke length, reducing rest times between sets or at turns etc.

▸ **Variation:** There are more examples of specific training forms for each training intensity in the previous chapter (see Tab. 24 – 28). One can exchange training forms of the same intensity to keep interest and excitement high.

▸ **Increasing fun:** It is always motivating to do workouts together with other crews side-by-side. If there are crews in different boat classes or of different performance levels, one should implement handicaps, which means that the faster crew should start their training piece at an appropriate time after the slower crew, assuming all crews start from the same location. The handicap should be set, so that the crews will be leveled at the very end of a piece.

▶ **Organizing test pieces:** Crews of the same club or rowing on the same stretch of water should organize time trials at distances that are appropriate to the training period where everyone can participate – essentially a local regatta. This reduces the effort that is needed to get a timing team set up, will keep the waterway free for the trial and increases motivation. Additionally, one can better monitor the performance of individual crews.

▶ **Training control:** Masters athletes should always take notes about their performance during training at each intensity. This valuable information can be used to answer some important questions – Are performance improvements consistent with training efforts? Which areas of the overall performance need special attention? Does the training program work? Is the time taken for recovery sufficient? Are there any skill improvements to register? Are the attempted strokes rates appropriate for the different training intensities and can they be sustained with proper technique over the entire piece?

7.3   TRAINING CAMPS

Training camps can provide wonderful experiences for masters rowers and have a very positive impact on rowers' performance. It definitely makes sense to organize a training camp even on a club basis. It is always better to plan for a larger group of rowers, which could include rowers of all ages. Such camps are also often run by associations, like college programs, but of course are also offered by professional training centers. Such professional training camps often offer additional perks, which an individual club or rower alone cannot provide: Specialized coaching, physiological testing, video analysis and technique training in groups are very helpful and guarantee very exciting experiences. Some training camps have made a name for themselves and are very popular. They are often located in unique, scenic parts of the country and normally provide specially protected water conditions. Such camps offer exciting practises and the qualified coaching staff will provide learning experiences for any level of rower.

Such camps are not only offered in North-America, but all over the world. You can find them easily through an internet search.

Many clubs also offer training camps that are geared towards the specific needs of their members. You can similarly plan your own camp with your rowing friends or families. You should obtain tips from experienced rowers or coaches to design such a camp and a training plan for the camp days should be carefully prepared. Of course you have a lot of time in a training camp and you are inclined to run as many training sessions and row as many miles as possible. This can be very successful, but one should exercise reason and caution. If some of the rowers for example are not used to rowing twice a day, it may very well quickly lead to some forms of overloading, especially with less experienced and less fit athletes.

The preparation for a training camp needs to begin at home some time before its start. One has to build up training volume to get rowers used to the load that the camp will provide. Besides the general conditioning, additional preparation is required. Hands, for example, must be ready to handle the increased mileage at the camp to avoid excessive blisters or strain that can sideline a rower after only a few days. Likewise, athletes need to learn how to protect themselves from more intense and prolonged exposure to sunlight, and replenishing larger amounts of fluids during longer workouts.

Longer training camps should not just consist of rowing. Supplementary sports should be part of a training camp and should involve the additional support staff such as chaperons or kitchen personnel. Recommendations from chapter 6 should be used for planning supplementary training. It is also important to plan social and cultural aspects where possible as these provide a nice balance to the athletic part of camp and contribute to participants' high spirits.

7.4   PREPARATION FOR RACES

Rowing races are inevitably something special and require greater care and planning to ensure the best possible experience. Preparations and interventions, such as sufficient recuperation and sleep, proper nutrition and a schedule that avoids unnecessary stress are the basic elements. Learning through experience when and what to eat before the start of the race, is one example of a seemingly small action with a significant impact on performance. For example, appropriate snacking and hydration throughout race day is essential to keep up energy levels. It is especially important where athletes are competing in multiple races since the last substantial meal can only be taken 3-4 hours before a race. Similarly, some rowers may not tolerate certain drinks like orange juice before a race, while others like to drink a coffee to get a little "wake-up kick" for the race.

On the evening before race day, a meal should be taken with sufficient carbohydrates and proteins, while on the day of the races light, fast-digesting meals are advised. Added to this should be a sufficient supply of liquid for which cool water or diluted fruit juices are best suited. After a race, carbohydrates and proteins should be taken in smaller portions as soon as possible - preferably in the first 30 minutes. This measure is known to accelerate regeneration.

Good race preparation also includes familiarizing oneself with the regatta facilities and specific race and traffic rules. Good things to consider include: How far the walk is from the trailer to the docks; where to place the oars prior to launching; where the bathroom facilities are; where to get drinking water; are boats called to the start; is photo ID needed to get on the water; where to row on the course to warm up etc. Regatta organizers must provide athletes and coaches with information of all regatta rules and maps of traffic patterns. They often also hold information meetings prior to racing where rules are explained. All rowers are expected to know these rules, to insure safe and fair competitions.

Equally important is the correct preparation of all rowing equipment. The boat needs to be rigged and checked along with the oars leaving plenty of time before the scheduled start. Even seemingly minor issues should be attended to. Checking the rudder function and fixtures, or the undisturbed movement of the seats in the slides, help to prevent situations that can either create stress on the water or even negatively impact the race results directly. Wind and water conditions should be assessed as a crew and any necessary adjustments to the equipment, such as necessary changes to oar length in strong winds. All preparations and checks should be completed about an hour before the start of the race. This leaves enough time for a last visit to the bathroom and getting dressed for racing. The rowers can now bring the boat to the water, giving them about 30 min to warm-up and get to the starting gates.

It is absolutely crucial to establish a race plan to which every single crewmember commits. This plan is such that everyone knows what to do in the race and when. The calls of the coxswain or the crew captain are determined and explained, so that everyone knows what actions follow specific calls. The start sequence, the number of sprint strokes, the way to transition into race pace at a given stroke rate, any action to take in certain circumstances (e.g.: "If we are leading, we lengthen the stroke and take the stroke rate down"), any specific focus pieces (e.g.: "at the 500 m mark, we will do 10 strokes emphasising the leg drive") and when to start the final spurt are determined. Of course the tactical measures should be adapted to the abilities of the team and weather conditions. The racing circumstances and opponents must be properly assessed and an interesting goal should be sought and agreed on. Competition is fun when challenging goals are met or exceeded. Therefore, it is necessary to have a more detailed process as a goal and not "we want to win" as the only goal. If some or all of the following outcomes are achieved, the crew will have a positive racing experience independent of the final outcome of the race:

- Clean strokes at a specified stroke rate during warm-up
- Powerful start with technically well executed, hard strokes
- Full team commitment to the sprint strokes at full stroke length after the start sequence
- Good boat run in the middle of the race
- United attack from every crew member for the last spurt strokes

Such partial and quite specific goals should be agreed on and then can be checked after the race. The final result of the race becomes one of the goals, but should not be the only objective. One needs to realize that the race result is partly dependent on factors that are outside of the rowers' influence. Particularly the performance level of the other crews in the race cannot be influenced by one's own team. The most exciting races are those that are fought against crews of equal abilities, but one can also learn a lot from racing a stronger opponent.

Having a number of goals that are influenced by one's own effort and performance is important to make racing experiences valuable. One-dimensional objectives are also contextualized in this way. So, it may be that a crew won the race, but the start was poorly executed. While satisfied with the final result, the crew can take the lesson from the race that the start needs improving. This means that they can focus more on this part of the race in training. On the other hand, it may also be that the race is lost, but the team committed very strongly after the start and has found a very solid race pace. Thus, this team can take something positive from the race, because sub-goals have been exceeded.

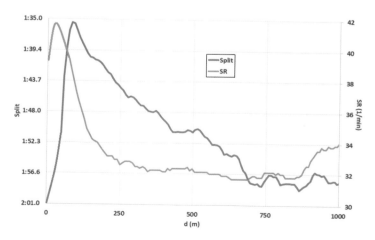

Fig. 67: Race data from stroke rate and splits of a high level 1,000 m Mix 2x race at Canadian Henley Masters Regatta 2017.

Fig. 67 shows the race data from the winner of the Mix 2x at the 2017 Canadian Henley Masters regatta taken from a Nielsen-Kellerman SpeedCoach® monitor and shows a typical race strategy which one could describe as "fly and die". This race strategy is ideal for 1,000 m races where it is important to start strongly and then try to stay as efficient and fast as possible for the majority of the race. A final sprint should be attempted, but can only have limited effect with the high lactate levels accumulated in the race. The crew in Fig. 67 increased the stroke rate in the last part of the race, but could only achieve a minimal increase in the boat speed.

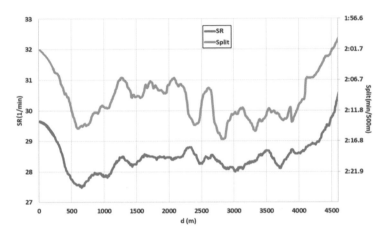

Fig. 68: Race data from stroke rate and splits of a MM 2x race at Head of the Charles Regatta 2019.

Race strategy and profile is different in a long distance race – see Fig. 68. The start is much less pronounced and the middle of the race stroke rate is maintained over the majority of the race. However, the sprint is more distinct, since rowers of course do not accumulate a lot of lactate during the race, so that there is still considerable capacity in the final stretch. While the stroke rate is quite constant, splits vary during the race because of steering and changing wind directions. Ideally, the rowers pass the start line at or just above race pace, transition quickly into race pace and then try to maintain a consistent stroke rate and pace just at the anaerobic threshold. The final sprint is started between 500 m-700 m before the finish line.

The warm-up procedure needs also to be learned and exercised. Once a procedure is established for a crew, one should use it exactly as planned in regular training before pieces at competition specific endurance intensity, so that every athlete knows its execution and the effect it has individually. Necessary changes can then be identified and implemented. If certain crew members for example need a longer time to warm up, they could individually go for a light run or sit on an ergometer before the crew gets together for their group preparation.

A normal warm-up should take about 30 min, which starts with light rowing to settle into the motion and includes a series of strokes around race pace that prepares the athletes from a tactile and mental point of view to the stress that will be experienced in the race. The athletes gain confidence that they are able to handle the water conditions and the intensity of the competition.

All intensive strokes should be finished 10 min before the official start time to make sure that any accumulated lactate is cleared out of the rowers' systems and all phosphate stores are replenished. Although it would be advisable to keep moving lightly up to the actual start, this is normally not possible or allowed by the race officials and the rules of racing. This is of lesser concern, since muscles will keep in a warmed-up, ready state for about 20 min, even if they do not move at all. If, however, a start is delayed for a longer time, rowers should try to adjust their warm-up accordingly and keep moving, if possible. In some instances, rowers are not allowed to leave the start zone and have to sit still for longer time periods. In this case, they need to do their best to adapt, stay positive and keep their muscles warm through clothing, light massages or shaking of their limbs.

Tab. 48: Example of a 30-min race warm-up on the water

TIME TO START	EXERCISE
30 min	Crew is on the water and ready to row
30 – 25 min	Light rowing (SR ~ 18 – 20) Possibly rowing half crew Executing some drills, like rowing with square blades
25 – 20 min	Rowing at intensive endurance pace (SR ~ 22 – 24)
20 – 10 min	Exercising a series of strokes around race intensity, like: 3 x 10 strokes @ SR 25/30/35 1 x 20 strokes; 10 strokes at SR 32; 10 strokes at maximum SR Start and 5 strokes Rest ~ 1 min after each piece
10 – 5 min	Approaching the start area to make sure possible commands of the starter can be heard Light rowing or waiting to be called into the gates
5 – 2 min	Affixing stern of the boat to the starting gates; remember: Boats have to be affixed to the starting gates 2 min before the official start time according to race rules
2 min	Ready to race; positioning the boat to the middle of the lane
0 min	Start of the race

Overall, it is important to view the entire process of participating in races as a learning experience that you can benefit from in any case. One can extract health, social and psychological benefits that individuals can be proud of and learn from.

With the right planning and the associated long-term preparation, racing can be fun and contribute to positive character development.

Bibliography

Adam, K., Lenk, H., Nowacki, P., Rulffs, M. & Schroeder, W. (1977). *Rudertraining*. Bad Homburg: Limpert.

Baltes, P. B. (1990). Entwicklungspsychologie in der Lebensspanne: Theoretische Leitsätze. *Psychologische Rundschau*, 41, 1-24.

Baltes, P. B. & Baltes M. M. (Eds.) (1990). *Successful aging: Perspectives from the behavioral sciences*. New York: Cambridge University Press.

Baltes, M. (1995). Verlust der Selbständigkeit im Alter: Theortische Überlegungen und empirische Befunde. *Psychol. Rundschau, 46*, 159-170.

Borg, G. (1985). *An introduction to Borg's RPE-Scale*. Michigan.

Boeck-Behrens, W.-U. & Buskies, W. (2002). *Gesundheitsorientriertes Fitnesstraining*. Lüneburg: Wehdemeier & Pusch.

Boeck-Behrens, W.-U. & Buskies, W. (2001). *Fitness-Krafttraining*. Hamburg: Rowohlt.

Brach, M. & Schott, N. (2003). Motorisches Lernen im Alter. In H. Mechling & J. Munzert, *Handbuch Bewegungswissenschaft – Bewegungslehre*. (S. 461-474) Schorndorf: Hofmann.

Canada Aviron Magazine, Victoria, 3, 18.

Conzelmann, A. (1994). Entwicklung der Ausdauer. In J. Baur, K. Bös & R. Singer (Hrsg.), *Motorische Entwicklung. Ein Handbuch* (S. 151-180). Schorndorf: Hofmann.

Conzelmann, A. (1997). *Entwicklung der konditionellen Fähigkeiten im Erwachsenenalter.* Schorndorf: Hofmann.

Conzelmann, A. (2004). *Zufriedenes Altern – welche Rolle spielen sportliche Aktivitäten?* Vortrag an der Christian-Albrechts-Universität zu Kiel. Dickhuth, H.-H., Mayer F., Röcker K. & Berg A. (Hrsg.). (2007). *Sportmedizin für Ärzte.*

Köln: Deutscher Ärzte Verlag GmbH.

Feldt, V. (1999). *Fit und gesund ab 30.* Aachen: Meyer & Meyer Verlag.

Franklin B. A., Fern, A. & Voytas, J. (2004). *Training principles for-elite-senior-athletes. Current Sports Medicine Reports,* 3, 173-179.

Friedrich W. (2008). *Sportvereine und Demographie.* Vortrag LSB Baden-Württemberg am 21.04.2008.

Fritsch, W. (1990). *Handbuch für das Rennrudern.* Aachen: Meyer & Meyer.

Fritsch, W. (Hrsg.). (1995). *Rudern – lehren, lernen, trainieren.* Wiesbaden: Limpert.

Fritsch, W. (Hrsg.). (1997). *Rudern – erleben, gestalten, organisieren.* Wiesbaden: Limpert.

Fritsch, W. (Hrsg.). (1999). *Rudern – informieren, reflektieren, innovieren.* Wiebelsheim: Limpert.

Fritsch, W. (2000). Rowing in daily life. In W. Fritsch. *Rowing.* Oxford: Meyer & Meyer Sport Ltd.

Fritsch, W. (Hrsg.). (2001). *Rudern – entwickeln, kooperieren, vermitteln.* Sindelfingen: Sportverlag Schmidt & Dreisilker.

Fritsch, W. (Hrsg.). (2003). *Rudern – erfahren, erkunden, erforschen.* Gießen: Sport Media.

Fritsch, W. (2004). *Tipps für Rudern.* Aachen: Meyer & Meyer.

Fritsch, W. (2005). *Das große Buch vom Rennrudern* (2. Aufl.). Aachen: Meyer & Meyer.

Fritsch, W. (2006). *Handbuch für den Rudersport.* Aachen: Meyer & Meyer.

Fritsch, W. (2015). *Rudern Basics.* Aachen: Meyer & Meyer.

Fritsch, W. & Willmann, T. (2005). *Skilanglauf. Methodik und Technik.* Aachen: Meyer & Meyer.

Grabow, V. (1995). Vergleich von Trainingsumfängen und – intensitäten bei Kader – und Altersklassenruderern. In W. Fritsch (Hrsg.), *Rudern – lehren, lernen, trainieren.* (S. 219-225). Wiesbaden: Limpert.

Grabow, V. (1997). Zwei Facetten des Erwachsenenruderns: Kondition und Technik. In W. Fritsch (Hrsg.), *Rudern – erleben, gestalten, organisieren*. (S. 116-121) Wiesbaden: Limpert.

Häfelinger, U. & Schuba, V. (2002). *Koordinationstherapie – Propriozeptives Training*. Aachen: Meyer & Meyer.

Hagerman, F. C., Fielding, R. A., Fiatarone, M. A., Gault, J. A., Kirkendall, D. T., Ragg, K. et al. (1996). A 20-yr longitudinal study of Olympic oarsmen. *Med Sci Sports Exerc,. 28(9)*, 1150-1156.

Hartmann, U., Mader, A. & Hollmann, W. (1997): Rudern von 8 bis 88 Jahren – wesensbestimmende Merkmale und Ausprägungsgrade einer Lifetime-Sportart unter besonderer Berücksichtigung des physischen Aspektes. In W. Fritsch (Hrsg.), *Rudern – erleben, gestalten, organisieren*. (S. 124 -135). Wiesbaden: Limpert.

Hohmann, A., Lames, M. & Letzelter, M. (2003). *Einführung in die Trainingswissenschaft* (3. Aufl.). Wiebelsheim: Limpert.

Hollmann, W. & Hettinger, T. (1976). *Sportmedizin – Arbeits- und Trainingsgrundlagen*. Stuttgart – New York: Schattauer.

Hollmann, W. & Liesen H. (1986). Höheres Alter und Sport. In W. Hollmann (Hrsg.), *Zentrale Themen der Sportmedizin* (3., neu bearb. Aufl.). (S. 342-357). Berlin: Springer.

Hottenrott, K. & Zülch, M. (1998). *Ausdauertrainer Radsport*. Reinbek: Rowohlt.

Journals of Gerontology. Series A, Biological Sciences and medical Sciences by E. J. Metter; zit. nach Spiriduso et al., 2005.

Kreiß, F. (1995). Sportlernen mit Erwachsenen. In W. Fritsch (Hrsg.), *Rudern – lehren, lernen, trainieren*. (S. 142-149). Wiesbaden: Limpert.

Kruse, A., Rott, Chr. & Schmitt, E. (1999). Einflussfaktoren der Kompetenz und Möglichkeiten der Kompetenzförderung im Alter. *Sportwissenschaft, 29* (3), 298-309.

Kuroda, Y. (1989). Sport und körperliche Betätigung beim älteren Menschen. In H. Dirix, G. Knuttgen & K. Tittel, *Olympiabuch der Sportmedizin*. (S. 281-288). Köln: Deutscher Ärzte-Verlag.

Lambert, C. (1999). *Über den Wassern*. Kreuzlingen: Ariston Verlag

Lamprecht M. & Stamm H. (2001). *Sport in der zweiten Lebenshälfte. Analysen zum Seniorensport in der Schweiz*. Sekundäranalyse der SOV-STG-Studie „Sport Schweiz 2000" im Auftrag des Bundesamtes für Sport, Magglingen.

Maharam, L. G., Baumann, P. A., Kalman, D., Skolnik, H., Perle, S. M. (1999). Masters athletes. Factors affecting performance. *Sports Med, 28 (4)*, 273-285.

Martin, D., Carl, K. & Lehnertz, K. (2001). *Handbuch Trainingslehre*. Schorndorf: Hofmann.

McNeely, E. & Royle, M. (2002). *Skillful rowing*. Aachen: Meyer & Meyer.

McNeely, E. (o. J.). *Strength goals for masters rowers*. Man.

Mechling, H. (1999). Training im Alterssport. *Sportwissenschaft, 29 (3)*, 288-297.

Mejia, M. (2008). *Muskeln maßgeschneidert*. Aachen: Meyer & Meyer.

Melges, T. & Fritsch, W (1999). Systemische Aspekte und empirische Befunde zur Selbststeuerung von Ausdauerbelastungen über das Subjektive Beanspruchungs empfinden.

In W. Fritsch, *Rudern – informieren, reflektieren, innovieren* (S. 229-242). Wiebelsheim: Limpert.

Meusel, H. (1999). *Sport für Ältere*. Stuttgart – New York: Schattauer.

Mosel, A. (1995). Altern, Leistungsfähigkeit und Training – Leistungsüberwachung und Gesundheit im Masterrudern. In W. Fritsch (Hrsg.), *Rudern – lehren, lernen, trainieren*. (S. 230-238). Wiesbaden: Limpert.

Murphy, M. (2008). *Der Muskelmanager. Powerwork für jeden Zeitplan*. Aachen: Meyer & Meyer.

Neumann G. & Hottenrott K. (1999). Sportartspezifiche Leistungsdiagnostik. *Sports Care 2*, 2-6.

Nilius, S. (2009). *Spiroergometrische Leistungsdiagnostik im Rudern. Vergleichende Analyse der Arbeits- und Technikökonomie auf dem Ruderergometer und im Boot*. Diplomarbeit, Sportwissenschaft, Universität Konstanz.

Nolte, V. (1982). Die Rudertechnik. In *Rudersport, 34*, Trainer Journal, I-XII.

Nolte, V. (1982). Die Stemmbretteinstellung und der Ruderwinkel in der Rücklage. *In Rudersport, 34*, Trainer Journal.

Nolte, V. (1984). *Die Effektivität des Ruderschlages*. Berlin: Bartels & Wernitz.

Nolte, V. (1984). Rudertechnik. In Nolte, V. (Red.), *Bericht zum 13. FISA-Trainer-Kolloquium*. (S. 31-41). Minden: Philler.

Nolte, V. (1989). Rudern. In Willimczik, K. (Hrsg.): *Biomechanik der Sportarten*. (S. 297-308). Reinbek.

Nolte, V. (1991). Introduction to the biomechanics of rowing. *FISA-Coach, 1*, 1-6.

Nolte, V. (2001). Drills from the experts. In Nolte, V. (Ed.), Coach boat view. *Rowing Canada Aviron Magazine, Victoria, 3*, 19-20.

Nolte, V. (2007). Golden years – more and more middle-aged athletes are winning on the world stage. *Rowing News, Vol. 14*, No. 5, 66-69.

Nolte, V. (Ed.). (2005). *Rowing faster*. Human Kinetics, Champaign, IL.

Oschütz, H. & Belinová, K. (2003). Training im Alter. In H. Denk, D. Pache & H. J. Schaller (Hrsg.), *Handbuch Alterssport* (S. 230-238). Schorndorf: Hofmann.

Ott, D. & Beckenbach, F. (2003). *Fit aber richtig* (2. Aufl.). Aachen: Meyer & Meyer Verlag.

Puggaard, L., Pedersen, H. P., Sandager, E. & Klitgaard, H. (1994). Physical conditioning in elderly people. *Scand J Med Sci Sports*, 4, 47-56.

Reifschneider, E. (2000). Rudern. In Klümper (Hrsg.), *Sporttraumatologie – ein Handbuch der Sportarten und ihrer typischen Verletzungen*. Landsberg: ecomed.

Rice, C. (2007). *Persönliche Mitteilungen*.

Rost, R. (1984). *Herz und Sport*. Erlangen: Perimed.

Roth, K. & Winter, R. (1994). Entwicklung koordinativer Fähigkeiten. In J. Baur, K. Bös & R. Singer (Hrsg.), *Motorische Entwicklung. Ein Handbuch.* (S. 217-237). Schorndorf: Hofmann.

Sayer, B. (2006). *Rowing and sculling*. London: Robert Hale.

Schaller, H.- J. & Wernz, P. (2008). *Koordinationstraining für Senioren*. Aachen: Meyer & Meyer.

Schmidt, H.-U. (2003). Zur Wechselwirkung von koordinativen Fähigkeiten, Technik und anderen Leistungsfaktoren im Rudern. In W. Fritsch, W. (Hrsg.). *Rudern – erfahren, erkunden, erforschen*. (S. 187-196). Gießen: Sport Media.

Schmidtbleicher, D. (1994). Entwicklung der Kraft und der Schnelligkeit. In In J. Baur, K. Bös & R. Singer (Hrsg.), *Motorische Entwicklung. Ein Handbuch* (S. 129-150). Schorndorf: Hofmann.

Schubart, A. & Bös, K. (1996). Zur motorischen Leistungsfähigkeit älterer Menschen.

Theoretische Grundlagen und Forschungsergebnisse. In H. Denk (Hrsg.), *Alterssport. Aktuelle Forschungsergebnisse* (S. 155-177). Schorndorf: Hofmann.

Seiler, S. (2003). *The master power – How were they, Who are they, and why are they still rowing?* S.A.F.F.E.-Congress 9.2.2003. http://www.worldrowing.com/insidefisa/reportsDownloads.sps?itype=7155&icustompageid=11122 (Zugriff am 10.01.2005)

Seiler K. S., Spiriduso W. W. & Martin J. C. (1998). Gender differences in rowing performance and power with aging. *Med Sci Sports Exerc. [30]*: 121-127.

Spirduso, W. W. (1997). Introduction in motor learning. Adaption and learning in old age. In G. Huber (Ed.), *Health, aging, activity and sports* (pp. 104-108). Werbach-Gamburg: Health Promotion Publication.

Spirduso, W., Francis, K. & MacKae, P. (2005). *Physical dimensions of aging.* Human Kinetics, Champaign, IL.

Strass, D. & Wilke, K. (2006). *Masterschwimmen.* Aachen: Meyer & Meyer.

Tittlbach, S. (2002). *Entwicklung der körperlichen Leistungsfähigkeit.* Schorndorf: Hofmann.

Trono, C. (2001). Think about your drills. In Nolte, V. (Ed.), Coach boat view. *Rowing Canada Aviron Magazine, Victoria, 3.*

Vernacchia, R. A., McGuire, R. T., & Cook, D. L. (1992). *Coaching mental excellence.* Dubuque: Brown & Benchmark

Weineck, J. (2000). *Optimales Training.* Balingen: Spitta.

Wiemeyer, J. (2003). Motorisches Lernen – Lehrmethoden und Übungsgestaltung. In H. Mechling & J. Munzert (Hrsg.), *Handbuch Bewegungswissenschaft – Bewegungslehre* (S. 405-428). Schorndorf: Hofmann.

Woll, A. (2006). *Sportliche Aktivität, Fitness und Gesundheit im Lebenslauf.* Schorndorf: Hofmann.

Yoshiga, C., Higuchi, M & Oki, J. (2002). Rowing prevents muscle wasting in older men. *Eur J Appl Physiol, 88,* 1-4.

Yoshiga, C., Higuchi, M & Oki, J. (2003). Lower heart rate response to ergometry rowing than to treadmill running in older men. *Clin Physiol & Func,* 58-61.

Yoshiga, C. (2007). The senior oarsman. In N. H. Secher, S. Volianitis (Ed.), *Rowing* (S. 115-123). Massachusetts/Oxford: Blackwell Publishing.

http://www.arrs.net/SA_Mara.html

http://www.concept2.com/us/training/records/2000m_records.asp

LIST OF FIGURES

LIST OF TABLES

CREDITS

Cover and interior design: Anja Elsen

Layout: Anja Elsen

Cover photo: © AdobeStock

Interior photos: Courtesy of Volker Nolte, Wolfgang Fritsch, and Drake Nolte

Chapter opener photos and illustrations: © AdobeStock

Managing editor: Elizabeth Evans

Copyediting: Qurratulain Zaheer

Translation: Alan Oldham